BEAD TALK

paskwāwi masinahikewina / Prairie Writing

ISSN 2818-1379

Brenda Macdougall and Robert Innes, Editors

paskwāwi masinahikewina / Prairie Writing series publishes books both academically rigorous and accessible to the public that relate to the contemporary experiences, histories, and knowledges of prairie Indigenous societies. It supports the work of new and established scholars who are examining how prairie Indigenous peoples understand and shape their own worlds.

1 *Bead Talk: Indigenous Knowledge and Aesthetics from the Flatlands,* edited by Carmen Robertson, Judy Anderson, and Katherine Boyer

BEAD TALK

INDIGENOUS KNOWLEDGE AND AESTHETICS FROM THE FLATLANDS

EDITED BY
CARMEN ROBERTSON, JUDY ANDERSON,
AND KATHERINE BOYER

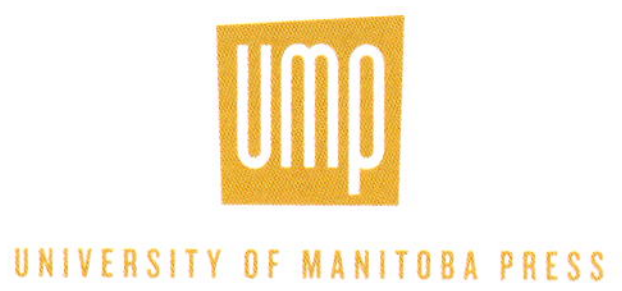

UNIVERSITY OF MANITOBA PRESS

Bead Talk: Indigenous Knowledge and Aesthetics from the Flatlands

28 27 26 25 24 2 3 4 5 6

University of Manitoba Press
Winnipeg, Manitoba, Canada
Treaty 1 Territory
uofmpress.ca

Cataloguing data available from Library and Archives Canada
paskwāwi masinahikewina / Prairie Writing, ISSN 2818-1379 ; 1
ISBN 978-1-77284-065-0 (PAPER)
ISBN 978-1-77284-066-7 (PDF)
ISBN 978-1-77284-067-4 (EPUB)
ISBN 978-1-77284-068-1 (BOUND)

Book Cover Concept: Carmen Robertson, Judy Anderson, and Katherine Boyer. Book Cover Photo: Katherine Boyer
Cover and interior design by Jess Koroscil

Printed in Canada

This book has been published with the help of a grant from the Federation for the Humanities and Social Sciences, through the Awards to Scholarly Publications Program, using funds provided by the Social Sciences and Humanities Research Council of Canada.

Funded by the Government of Canada | Canada

CONTENTS

FOREWORD

BRENDA MACDOUGALL

When I was asked to write a foreword for this volume produced by the Auntie Collective and their young relatives—nieces, sisters, cousins—I was equal parts honoured and nervous. I have been fortunate enough to know, and even count as friends, some of the beadwork artists in this collection, while others I have not yet met in person even as I've become familiar with their work. When they asked me to join this volume, it felt like being invited to hang out with the cool kids in the smoking area but instead of drawing me in with idle chatter punctuated by wafts of smoke from expertly wielded Players and du Mauriers, this group lured me with delica, miyuki, and charlotte seed, along with bugle and pony, beads in a startling array of colours and cuts with milky, flat, matte, and sparkly finishes. I admire these cool kids, Indigenous beaders, for their swagger, talent, and ability to bring beauty into the world, giving life to intricate patterns rich with contours, perspective, depth, and shape. So here it goes, I am hoping I don't screw this up and embarrass them all as I write this foreword to their beautiful book shaped by so many conversations and the production of art steeped in the traditions of beading and cultural teachings.

These prairie, plains, Flatland-born or -based artists came together to talk and write about beading to explore and deepen understandings around the practices, processes, and philosophical questions that fuel their work. Like all Indigenous artists, these beaders are out in front of the rest of the Indigenous academic pack, breaking trail by formulating and expressing cutting-edge ideas, theoretical perspectives, and methodological processes rooted in, and expressive of, our values, our ideas of being human, and our concepts of home and territory—all part of our intellectual traditions. They also, in their special language of beads and stitches, critique and challenge settler colonialism, systemic racism, and epistemic violence. The work of the artists in this volume is grounded in our traditions, world views, values, and philosophical constructions of Indigenous peoples, laying the foundations for the rest of us to (re)build and produce histories, political philosophies, and legal orders based on their insights and invaluable contributions. Artists, through their intuitive gifts of expression and emotion, give the rest of us the power needed to defend ourselves against the forces of oppressive discriminatory practices and beliefs that seek to hold us back. They remind us that we have the creativity and imagination to produce scholarship steeped in the beauty of our traditions as they do. Our lives are the richer when we are surrounded by the colours, textures, and patterns—particularly those produced in beads—that are, in effect, the visual expression of our emotions, our sense of self, and our relationships to one another and the world around us.

This collection of essays and conversations introduces and connects us to the teachings of kiyokewin—visiting—the act of spending time with others talking, listening, and sharing. Kiyokewin is a verb, it requires the active presence of, and engagement with, the gifts of speaking, hearing, and participating. It is through the act of visiting that we create, reinforce, and maintain wahkotowin (family, kinship, relationships) amongst ourselves, to our land/territory, and to the beings that inhabit the world around us. It is through the act of visiting that we learn and teach, inspire and create, understand and grow. It is through the act of visiting that we share knowledge and, in effect, share ourselves with others. Kiyokewin is a process that, much like making art, takes time, effort, patience, and, importantly, requires an active presence. Kiyokewin requires us to take, and make, time and space for one another. I learned the teachings of wahkotowin and how to bead through kiyokewin but also through a form of inter-generational mentorship that is the foundation of a teacher/student relationship rooted in love and friendship. We visit with, and learn from, one another across generations, across genders, and across species and natural and spiritual realms. I am still learning how to express these ideas about kiyokewin and wahkotowin and any failure to do so well, or properly, or accurately is mine alone. I am, much like these bead artists, a work in progress on the path to claim and reclaim cultural traditions. But it is clear that the teachings and values embedded within wahkotowin and kiyokewin about how to live in the world exist as an active presence in the lives of these artists, these relatives who come from, or live and work in, my homeland, described by them as the prairie, plains, and flatland. They have used this medium of beading to translate cultural teachings and construct a visual language that serves to express our humanity, because, in the end, all of our teachings point us towards what it means to be and become human. Their artistic expressions encode and inscribe kiyokewin, wahkotowin, and other traditional teachings on our hearts and minds so we often feel them before we can find the words to articulate them properly.

In March 2020 when the world shut down, I was struck by the beauty of the stillness that surrounded us all. In and amongst the stressful realities of enforced and necessary isolation and the daily news of death and illness in horrifying and unprecedented numbers, and as we collectively faced an uncertain future, we experienced, however briefly, a world renewed. In my downtown Ottawa neighbourhood I was awestruck listening to the breathtaking songs of birds who were no longer drowned out by the incessant thunder of cars and trucks and a happy witness to wildlife moving freely without fear of traffic, people, or pets. Like everyone, I felt the general pace of life slow down as we all caught our collective breath and tried to reorient ourselves to who we could be if we actively chose to be something different. Deeply suspicious of social media, I have resisted Facebook and Twitter in large part because they appeared to breed and reproduce insidious forms of negativity and toxicity (a problem made worse by the COVID-19 pandemic). Yet it was COVID itself that convinced me to finally take the plunge and I joined Instagram, a platform that struck me as being filled with light and happiness. This was a deliberate decision grounded in a need to find and follow Indigenous artists—creators using beads, birchbark, clay, quills, gemstones, silver, wool, silk, hide, fur, velvet, and stroud to fabricate and design jewellery, clothing, textiles, and vessels. I have followed beaders along with traditional tattooists, potters, painters, and sculptors. Whatever the form or medium, Indigenous artists have demonstrated their versatility, resilience, and commitment to their art, their traditions, and most especially their families, honouring their people's values and insights about the world through their labour. I am in awe of it all but most especially of the work of bead artists—those people able to produce the most spectacular wearable, functional, and displayable art grounded in tradition but with contemporary flare. Instagram has introduced me to a whole new group of artists—Indigenous makers spread out across the continent committed to perfecting their abilities to create and inspire, who are in no way limited by their circumstances or imaginations. For me, Instagram became a way to think about wahkotowin and kiyokewin and actively practise the art of being human because it calls on me to remember the beauty that we are capable of creating. Now that the world is reopening, it is my hope that we can experience and live these teachings safely again in person but also that we do not forget the teaching we were gifted about needing to live differently so that we can have a world where the beauty of birds, wildlife, land, water, sky, and earth can continue to thrive and inspire. This collection of voices, each of which represents an immense and profound artistic talent, points us towards that world, and I look forward to the new teachings and inspiration that art and artists will gift to the rest of us.

WHO WE ARE

Visiting is a key aspect of the beading process. To visit we need to introduce ourselves. We've arranged our introductions in alphabetical order for no other reason than it is as equitable as any other way to tell you about ourselves.

JUDY ANDERSON is nêhiyaw from Gordon First Nation, Saskatchewan. She is a professor of Canadian Indigenous Studio Art in the Department of Art and Art History at the University of Calgary. Her practice includes beadwork, installation, three-dimensional pieces, painting, and collaborative projects; her work focuses on issues of spirituality, family, colonialism, and nêhiyaw ways of knowing and being. Her current work is created with the purpose of honouring people in her life and nêhiyaw intellectualizations of the world.

KATHERINE BOYER (Métis/settler) is a multidisciplinary artist, whose work is focused on methods bound to textile arts and the handmade—primarily woodworking and beadwork. Boyer's art and research encompasses personal family narratives, entwined with Métis history, material culture, and architectural spaces—both human made and natural. Her work often explores boundaries between two opposing things as an effort to better understand both sides of a perceived dichotomous identity. This manifests in long, slow, and laborious processes that attempt to unravel and better understand history, environmental influences, and personal memories.

RUTH CUTHAND was born in Saskatchewan and is of Plains Cree and Scottish ancestry. She grew up in Alberta near the Blood Reserve, where at the age of eight she met artist Gerald Tailfeathers and decided that she too wanted to be an artist. Cuthand studied at the University of Regina in 1977 before completing her Bachelor of Fine Arts in Saskatoon at the University of Saskatchewan in 1983. She later pursued post-graduate studies at the University of Montana (1985) before completing her Master of Fine Arts at the University of Saskatchewan. During her school years, Cuthand worked in printmaking but switched to painting after developing a severe allergy to one of the chemicals used in making prints. Cuthand also works in drawing and photography. Since the early 2000s she has reshaped directions in beading. Her art addresses themes such as colonialism, Indigenous representation in mainstream media and in Canadian politics, and the history of abuse in residential schools.

DAYNA DANGER is a Two-Spirit, Indigiqueer, Métis-Saulteaux-Polish visual artist. Danger was raised in Miiskwaagamiwiziibiing, Treaty 1 territory, or so-called Winnipeg. They are currently based in Tiohtiá:ke/Mōniyāng, or so-called Montreal. In 2021, they began a doctorate at Concordia University that focuses on hide-tanning stories, bush skills, and culture camps that were passed down from their Saulteaux great-grandmother, Madeline McLeod (Campbell).

SHERRY FARRELL RACETTE (Métis/Algonquin/Irish, @artistteach) is an interdisciplinary scholar with an active arts and curatorial practice. Born and raised in Manitoba on the Winnipeg River, she is a Bill C-31 member of Timiskaming First Nation in Quebec. Her principal areas of interest are Métis history and visual culture, traditional media in contemporary art, and visual storytelling. She has worked extensively in archives and museum collections to retrieve women's voices and recover aesthetic knowledge. Beadwork and stitch-based work are increasingly important to her artistic practice, creative research, and pedagogy. She is currently teaching in the Department of Visual Arts, University of Regina. She recently co-curated *Radical Stitch,* which was mounted at the MacKenzie Art Gallery in 2022 with Cathy Mattes and Michelle Lavallee.

MARCY FRIESEN is of Swampy Cree and Welsh ancestry and currently resides on a mixed farm with her family near Carrot River, Saskatchewan. Marcy comes from a long line of traditional master beaders and talented creative family members. Marcy has always felt the need to create and has focused her career starting her Trapline Creations business where she makes utilitarian pieces. Marcy now also uses beads, leather, and fur in new and exciting ways that open discussions on mental health issues and racism. By pushing her boundaries and through self-exploration, Marcy is finding that art isn't as "useless" as she first thought, and recently completed an artist residency at Wanuskewin, outside of Saskatoon, Saskatchewan.

FELICIA GAY is muskego inninu iskew from waskiganeek (Cumberland House, Saskatchewan) and a member of the Opaskwayak Cree Nation, Treaty 5 territory. Gay's practice as a curator began in 2004. In 2006, Gay and fellow cultural worker Joi Arcand co-founded the Indigenous-led artist-run centre The Red Shift Gallery in Saskatoon, Saskatchewan. In 2018, Gay was awarded the Saskatchewan Arts Award for Leadership in recognition of her work in curation and advocacy for the creation of safe and productive spaces for Indigenous artists. Since 2019, Gay has lived in Regina, Saskatchewan, and was the MacKenzie Art Gallery's first Mitacs Curatorial Fellow, a position created in partnership with the University of Regina's Faculty of Media, Art, and Performance. In 2020, she received the SSHRC Joseph-Armand Bombardier Scholarship for her research as a doctoral candidate. Her insights as a curator have been featured in public presentations, including a keynote at the Canadian Arts Summit and in catalogue essays and articles for *Canadian Art*, *BlackFlash*, Dunlop Art Gallery, PAVED Arts, and Mercer Union, among others. Her curatorial projects include *Miskwaabik Animiiki Power Lines: The Work of Norval Morrisseau*, MacKenzie Art Gallery, Regina; *Beads in the blood: Ruth Cuthand, a Survey*, College Art Galleries, University of Saskatchewan, Saskatoon; *Touching Earth and Sky*, MacKenzie Art Gallery, Regina; *borderLINE: 2020 Biennial of Contemporary Art*, Art Gallery of Alberta, Edmonton, Alberta, and Remai Modern, Saskatoon;

and *Give her a face*, PAVED Arts, Saskatoon, and Grunt Gallery, Vancouver, British Columbia.

FRANCHESCA [FRAN] HEBERT-SPENCE is currently residing in Inuvik, the Inuvialuit Settlement Region, and is Anishinaabe (Sagkeeng First Nation) from Winnipeg, Manitoba. Her grandmother Marion Ida Spence was from Sagkeeng First Nation, on Lake Winnipeg, Manitoba. Hebert-Spence has worked as a cultural producer with a background in making, curating, research, and administration. She has described her curatorial practice as "snacks and chats." The foundation of her creative practice stems from Ishkabatens Waasa Gaa Inaabateg, Brandon University Visual and Aboriginal Arts program. She is an independent curator and previously served as adjunct curator, Indigenous Art at the Art Gallery of Alberta, as well as a curatorial assistant within the Indigenous Art Department at the National Gallery of Canada. She is a PhD student in Cultural Mediations (Visual Culture) at Carleton University and will examine the presence of guest/host protocols within Indigenous methodological practices with a focus on visual art in Canada.

CATHY MATTES (Southwest Manitoba Michif) is a curator, writer, and art history professor based out of Sprucewoods, Manitoba, Canada. Her curation, research, and writing centres on dialogic and Indigenous knowledge-centred curatorial practice as strategies for care. She has a PhD in Indigenous Studies from the University of Manitoba, and currently teaches at the University of Winnipeg in the History of Art and Curatorial Studies programs. Mattes has been beading since she was twenty years old and has taught beading and moccasin-making in workshops, university courses, and around her kitchen table with family and friends.

AUDIE MURRAY is a visual artist who works with a multitude of mediums such as sculpture, media, beadwork, and drawing. Her practice is informed by the process of making and visiting to explore themes of contemporary culture, embodied experiences ,and lived dualities. These modes of working assist with the recentring of our collective connection to bodies, ancestral knowledge systems, and relationality. Murray is Cree-Métis from the Lebret and Meadow Lake communities located on Treaty 4 and 6 territories and is currently based in Oskana kâ-asastêki (Regina, Saskatchewan).

CARMEN ROBERTSON is an auntie and mother, a teacher, and not a very good beader. Born and raised in Treaty 4 territory in and around the Qu'Appelle Valley, the Scots-Lakota professor holds the Canada Research Chair in North American Art and Material Culture at Carleton University in Ottawa. Before joining Carleton, she taught at University of Regina and First Nations University of Canada in Saskatchewan for seventeen years. While leading the Morrisseau Project: 1955–1985 that studies the art of Anishinaabe artist Norval Morrisseau, she also passionately researches beadwork on the prairie and has written curatorial essays for *Catherine Blackburn: New Age Warrior* and *Wâhkôhtowin: Carrie Allison*, and the 2017 essay in *RACAR*, "Land and Beaded Identity: Shaping Art Histories of Indigenous Women of the Flatland." Robertson also maintains an independent curatorial practice and co-curated *Medicine Currents: The Art of Norval Morrisseau* with Danielle Printup for the Carleton University Art Gallery in 2023.

BEAD TALK

INTRODUCTION

CARMEN ROBERTSON, JUDY ANDERSON, AND KATHERINE BOYER

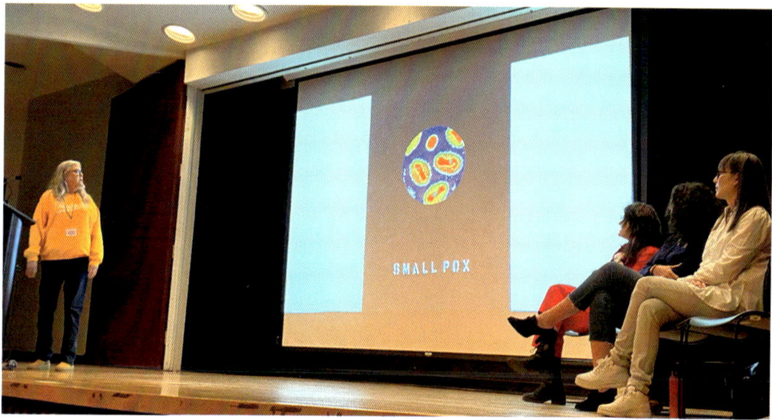

FIGURE 0.1. Ruth Cuthand at "Knowledge Transmission: When the Lines are Broken," panel discussion at the Ziigimineshin Winnipeg 2020 beading symposium. From left to right: Ruth Cuthand, Katherine Boyer, Carmen Robertson, Judy Anderson. Photo courtesy of Linda Grussani.

This is a sharing of stories of ourselves, our families, our homes, and our love of beading. We began to talk about beading as a group of friends who have worked together and known each other mostly during our time in Saskatchewan in the early to mid-2000s. We began to call ourselves, informally, the Aunties Collective in about 2017, and then invited others to join our circle. With this book, a project that got underway in 2016, we set out to ask a series of questions about Indigenous beading that we sought to engage with through visiting. Our conversations and ideas have been focused on beads and the stories they hold. We came together to write about beading on the Prairies or the Flatlands region of Manitoba, Saskatchewan, and Alberta, hoping to deepen our understanding of beading practices, processes, and philosophical questions about ways of knowing and beading in the Flatlands.

Through a series of wide-ranging discussions, essays, and beaded works, we offer textual and visual insights into how beading embodies epistemological concepts such as reciprocity and respect and the ways they are interconnected with storied intergenerational knowledge transmission. Each of the contributors to this project is from the Prairies, the Flatlands, the Plains. Collectively, we wear a lot of hats, and the pandemic took its toll on each of us. Some of us are expert beaders, some of us are not, some of us are teachers, some of us are not, some of us grew up in our communities, some of us did not, but we all feel connections to one another and to our land, and beading is an important link. Teaching and learning are back-and-forth processes that go beyond formal educational settings, yet many of us continue to find intersections through educational institutions. Relational connections shape the stories that impact the way we understand beading as part of an embodied process of active presence.

CLEARING BEADING PATHWAYS

Indigenous beading in North America was once thought of as artifact, understood outside Indigenous circles through an anthropological lens, a frozen-in-time object relegated to ethnographic archives. Beaders defy such one-dimensional understandings, embracing glass beads as a new technology that offered innovations and opportunities to expand visual storying. Seemingly a solitary task, the process of beading involves community support and connection, either digitally or in person, to facilitate a fluid intergenerational transmission of skill and pattern. Glass beads therefore naturally foster and care for Indigenous ways of teaching and learning. Beads, themselves, are beings that claim space and cultural identity; they hold stories and serve as a medium of resilience. While this book focuses on the work of a small group of beaders, it is important to note that Indigenous beading on the Flatlands is richly represented in many ways; it is not our intention to do a survey of this art form—a book that also needs writing! Trying to quantify the number of beaders on the Plains would be impossible. Even qualifying beaders is difficult since there are so many different forms of beaded expressions that thrive on the Flatlands. Rather, we hope to share our own experiences in ways that may open deeper understandings beyond the beaded works included here.

In 2005, Sherry Farrell Racette and Carmen Robertson curated *Clearing A Path: new ways of seeing traditional Indigenous art* for the Saskatchewan Arts Board as part of the centennial celebrations underway in the province. From the start, this exhibition defied expectations. It was unusual at that time to view Indigenous beadwork in a gallery setting, and artists included in *Clearing A Path* received the first rounds of grants from the Saskatchewan Arts Board as part of a new project to support Indigenous artists. Not all the artists included in the catalogue were beaders, but artists such as Robert and Bernadette Badger, Marcia Chickeness, Hilary Harper, Stella Johnstone, Caroline Montgrand, Rose Morin, Minnie Ryder, Sylvia Sewap, Ida Bella Tremblay, Flora Weenonis, and Alicia Yuzicappi created works that challenged barriers and confining classifications that positioned their work as something lesser and unsuitable for gallery spaces. Combining traditional knowledge and individual creativity in relation to family and community, these artists push their arts in new directions—as Indigenous artists have always done. Caroline Morin's sneaker moccasins, for example, featured on the cover of the exhibition catalogue (Figure 0.2), defy the problematic stereotypes of the "Imaginary Indian" that had long relegated Indigenous arts and Indigenous peoples to a frozen-in-time drawer in a museum vault.[1] Morin's work demonstrates some of the innovative ways that beaders create new forms. Like the many works included in *Clearing A Path*, works by prairie beaders featured in this book reflect movement and active engagement with the past, present, and future.

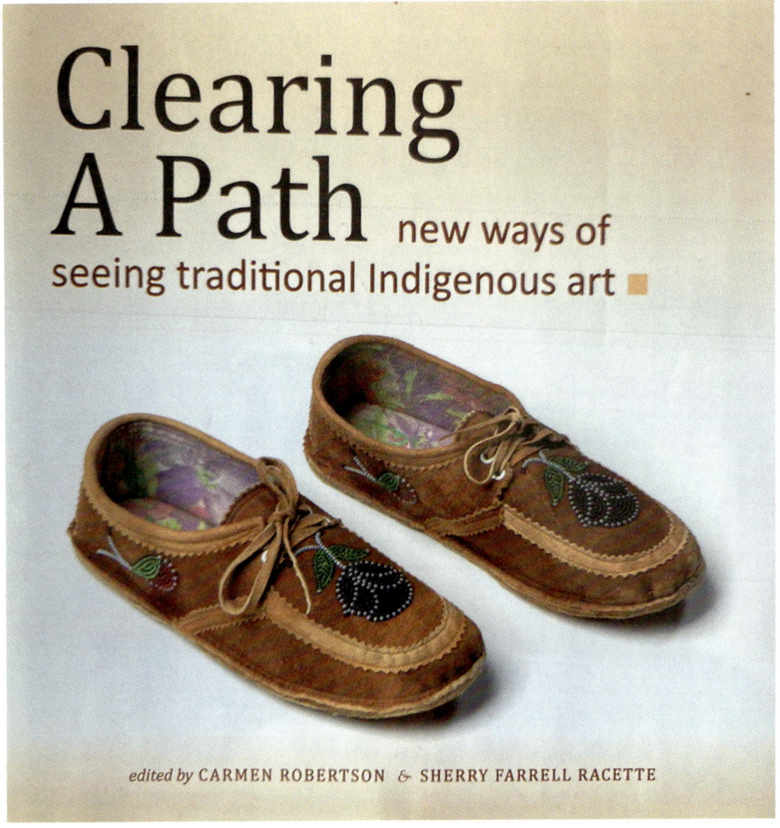

FIGURE 0.2. The book cover for *Clearing A Path: new ways of seeing traditional Indigenous art*. Courtesy of University of Regina Press.

During the five or so years after the initial exhibition was held in the art gallery at First Nations University of Canada, this exhibition toured the province and gained momentum. Gallery audiences, unaccustomed to seeing beadwork, began to better understand the agency and energy of beads that share stories of this land, and of all living beings.[2]

In the almost twenty years since *Clearing A Path*, interest in beading has exploded with beaded works included in exhibitions and collected by private and institutional collectors. Countless beaded artworks made by artists on the Flatlands are not featured in this book, yet their ideas and beading remain part of the creative force that inspires us. Dene artist Catherine Blackburn, from English River First Nation in Saskatchewan, for example, routinely pushes beading in fresh directions in gallery spaces and also in the world of fashion. Her unorthodox beadwork and the use of plastic perler beads shown in *New Age Warriors*, mounted at the Mann Gallery in Prince Albert in 2018 and that toured extensively until 2022, repositions wearable beaded garments for a future generation. Other recent group and solo shows in Regina, Saskatoon, Winnipeg, Ottawa, and Montreal extended understandings of her beaded work. In the exhibition essay for the 2020 exhibition *Catherine Blackburn: With these hands from this land*, Saskatchewan-born Cree and Saulteaux arts scholar Jas M. Morgan contends, "We are living a future we were never supposed to realize, birthing new possibilities for Indigenous joy and freedom on the Plains, with the help of our material cultures, technologies and objects that ground us radically in the Indigenous present."[3]

Like Blackburn, Cree artist Carrie Allison, who lives on the east coast but whose family is from Alberta, creates beaded projects that shape new directions in galleries. Allison explains, "I bead to connect, to spend time with, and share space with my Ancestors, family, community, and myself."[4] In 2018, she created *Heart River,* one of three rivers she has beaded. Using Google Maps as a guide, her eleven-metre-long piece, four strands of glass beads wide, follows the undulating path of a northern Alberta river and was mounted onto a gallery wall at the Owen's Gallery to honour her family's territory. The following year, Allison beaded *Red River,* which was mounted at Urban Shaman Gallery to coincide with Ziigimineshin. More than geographic locators, the importance of water, territory, and the flow of the river, in tune with the heartbeat of Mother Nature, is conjured by this meandering collection of beads.

SEWING TOGETHER STORIES

This book fits within a larger art movement of Indigenous beading across North America and beyond, evidence of which can be found in art gallery exhibitions. The incredible beaders from the Flatlands who create regalia, clothing, beaded moccasins, cradleboards, COVID-19 masks, and gallery works have shifted broader understandings of beadwork practices and meanings. Just looking at the earring collections on Instagram is overwhelming. Beading practices of all shapes and sizes are flourishing as beaders take their places alongside other Indigenous artists. The contributors to this collection of conversations and essays have also contributed to the growing interest in beading through their curatorial and artistic efforts.

Most importantly, Métis curators Sherry Farrell Racette, Cathy Mattes, along with Anishinaabe-kwe curator Michelle Lavallee, mounted a "big ass" beading exhibition, *Radical Stitch,* at the MacKenzie Art Gallery (MAG) in Regina, Saskatchewan, from April to September 2022, that has helped introduce beadwork to new audiences—the exhibition will tour across parts of North America, including the National Gallery of Canada, through 2024. Showcasing the work of about fifty artists from all parts of Turtle Island who were selected to reflect current and future directions of some of the most impressive beading practices in Canada and the United States, the exhibition includes a wide range of works described as "from the customary to the contemporary."[5] Several artists included in this collection are featured in the exhibition, along with the work of several other prairie beaders such as Marcia Chickeness, Catherine Blackburn, and Kristen Auger in addition to artists featured in this book who include Ruth Cuthand, Marcia Friesen, Audie Murray, Judy Anderson, and Katherine Boyer.

A recent exhibition, co-curated by Sherry Farrell Racette and Cathy Mattes, speaks to the cultural significance of beading as part of the cultural history of the Métis. *Kwaata-nihtaawakihk: A Hard Birth* at the Winnipeg Art Gallery (2022), for example, commemorated the 150-year anniversary of the founding of Manitoba from a Métis perspective and included a wide range of beading by several artists. The large-scale beadwork frame by Métis artist Jennine Krauchi that helps define an iconic 1870 photograph that depicts Métis leader Louis Riel and members of his provisional government is central to the exhibition. Considering this exhibition, Michif curator Cathy Mattes states, "For me personally, the key theme . . . is recognizing the importance of kinship ties, and how continuance and continuum is present in ancestral and contemporary art."[6]

Beading also played a key role in the global Indigenous art blockbuster exhibition *Abadakone/Continuous Fire/Feu continuel* at the National Gallery of Canada in 2019, with works by Ruth Cuthand, Dene artist Catherine Blackburn, and Dayna Danger included. Other notable recent exhibitions include *Beads, they're sewn so tight, Their Breath in Beads, Beading Now!, mazinigwaaso/to bead something—Barry Ace's Bandolier Bags as Cultural Conduit, Endurance . . . Patience, Wâhkôhtowin: Carrie Allison*, and *Catherine Blackburn: New Age Warrior*, just to name a few.[7] With the pandemic lockdowns came virtual beading circles, YouTube video sharing, Instagram accounts, and even more interest in beading.

One significant transformational event that inspired beaders from across Turtle Island and was internationally positioned outside the conventional gallery system was Christi Belcourt's pivotal *Walking With Our Sisters*.[8] The commemorative art installation was considered as a traditional lodge space rather than a gallery exhibition, complete with traditional protocols overseen by Elder Maria Campbell and Elders from each territory where the project travelled. The project, which toured across Canada from 2012 to 2019, was designed to remember and honour the Missing and Murdered Indigenous Women and Girls from Canada. An outpouring of support and beading led to more than 1,765 moccasin vamps, the uppers or tongues that were intentionally not sewn into moccasins, being donated to the project.

Gallery exhibitions involving beading have been extended in ways that highlight the process of beading, visiting, and making. Such gatherings have made a major impact on the concept of bead talk. A 2022 symposium linked to the exhibition *Beading Together: Radical Stitch*, hosted by the Shushkitew Collective at the MAG, brought together beaders from Montreal to the Prairies at the MacKenzie Art Gallery to further activate the exhibition through making and sharing in the beading process. This event was part of a recent and significant trend in Indigenous-designed gatherings established in 2017 in Toronto by Anishinaabe curator and scholar Lisa Myers to extend the exhibition *Beads, they're sewn so tight* at the Textile Museum of Canada in Toronto. Myers's concept of visiting and beading was further extended and expanded with Ziigimineshin Winnipeg 2020, a pivotal gathering at the Manitoba Museum, organized by Franchesca Hebert-Spence and discussed in Chapter 4.

TALKING ABOUT BEADS

Over the years, we have had plenty of time to talk while visiting and beading. Our visits and talks led us to sharing our conversations captured in this book. In this text, we celebrate beading by focusing directly on a form of visiting between a small group of beaders and people who write about beading who came to know each other through teaching and learning experiences on the Flatlands. First Nations University of Canada (FNUniv) has been a touchstone for many of us over the years, while gatherings and exhibitions provide opportunities to reunite as some of us moved further apart geographically. Beading reminds us that the big skies and the expansive flatlands are never far away.

Bead Talk took shape to celebrate stories—visual stories and shared conversations that come about through the processes of making. Conversations between beaders, curators, and scholars are meant to further activate the processes as collective community and individualized processes shaped through relational ways of knowing. Stories held by the beads in this collection draw from the past, connect to our present realities, and help to inspire future stories.

We all look to the groundbreaking work that nêhiyaw/Scottish artist Ruth Cuthand from Little Pine First Nation in Saskatchewan has done to shift how people in Canada and beyond respond to beadwork in galleries. Her work is foundational to the shifts that have taken place on the Flatlands. Ruth's body of work informs the design of this book project.

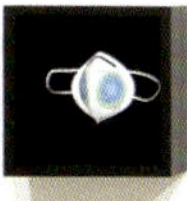

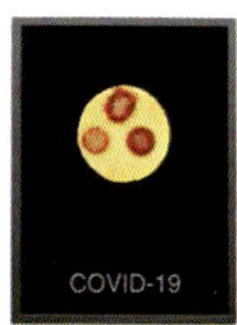

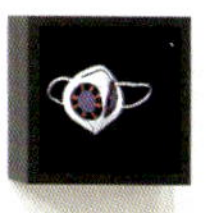

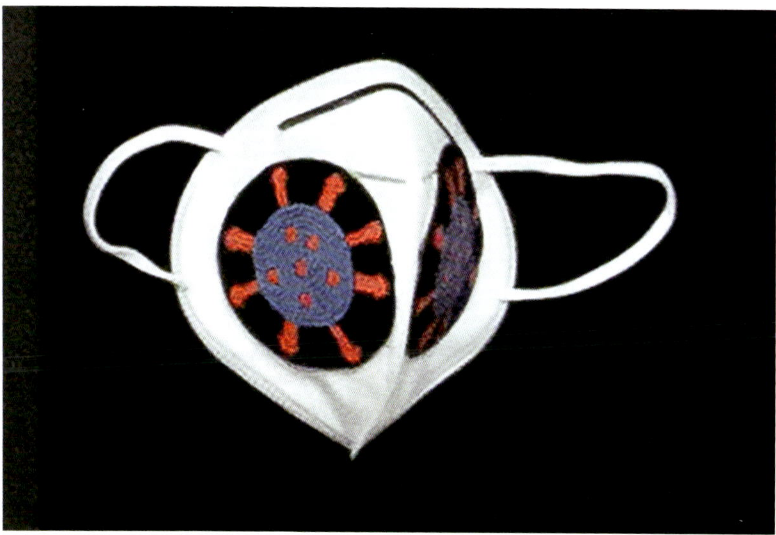

FIGURE 0.3A AND B. Ruth Cuthand's *Surviving: COVID-19* series (partially displayed), from her exhibition *Beads in the blood: Ruth Cuthand, a Survey* (2021), at College of Art Galleries, University of Saskatchewan, Saskatoon, Saskatchewan. Photo courtesy of Carey Shaw. Also see Figure 5.3 and Figure 7.1.

For us, Ruth is *Queen Bead!* Ruth taught at the FNUniv campus in Saskatoon for many years, and our paths intersect in many ways. She leads the way as an artist who expanded the ways Indigenous beading on the Flatlands is understood, in part through her *Trading* series (2009). Cuthand began the *Trading* series in 2008, rendering magnified images of diseases that were introduced to Indigenous populations by Europeans, such as pneumonia, tuberculosis, Spanish flu, and smallpox, in glass beads. This powerful series became part of a three-part project of beaded diseases that included the *Reserving* and *Surviving* series. Cuthand describes the process of "budding," in which a disease replicates and exhausts a host cell, as aligned with the process of colonialism. *Don't Drink, Don't Breathe* extended her commentary related to colonialism to tackle serious housing and infrastructure problems facing First Nations communities in northern Canada situating beads as pathogens. This iconic installation was created in 2016 and since then Cuthand has completed a related series of smaller groupings of drinking vessels using beads and resin to mimic unsafe drinking water titled *Boil Water Advisory* that extends important contemporary conversations about living conditions on reserves.

Cuthand continually uses beads as a means of remembering and enacting survivance. Her noted beadwork series are held in collections at the National Gallery of Canada in Ottawa, the Whitney Museum of American Art in New York City, the Art Gallery of Ontario in Toronto, and the MacKenzie Art Gallery in Regina, to name only a few institutions that stretched their collections in ways that open doors to beads. A teacher, a mentor, and a trailblazer for beading, Ruth is also a friend and art star to everyone involved in this book project.

Coyote constantly plays tricks on nêhiyaw artist Judy Anderson. She thought she was headed toward a painting career in the arts when her friend and mentor Ruth Cuthand beaded the *Trading* series. Coyote whispered melodic words about beading into her ear, and she now finds

FIGURE 0.4. Judy Anderson (left) and Cruz Anderson (right) standing before their *Exploit Robe (Toying Around)* (2012) at the *Beading Now!* exhibition, La Guilde Gallery, Montreal, Quebec (2019).

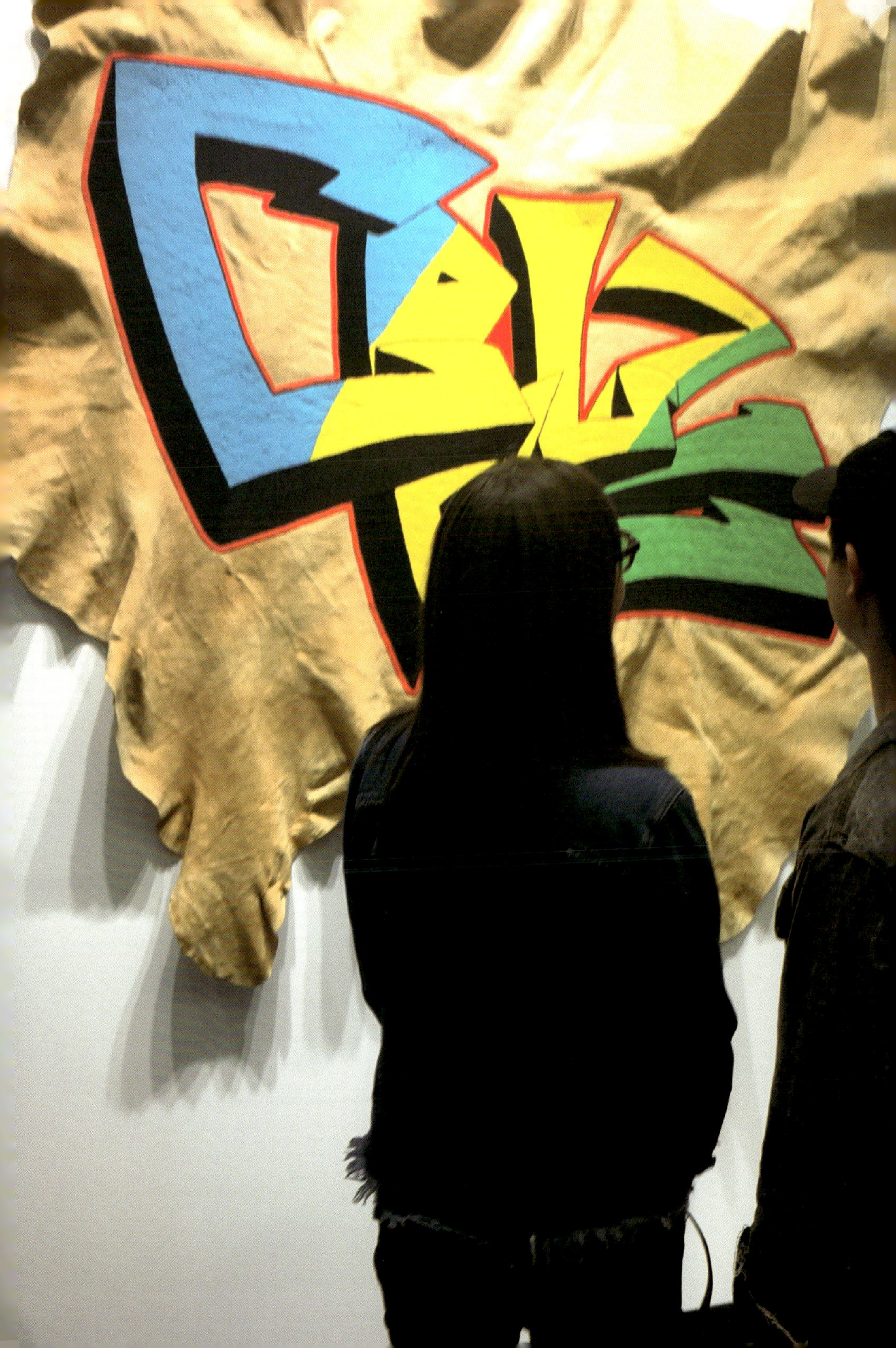

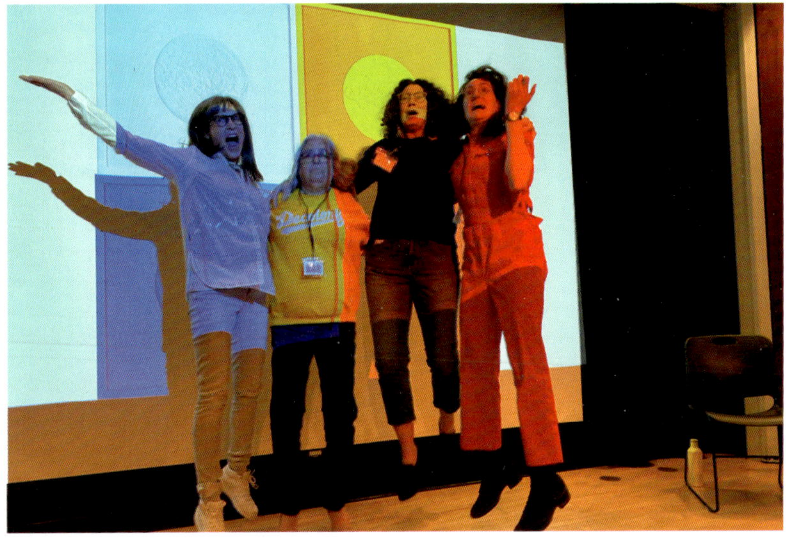

FIGURE 0.5. From left to right: Judy Anderson, Ruth Cuthand, Carmen Robertson, and Katherine Boyer, at "Knowledge Transmission: When the Lines are Broken" (presentation given at the Ziigimineshin beading symposium, Winnipeg, Manitoba, 2020). Photo courtesy of Linda Grussani.

herself honouring friends and loved ones in beadwork. Stories of family, community, and nêhiyaw traditional beliefs infuse her beading process, which often includes collaboration.

Métis/settler artist Katherine Boyer was raised between big prairie skies, hot dusty rural back roads, and the city. In her work, she has been interested in the intersection of land and plant knowledge, constructed environments, and identity. Katherine's practice is as much sculpture as it is beadwork: tumplines, or straps to carry heavy loads, and vests resonate with stories of homelands. Katherine wishes her introduction could be as charming as Carmen and Judy's, but instead it is very serious.

Carmen Robertson is intimidated by the profound beading done by everyone in this project. A Scottish/Lakota scholar from the Qu'Appelle Valley, in Saskatchewan, Carmen is an Indigenous art historian and a curator who struggles to complete a lane-stitch conceptual project about her kinship ties in the valley and at the same time she realizes the importance of being a maker in order to be a better thinker.

In 2016, Carmen met with Ruth, Judy, and Katherine to write an essay on beading on the Flatlands that was published in the *Revue d'Art Canadienne/Canadian Art Review* in 2017.[9] Around this time, Judy left FNUniv and Regina for a faculty position at the University of Calgary, Katherine left for grad school at the University of Manitoba in Winnipeg, and Sherry Farrell Racette came back to the University of Regina. Cathy Mattes left Brandon University for a position at University of Winnipeg as she finished her PhD. In 2018, Carmen headed off to Carleton University in Ottawa. Yet, even with all our moving around we found ways to reconnect in non-prairie places like Halifax, Tulsa, Minneapolis, Ottawa, Montreal, and Quebec City. Along the way, and after scouring Google for what's out there related to beading (there isn't much beyond how-to-books), we got serious about imagining this book project. "Beading Back and Forth," a conversation between Cathy Mattes, Ruth, Judy, Katherine, and Carmen about beading while beading at the University Art Association of Canada conference in Quebec City in 2019 (Figure 0.5), gave focus to our ideas. And our visiting at Ziigimineshin in Winnipeg just before the pandemic hit solidified our vision.

Often our visits (pre-COVID-19) involved trips to beading stores, shoe stores, and outlet malls—mostly in that order. Besides spending way too much money on bling and beads, we found some great additions to our wardrobes. Ruth bought some amazing yellow shoes in Quebec City, and Katherine bought a fabulous red jumpsuit in Minneapolis. When we were invited to come together again as a panel at Ziigimineshin, it made sense to dress in the four-direction colours for our panel discussion, "Knowledge Transmission: When the Lines are Broken." This powerful gathering took place just before the pandemic hit. We were flying high (literally) at a gathering that celebrated so much of what is meaningful to members of the Indigenous beading community (Figure 0.5). It is hard to convey the creative pulse present at the beading tables that week. Ziigimineshin (Figure 0.1) paired artists in conversation and practice and reflects the interconnected ways that theory and practice are interwoven as an extension of kinship and visiting to strengthen future directions related to beading through art. Together these beaded conversations help us understand that beading and beadwork go beyond simply beautiful objects.

At its heart, this is a book about sharing and visiting—bead talk means bead love. Métis scholar and artist Dylan Miner relates how Anishinaabe Elders shared with him that contemporary life leaves "precious little time to visit."[10] These words carry real weight for each of us involved in this project. Finding time to visit became especially difficult during the pandemic. Still, visiting is a practice we all hold dear. Visiting was a method for the creation of this book and holds the key to our efforts. Yet, we quickly realized how difficult it is to put visiting into practice in book form and tried to imagine how to replicate such processes on a page. We view this book as an opportunity to visit with one another while savouring and sharing ideas, stories, and especially works of art. The foreword is by Metis scholar Brenda Macdougall from the Prairies; she writes about how traditional Métis kinship systems are lived and expressed through social and material relationships as well as political action. She sets the stage for our own active processes of belonging on the Flatlands. She is the Chair of Metis Research at University of Ottawa, whose book *One of the Family: Metis Culture in Nineteenth-Century Northwestern Saskatchewan* documents connections and relationships.

We include a number of conversations between artists and curators to offer insights into processes around beading. This book begins with a series of conversations and visual images and ends with essays. Our aim was to create intergenerational visits that demonstrate experiential practices of teaching and learning, which are at the heart of beading processes. The conversations were mostly held online using Zoom, a digital platform, and recorded to capture an audio transcript, which we had to edit because when Zoom hears *beads*, it records it as *beats*. Still, we like the link to Mother Earth.

Ruth Cuthand and Marcy Friesen engaged in a wide-ranging conversation about beading and mentoring. Marcy benefited from having Ruth as a mentor, first formally through the Canadian Artists Representation (CARFAC) mentorship program in Saskatchewan and afterwards as they continued to share and work through ideas. Talking about process, materials, and how Marcy drove from her farm to her photography studio with her face covered in beads, Ruth and Marcy also share how mental health has been a focus of their arts practices.

Carmen Robertson and Swampy Cree curator Felicia Gay met to discuss Felicia's experience of working with Ruth, someone she has a long and important relationship with, when curating *Beads in the blood: Ruth Cuthand, a Survey*, the 2021 exhibition held at the Kenderdine Art Gallery at University of Saskatchewan in Saskatoon, Saskatchewan (Figure 0.3). Sadly, few people were able to visit this amazing exhibition because of the COVID-19 lockdown, so we are grateful that Felicia agreed to share aspects of her curatorial process of working with Ruth, whom she has known for years, to realize this important solo beading show.

Judy Anderson and Audie Murray first met in 2019 when Audie was a finalist for the Salt Spring National Art Prize. After a series of conversations, Audie decided to work on a master's of fine arts degree at the University of Calgary with Judy as her supervisor. They shared a set of open-ended questions that led to a wide-ranging conversation about how and why they bead.

Katherine Boyer and Dayna Danger have used this opportunity to not only lay bare the project planning process, but to explore questions around gender fluidity and Two-Spirit identity in and through beading. Readers will follow the development of a beaded vest in their parallel conversations about design creation, colour choices, and regenerating queer and Two-Spirit knowledge.

Anishinaabe-kwe curator and PhD student Franchesca Hebert-Spence and Carmen Robertson revisited the visiting process that took place at Ziigimineshin. The gathering, which included nearly all the contributors to this book, provided a meaningful occasion to celebrate all aspects of the beading process. The process that Fran engaged in to pull off such a powerful experience was the subject of their visit.

This book includes a wide range of full-colour reproductions of beadwork with details and photographs of process. The images are more than simple illustrations of work and process, however. The beaded works reproduced in the book serve as part of the visual storytelling process enacted by the beads. The beaded works hold stories about the past, present, and future, expressing and sharing ideas that are not always easily communicated in text.

In addition to the series of visual images and reproduced oral conversations, we include essays to further situate the works of art included in this book. Michif curator and scholar Cathy Mattes and the Beading Babes from Brandon University (BU) share their unique relationship of beading and visiting in "'Until We Bead Again': The BU Beading Babes and Embodying Lateral Love and Generous Reciprocity." Their essay offers a snapshot of the supportive circle created by coming together to bead and was written with the help of Fran Hebert-Spence, Debbie Huntinghawk, Albyn Carias, Christine Tokohopie, Justine Hutcheson, Jenna Brisson, Kevin McKenzie, Barb Blind, Eleanor Daniel, Kimmi Charlton, and Jessie Jannuska. "I consider the quotes as beadwork stitches that hold the body of writing together," says Mattes about the sharing of ideas included in this essay.[11] Métis artist, scholar, and curator Sherry Farrell Racette's essay, "If the Needles Don't Break and the Thread Doesn't Tangle: Beading Utopia," situates beading as utopias. Bringing into conversation the beading of many artists, including a wall pocket by Saskatchewan Métis artist Rosalie LaPlante Laroque (1843–1910) with Katherine Boyer's beaded vests, she situates beading as living objects. Carmen Robertson's essay, "Visiting Kin: Indigenous Flatland Beading Aesthetics," posits beading as a practice understood beyond the ways that art institutions present beading. Rather than seeing static objects, Robertson observes beads as story keepers as she engages with works by each of the artists featured in this book, drawing on ideas advanced by Farrell Racette. Understanding beads as kin shifts understanding away from considering beads as decorative objects and invites viewers to appreciate not just the finished product but also the amazing process involved in making beadwork.

Together, the many images, conversations, and essays are meant to extend understandings of visiting and sharing beyond our own beading circle, inviting readers to visit with the stories included in this book. We hope that the processes of beading and understandings of beads as beings, rather than as things, will help to reshape how beads are perceived and viewed in galleries. Sherry Farrell Racette reminds us there is no one way to bead: "Some use two needles, others only one. Some double the thread, others don't. Some start in the middle of each motif and work outward, while others bead the outline of the shape and fill it in.... Most of us follow the way we were taught, with a few personal modifications, and that way the styles and the techniques of generations of bead-workers pass from one pair of hands to another."[12] We all enter the beading circle with different skills and gifts. Yet whether we sit around an actual table or connect via a virtual beading circle, stories and laughter connect us all to generations of artists who came before and to generations that will follow us.

NOTES

1 For examples of problematic representations of Indigenous Peoples in Canadian culture, sometimes referred to as the "Imaginary Indian," see Daniel Francis, *The Imaginary Indian: The Image of the Indian in Canadian Culture* (Vancouver: UBC Press, 1992); Mark C. Anderson and Carmen Robertson, *Seeing Red: Natives in Canadian Newspapers* (Winnipeg: University of Manitoba Press, 2010).

2 Carmen Robertson and Sherry Farrell Racette, eds., *Clearing A Path: new ways of seeing traditional Indigenous art* (Regina: Canadian Plains Research Center, 2009).

3 Jas M. Morgan [Lindsay Nixon], "If You Don't Handle Me at My Best, You Don't Deserve Me at My Worst," in *Catherine Blackburn: with these hands, from this land*, 7 February–18 April 2020, Kenderdine Art Gallery, University of Saskatchewan, https://kagcag.usask.ca/exhibitions/2020/catherine-blackburn_with-these-hands,-from-this-land.php.

4 Carrie Allison, http://www.carrie-allison.com.

5 *Radical Stitch,* exhibition description, MacKenzie Art Gallery, 2022, https://mackenzie.art/exhibition/radical-stitch/.

6 Cathy Mattes, *Kwaata-Nihtaawakihk: A Hard Birth*, interview, Winnipeg Art Gallery, 2 May 2022, https://www.wag.ca/art/stories/kwaata-nihtaawakihk-a-hard-birth/.

7 Lisa Myers, *Beads, they're sewn so tight*, Textile Museum, Toronto (touring), 2018; Jean Marshall, *Their Breath in Beads*, Thunder Bay Art Gallery, 2019; Karine

Gaucher, *Beading Now!*, La Guilde Gallery, Montreal, 2019; Lori Beavis, *mazinig-waaso/to bead something—Barry Ace's Bandolier Bags,* Concordia University Gallery, Montreal, 2019; Daina Warren, *Endurance . . . Patience,* Urban Shaman Gallery, Winnipeg, February 2020; Emily Falvey, *Wâhkôhtowin: Carrie Allison*, Owen's Gallery, Mount Allison (touring) 2019; Jesse Campbell, *Catherine Blackburn: New Age Warrior* (touring), 2018; *Nico Williams: Chi miigwech,* Never Apart Gallery, Montreal, 2021; Sophie Lavoie, *Cassandra Cochrane: Nindinawemaaganag: My Relations,* Muse Gallery, Kenora, 2020.

8 For discussion of their hosting of *Walking With Our Sisters (WWOS),* see, Mattes et al., "Until We Bead Again," this volume, 113; also see, Farrell Racette, "If the Needles Don't Break," this volume, 152.

9 Carmen Robertson, "Land and Beaded Identity: Shaping Art Histories of Indigenous Women of the Flatland," *Revue d'art canadienne/Canadian Art Review* 432, no. 2 (Fall 2017): 13–29.

10 Dylan A. T. Miner, "Mawadisidiwag Miinwaa Wiidanokiindiwag//They visit and work together," in *Makers/Crafters/Educators*, eds. Elizabeth Garber, Lisa Hochtritt, Manisha Sharma (New York: Routledge, 2018), 131.

11 Cathy Mattes, email correspondence with Carmen Robertson, 14 October 2022.

12 Sherry Farrell Racette, "Historical Overview," in *Wapikwaniy: A Beginner's Guide to Metis Floral Beadwork,* eds. Gregory Scofield and Amy Briley (Saskatoon: Gabriel Dumont Institute, 2011), 5.

PART I:
CONVERSATIONS

1.

MENTORING AND BEADING

RUTH CUTHAND AND MARCY FRIESEN

Ruth Cuthand and Marcy Friesen talked via Zoom on 20 October 2021 about their beading practices, their mentoring relationship, and the significance of mental health issues in relation to their beading practices. The following is an edited transcript of their conversation.

RUTH CUTHAND: Marcy and I have known each other for a while now. I was a mentor to Marcy Friesen through CARFAC [Canadian Artists Representation] on a mentorship program and I think that was 2019, right, Marcy?

MARCY FRIESEN: Yes, that's right.

RC: I met Marcy through a jury at the Saskatchewan Craft Council in Saskatoon. I'd been looking for somebody to mentor, and when I met Marcy, I was really impressed because I did a critique of her work and she actually listened, and she didn't get cranky, and she didn't pout, so I thought this woman has a lot of knowledge, I could work with her and then see what would happen. I asked her if I could be her mentor and she said yes and CARFAC said yes, and we started on our mentorship.

MF: Ruth is my mentor. As an artist I knew how important it was to be judged by professional artists. I really wanted to get into the Saskatchewan Craft Council, I wanted to be a juried member, which means having a professional designation given to artists creating exceptional hand-made contemporary and traditional works. In order to get this designation, I would need to first have my work reviewed and approved by a jury. When I got there, they were pretty excited and told me that Ruth Cuthand was going to be one of the people jurying my work! At that time, I didn't know anything about the art world at all, and I remember I was so nervous having people look at my work, having someone look at my work and tell me different things about it makes me nervous. Up until I met Ruth, I had never had anybody ever give me constructive criticism before about my art, and I think I was really craving that.

Previous to Ruth looking at my work, it was all my family members and people purchasing from my business, and everyone loved my work. I wanted to grow, I wanted to do more, I wanted to do so much more, and so when Ruth was giving me her thoughts and ideas on my beadwork, I remember questioning her on everything. Why didn't you like this, or what could be better about this? Ruth shared her thoughts honestly, she critiqued my work, pushed me and prodded me, and also gave me different ideas.

She asked if she could be my mentor and I could be her mentee! Oh, I agreed fully. That is something that I wanted so bad, and I didn't even realize how bad I wanted it. When I got home that night, I searched up Ruth Cuthand. Who is this woman that didn't like my beadwork? Because everybody liked my beadwork up until then. I googled you, Ruth, and the first thing I read on your website said, "I'm not the Indian you're looking for," and this just blew me away! This is one brave woman, and I really need to get to know her. What is going on in her mind?

Then I researched what she does, and she was beading viruses, and that is just something I've never ever heard of before. For me, I always made things with a really utilitarian value—they had to be super useful, otherwise I struggled making things. And so yeah, getting to know you, Ruth, through our mentorship was amazing.

RC: I remember when I started working with you and you were beading flowers the size of, I don't know, maybe three inches across. I kept pushing you to go bigger and you were really unsure of how to go bigger, and I remember you were frustrated. But one of the things you wanted to work on was a moccasin where the inside was beaded. And you did a flower, of course, and you wanted to know what to do about the background, and so I remember telling you that I used to just mix beads up and use them as a background. Then you got all excited and you're like bead soup! I remember you used bead soup for the background, and it was just like watching every step that you took on your way to become this incredible creative person that you are! I know you still kind of hang on to your business, Trapline Creations,[1] working with furs. I kept trying to push you to stop taking orders and just, you know, make art. I must say, when you finally did, you exploded! All the work you did was incredible.

I know one sort of thing that we both work on through beadwork is mental health related. I do it through brain scans using glow in the dark beads [Figure 1.1].[2] [See also installation image of this work in Chapter 5.] Maybe you can talk about the approach that you take?

MF: Oh sure, I always say I've known what mental health was my whole life, I just didn't know it was called mental health. Just hearing different stories from my own family. Some of my friends and family members suffer with or live with mental health issues.

So for me, the very first project that I made through CARFAC with you, Ruth, was where I did *Soft Soul (Mental Health Moccasin)* [Figure 1.2]. The very first one has a flower, it's got the exploding flower, and I remember telling you I could bead flowers and feathers all day long and you pushed me to be more, you're like, "bead something else."

After that, I made another one called the *Depression Moccasin* [Figure 1.3] and yeah, they're all made with specific purposes and reasons in mind. On my *Depression Moccasin* you'll be happy to find that there's

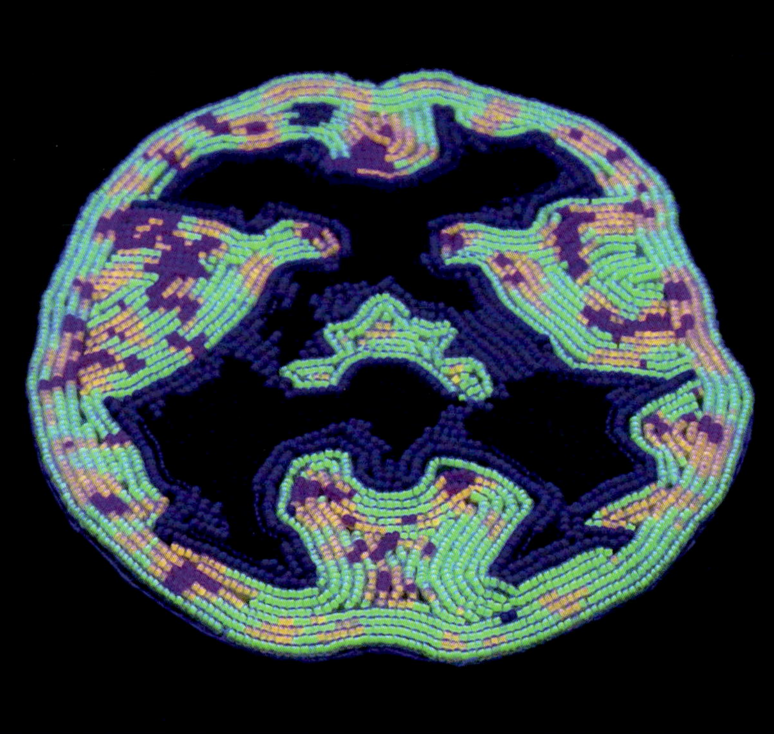

a big tree on the top of it! I didn't do a flower, I wanted to do another exploding flower but I'm like, no I think I'll do a tree. And yeah, those are fully beaded! I'm pulling from stories from my past. I also did one called *Grannies Soup*, and that has a family story that goes along with it. Yes, that story comes from her through my mom, about her mom.

Yeah, that's how it's been for me. I've done a few other things as well for mental health. I guess one of the first ones I had in an exhibition. Ruth, you're the one that got me into that exhibition during our mentorship and that was Montreal's Contemporary Native Art Biennial or BACA and the piece was called *Muskrat Tears* [Figure 1.4].

And so, *Muskrat Tears*, I guess, was my very first completed piece that went into an exhibition on mental health and I was able to make it because of a micro grant from the Saskatchewan Arts Board. For BACA in 2020, I included this statement with the art:

> Muskrat Tears
>
> Depression
>
> Little muskrat is swimming in a puddle of its own tears. The silent crying continues as the puddle begins to overflow and the tears hit the floor.
>
> Little muskrat is brave as he slowly swims ever moving forward. Too tired to look back, too tired to hop out. Too tired.
>
> Little muskrat perseveres with a strength not his own.

Ruth, I remember, I think I took it to you, and I showed you and I didn't get a reaction that I thought I might! I thought you would really love it and I don't think you did. But I got home, and I put it on the

FIGURE 1.1. Ruth Cuthand, *PTSD* (2020), glass beads, thread, backing, 5 x 5 x 10 cm. College Art Galleries, University of Saskatchewan, Saskatoon. Photo courtesy of Carey Shaw.

floor, and I showed my girls. I'm like, this is it, what do you think? Even from them, they kind of hemmed and hawed, and I'm like, okay, I'm not done this yet. So, I strung beads and strung beads and strung beads. And then, it was done! You know, that's what I find with a lot of pieces right now. I'll think they're done but they're not. There's always something more a person can add to make them better.

RC: That's true. I remember you used not only beads but studs! You know, you have like a moccasin, and it's beaded and then you look inside and there are studs sticking up! You know that obviously you can't put your foot in there, you know, you'd cut it all up! Can you talk about the use of those studs in this project?

MF: Oh, for sure! The very first time I started using studs was when I made this beautiful beaver fur cushion. And it kind of goes back to my first time visiting an art gallery, and leaving, I kind of laughed and I thought art is so useless. And then I thought I really want to do it. I want to make art so bad, and I want to know what's going on in Ruth's mind when she's making things. So, when I was making this cushion, I thought, how can I make a cushion unusable. And it came to my mind. I will put studs on it. The first thing you want to do when you see a cushion or a moccasin is, you know, feel the comfort of it, but I wanted to make it uncomfortable. I wanted to make it so that maybe it makes people uncomfortable seeing things like that. Well, I wanted viewers to ask what is going on in her mind that she needed to put spikes in that? Spikes take it to the next level for me. And make it not comfortable.

I guess, I kind of, my whole life, I've never wanted to feel uncomfortable outwardly, but inwardly I was always uncomfortable. I have talked about being uncomfortable in my brown skin. For years I was, and probably it was not till I was in my thirties when all of a sudden, I embraced myself, I embraced my brownness. But it's true that this is

FIGURE 1.2. Marcy Friesen, *Mental Health Moccasin* (2020), glass beads, beaver fur, mirror, pellon, thread, 25.4 x 12.7 x 6.35 cm. Photo courtesy of Fazakas Gallery, Vancouver, British Columbia.

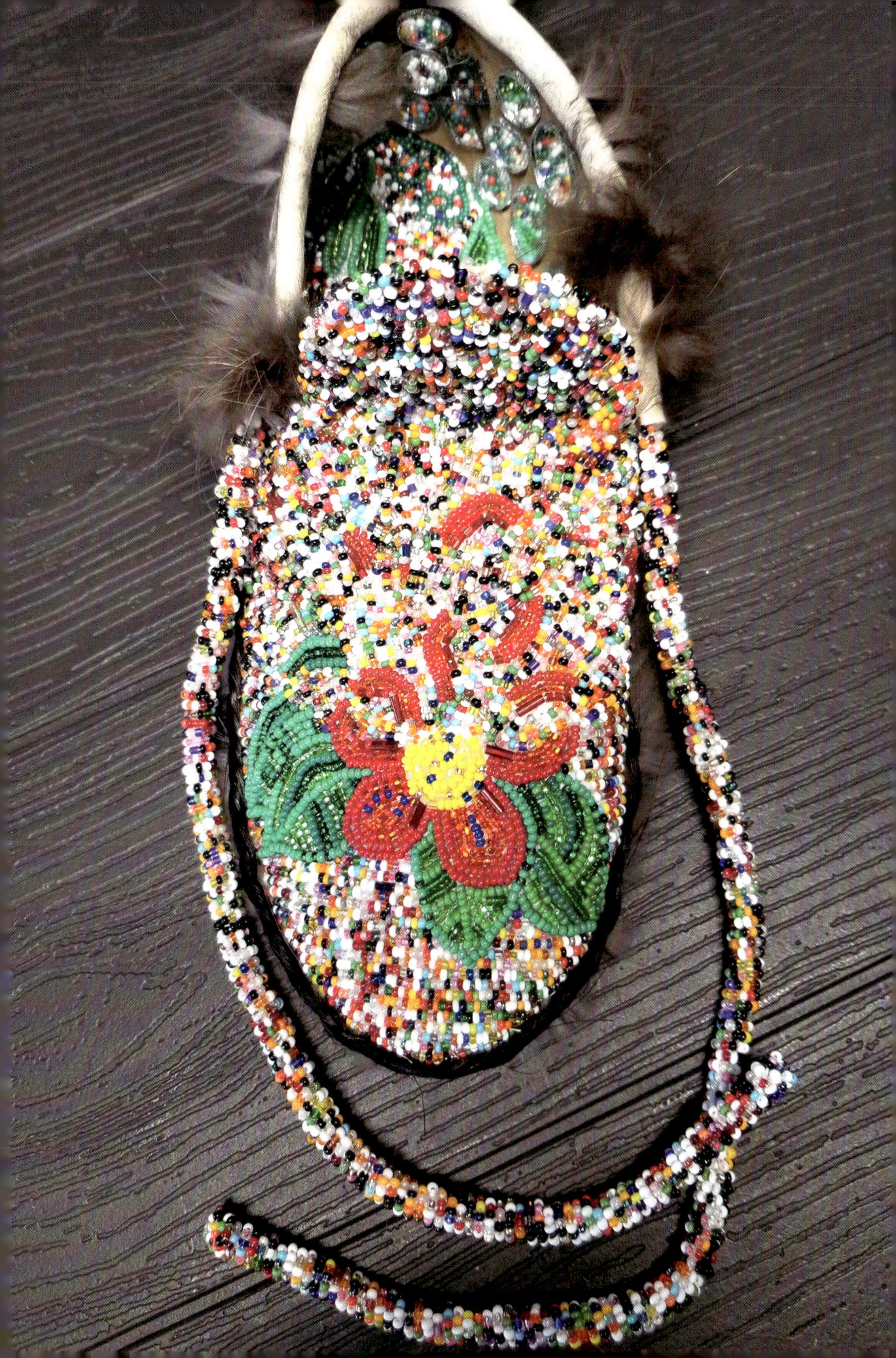

all part of the process of pulling stories from the past. Yeah, I love using spikes for that purpose.

RC: When I look at that work, I especially think about residential schools and the process of looking for bodies and all that kind of thing. It seems to me that those spikes are like the Indigenous and Canadian experience. Our relationship is uncomfortable. We have the fur trade and all that wonderful stuff but, at the same time, our relationship is spiky, and so that's what I get out of that work. It's so beautiful.

MF: Oh, thank you, Ruth! I can see that as well. So yeah, and a part of it, for me, is I'm enjoying making art because it's making things that people don't expect of me as an Indigenous woman. I want to make pieces that people have never seen before. Ruth, you've paved the way for so many Indigenous women in the art world and out of the art world. You supported me and so many more women, your nudging me, and supporting me, and giving me permission to make art. It's been huge.

RC: I remember when I first started beading, I was trying to think of a way to move beading into contemporary Indigenous art. When I finally did those viruses, I made a breakthrough. What I loved about them was on the microscopic level they're so abstract. Using beads makes them so gorgeous. But then, at the same time, they're diseases that caused so many deaths and . . . when I got on to them, I thought, you know, this is really great work, which I usually don't say about my work, but I thought, you know, there's something here [Figure 1.5].

So I think I'm going to keep working with it and then I—you know I don't want to sound like I have a big head—but it really did lead to this massive revival of beading and beading in a different way for so many women.

Everybody had new ideas of what they were going to do with beads, and I just love watching the growth of contemporary beadwork. And what I really love is all the beading sites on social media where women are showing what they're making. Man, those earrings are getting so big, it's

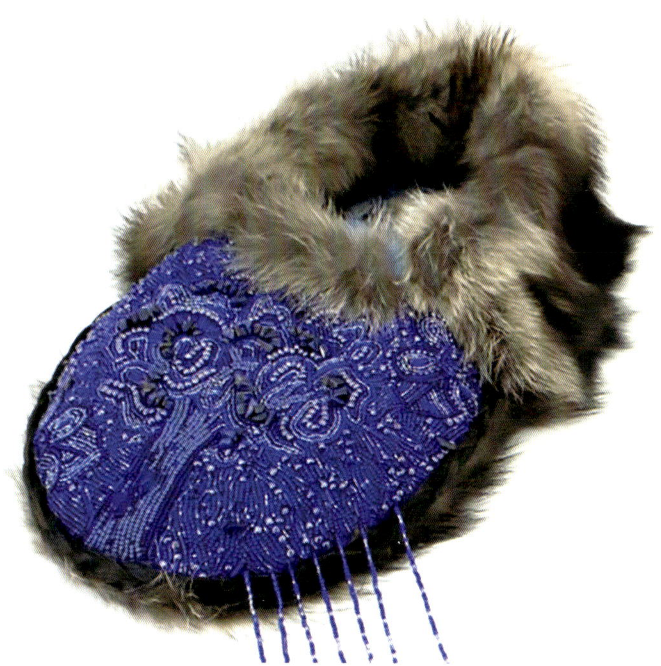

FIGURE 1.3. Marcy Friesen, *Cleansing Tears (Depression Moccasin)* (2020), glass beads, fisher fur, leather, thread, dental floss, horsehair, pellon, 40.6 x 22.9 x 7.6 cm. Photo courtesy of Fazakas Gallery, Vancouver, British Columbia.

like two-pound earrings! Looking at them, I'm like, I couldn't wear those. It would hurt so much! But yeah, I'm just blown away by what's happening across Canada and the United States.

MF: It's amazing to see, isn't it. It is inspiring and it's quite something, and yeah, I know, had I not met you and worked with you, I wouldn't be making art like I currently am, there was a really good chance that I wouldn't be because I might not have gotten the support that I needed to do it and the nudge and the permission. The right people were placed in my life at the right times.

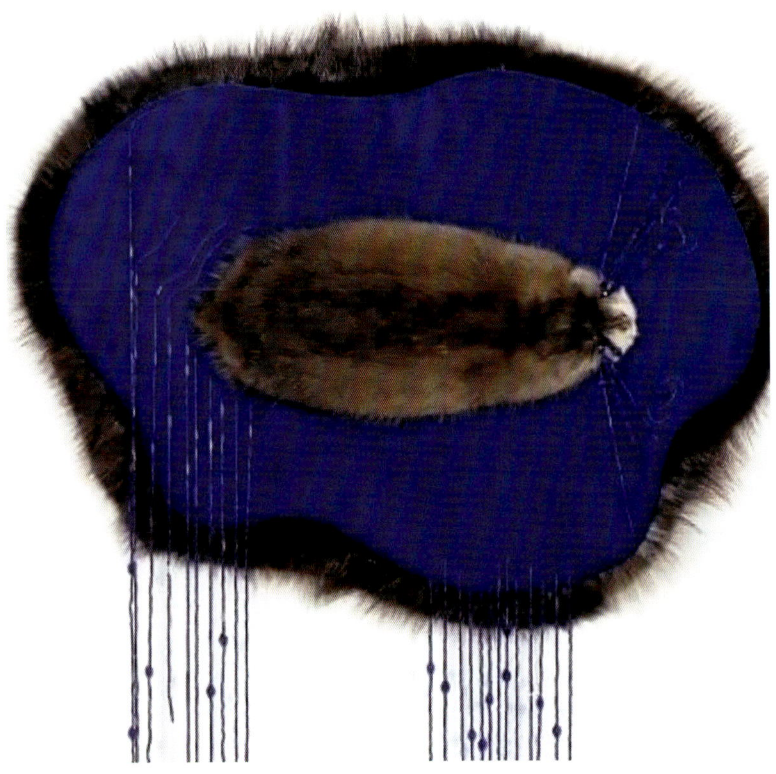

FIGURE 1.4. Marcy Friesen, *Muskrat Tears* (2020), beaver pelt, muskrat pelt, thread, glass beads, plastic beads, velveteen, felt, wooden strip, 63.5 x 183 cm. Photo courtesy of Michael Patten.

RC: I think it's hard for women to make art, especially Indigenous women, because we have so much community that really depends on us, and we have so many familial relationships to take care of that when we want to carve out time to make art, which, well let's face it, people see it as useless. You really need a lot of support to be able to just take time and do what you want to do, which is really hard for Indigenous women to carve that out, but you have, and you have done so much so quickly. Watching your growth from when I first met you to where you are today is truly amazing! I was doing a beading workshop at the Remai Modern and the guides were telling me: "holy smoke that Marcy Friesen, she's just zooming ahead!"

MF: Well, a lot of that does have to do with you, Ruth, because I'm trying my hardest to use these beads and supplies that I have in different ways. In ways that have never been done before, never been seen before. And it's so fun and it's so freeing. Quite honestly, I think part of it, too, for me, is like I still go back to my Trapline Creations business. I'm still doing that, because I need the income, you know. And I do still enjoy making full fur hats and full fur gauntlets. But sometimes when I'm making the hats and the gauntlets, I think I should be creating art. I ask, what am I doing? I should be creating art but it's like at the same time, I have bills. I'm starting out, I'm new, and I'm trying to make my way through this art world. Yeah, I'm getting it all figured out and doing what I need to do still to get by every day.

RC: Well, you know the great thing about working with you is that your mind knows how to do it right so and you're very competent at it, so it actually frees up the creative part of your brain where that will just start thinking about the next thing, the next project, you know, and so I think it's great that you're still working on your furs—and if anybody ever wants a pair of beautiful skunk gauntlets that's the woman to get them from. That skunk fur is so beautiful!

MF: Yeah, it's just gorgeous fur, and you know I find if I have something in my workshop here that sits too long it all of a sudden becomes a piece of art! I stare at it long enough and I'm in here thinking and thinking and thinking and then all of a sudden, yeah! Or, if something doesn't sell, it's like, Oh, I know what I'm going to do to it now. I make something.

RC: I like that. Like the mitten that's on the cover of the Saskatchewan Arts Board annual report. Do you want to talk about that a little bit?

MF: Oh sure, that gauntlet stemmed from trying to make things that are no longer fully utilitarian. I named it *Flourish*, it was actually when COVID first hit and each of the three flowers beaded on it represent my kids who were all of a sudden at home, and I thought, how can I make a gauntlet that is . . . I'm going to use the word *useless*. I know, art isn't useless, there's such a purpose to it, but I thought, how can I make a pair of gauntlets useless? I thought, well for starters, I'll make only one, and then I thought I'm going to bead the palm instead of the back of it. That's where that one came from. I've made a few more since then, mostly child-sized ones, but the idea for that was stemming from you, Ruth, pushing me to bead something bigger. So, I beaded a full palm!

You don't know how often I think about you when I'm in my workshop here, making art. And I know I still have it in my mind to bead something bigger, something better, constantly. You're right that when we met, I was beading a flower on a moccasin vamp. That was about the biggest thing I'd ever beaded. Now I think it's my face! My face is the biggest piece that I've beaded, but yeah, bigger things are coming yet.

RC: I really love your beaded faces and your photographs of your beaded faces [see Figure 7.5 and 7.6 in Chapter 7]. Those are so fresh and a whole new way to use beads! I think the first one you did was with tears running down your face, right?

MF: You know what, the very first one, I used bead soup. The very first one was solid bead soup, and then I thought, "Okay, I need to advance that now." So, then I think I might have put tears on all of them. The second one was floral—you know me and flowers. Yes, I think I put flowers on pretty much every single one, other than some for the residential school and for the mental health with tears. I have a different one in mind now that I will be doing next.

RC: I just love the beaded faces, and the furs that you wrapped yourself in or you were wearing a fur hat. I really like the way the photograph is lit

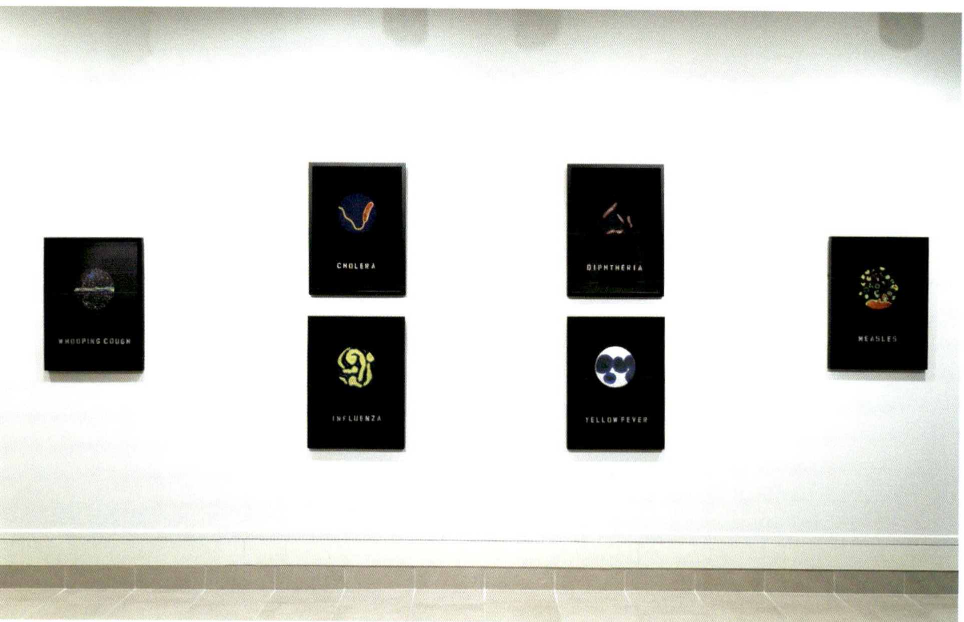

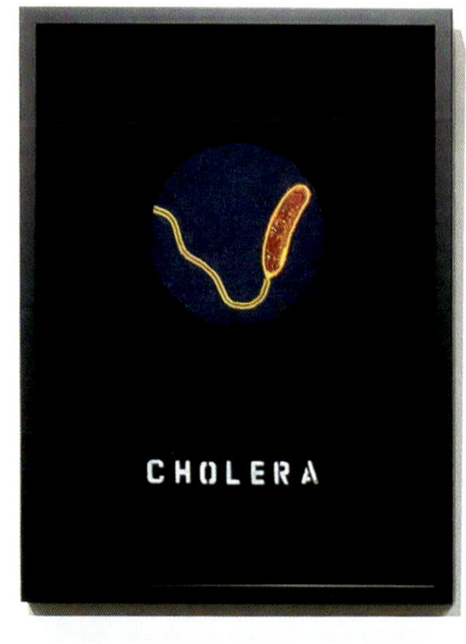

FIGURE 1.5A. Ruth Cuthand (clockwise from left), *Trading: Whooping Cough, Cholera, Diphtheria, Measles, Yellow Fever, Influenza* (2009), beads and acrylic on suede board, 61 x 45.7 cm. College Art Galleries, University of Saskatchewan, Saskatoon. Photo courtesy of Carey Shaw.

FIGURE 1.5B. Ruth Cuthand, close-up of *Cholera* (2009).

so the background is just black and you're just this beaded face emerging. They're fantastic!

MF: Oh, thank you, Ruth! They're really fun to make and a part of it all stems from my past of just wanting to fit in for so long and not wanting to be different. But right now, I'm like, bing bang boom, here I am, and my face is beaded. That's how Indigenous I am [laughter], my face is beaded. I just embrace it. Be who you are and just embrace it.

RC: I think of you driving your car from your farm to your photographer with the beaded face!

MF: I know, and I live on a country road, and one of the first ones I did it felt like everybody was out walking on the road that day. And I'm like, you're kidding! I put my visor down and hoped no one noticed. At first it was, like, all these people are going to think I'm crazy and I can't smile, and I can't talk or laugh. It was kind of unnerving at first. I had to drive through Carrot River and go all the way to the other side of town. It's about a half-hour drive from where I live. But by the time of my fifth and sixth face came around, I didn't care anymore.

RC: When you have your face beaded, can you talk or no?

MF: No, no, you can't talk at all. You have to stay calm, not move your face, and control your breathing too. When I'm driving to the photographer's, the beads are so close to my eyes and right up to my nostrils, and so it's just slow breathing through the nostrils. I have to be pretty controlled, yeah. By the time the photo shoot is done, it's already loosened up in some places. When it starts to come off, it's pretty strong, it'll take a few hours.

RC: That's amazing! I remember you told me that you can actually, like, pull the face off and have it still be together. Now that would be really interesting, to show some of those beaded faces that are empty and maybe caving in. I think that'd be really interesting.

MF: Yeah, I was actually able to pull two of them off, so I do have them here. They're stored for the purpose of framing them in the future to maybe to go along with an exhibition of the photographs. That type of thing. They're so pretty.

Ruth, what are you busy working on now?

RC: Well, my work has taken a really unexpected turn into public art just recently. I've never considered myself a sculptor or had any interest in 3-D, but I was approached by Jen Budney, who was a curator working with the City of Saskatoon to create public art for their Placemaker Project.[3]

Well, it started off as a mural but that got all changed. They want an Indigenous person to work with a person from West Africa, and they wanted us to create some public art for three neighbourhoods in Saskatoon. I met with Suada Jailan, a henna artist from Kenya, by way of Somalia. I actually learned a lot about henna, there's henna from India and from Somalia, where she's from, and they all have very different designs. Anyway, we were trying to think of some commonality, she was showing me her henna designs. They're very, very floral and there's plants leaves and things, and so I said why don't we do flowers! We could use some of your designs and I could use some beadwork designs—floral beadwork. We were working with Henry Lau from the city and he's an architect, and so he got the designs, and we glued them on to try to figure out the composition and planned to have it fabricated. Then COVID started, so he went to a Hutterite colony because all the big manufacturing firms were closed. They actually laser cut aluminum for our sculptures called *Saadat Qalbi/Miyawâtam 1, 2, and 3*, which translates roughly as "they are joyful." It's very interesting, and then they delivered it into my backyard one at a time, and I painted with Suada a little bit. She's so used to painting on little hands, and these were such a big scale, so it ended up that I painted them. There's one at White Buffalo Youth Centre and there's one on Second Avenue, and those are henna design, with two flowers on it. I just finished the one for Broadway Avenue, and it has flowers on it.

Then Henry and I started over the winter talking about continuing to create public art together because he knows materials and he could cut anything with an x-acto knife, making little tiny designs and everything. We submitted to the City for this year, and we actually got another sculpture for the City of Saskatoon and it's on Avenue B and 20th Avenue, where they used to stack the buffalo bones that were being shipped over to England. So, I have buffalo and the cut-outs on the buffalo are in the shape of the skeleton of the buffalo. The buffalo is painted red and then the cut-outs, or the inside of them, are painted white so as you move past the work, bones will kind of pop out. Crossways from the mother is the buffalo calf, and the calf is yellow, and he has little triangular cut-outs and the inside of those are green to sort of talk about renewal and how the buffalo is coming back. In Saskatchewan there are a lot of reserves that are getting their own private buffalo herds, and then they will cull for ceremony and feasts, yeah, back to the way it used to be.

Next year [2022], we [Ruth and Henry] have a public commission submission into Edmonton and one into Toronto. It's totally different work than I've ever done, but it's amazing. They're all about animals and plants, so we'll see what happens. It's been really interesting working with totally different materials. It's amazing when you find somebody who knows so much, and it just opens a whole different part of your creativity.

MF: Oh, I bet it's like, the sky is the limit!

RC: And you don't have to worry about how is this going to work, he'll figure it all out because he knows all about materials. We were talking about working with tamarack wood if we ever get to do an interior.

Henry says, "if you dream it, I can make it," and so we're actually talking about installing giant beads on the side of the building that we would light up, and I think we're going to submit one, I think we found a place that we could submit that one to. If you ever see a really blank government building, let me know and I'll put beads on it!

MF: Okay! And I'll be on the lookout next time in the city to see your sculptures. I actually did see one of your flowers when I was in Saskatoon a while back, and oh, I just knew it was yours. I pointed it out and said, "look, Ruth did that!" I get a real feeling of a sense of pride when I see First Nations art in cities. It's so nice to see.

RC: Oh yeah, I've been thinking about cities and Indigenous people who live in cities, and they need something that they can relate to it. With the flowers sculpture at White Buffalo, it's so great, because it's on a tiered pedestal and every time I go by there are Indigenous men sitting there visiting. The base of it is sloped on one side, facing south, and there's always somebody laying there, you know, in the sun, and they're all just visiting and enjoying themselves. I just love it. It's like they have claimed it and know this is part of us [Indigenous peoples], and that's what I love about public sculpture.

MF: Oh yes, for sure, that's so neat that you can now see that.

RC: I saw the buttons that the Remai Modern commissioned you to make. Are they *Every Child Matters* buttons in beads, and then made in metal, too?

MF: Yeah, they had wanted to do something for National Truth and Reconciliation Day in September, and so they approached me because I have other beaded things and jewellery in their gift shop. They asked me to do up some pins that could be worn on jackets. I have done little orange shirt pins in the past, so I did one up and I thought, "Oh, I think I want to do it a little bit more." I came up with a little bit of a bigger one with the blue background, some of the white background, and they sold out. I will never mass produce something, that's just not my thing.

And I'll never make identical pieces, I just can't for some reason. To make identical things takes away so much from it in my mind. There's no way I will mass produce, and I don't want to make an income off of these pins at all, so it's just all donated. If I'm doing it, I'll donate the proceeds.[4]

RC: Can you think of anything else we need to talk about?

MF: I think we covered so much, I think we've covered everything, Ruth.

NOTES

1 See http://www.marcyfriesen.ca/traplinecreations.html.

2 For images of all six brain scans see https://www.ruthcuthand.ca/brain-scan-series/.

3 See Image 23, https://storymaps.arcgis.com/stories/531ae814f21f4f789d8d79d66853205a.

4 See https://shop.remaimodern.org/products/orange-shirt-enamel-pin.

2.

MÎKISISTAHÊWIN (BEAD MEDICINE)

JUDY ANDERSON AND AUDIE MURRAY

The following is an edited transcript of a conversation between Judy Anderson and Audie Murray that took place in late 2021 via Zoom, moderated by Carmen Robertson.

JUDY ANDERSON: Audie, what brought you to beading, and who taught you?

AUDIE MURRAY: I took Indigenous studies classes at the university and needed to make a cultural object for an assignment. I decided to make moccasins but didn't know how. One student knew how to bead, Brandi Cyr, and she showed a few of us how to do a one-needle stitch. We started with a circle, and I figured it out from there. I left it for a little bit and picked it up again when I went to art school because I was making work about my positionality. Because of that, beads were an instinctual material for me to move toward.

CARMEN ROBERTSON: Audie, do you remember when I had hired you as my research assistant when you were studying at University of Regina? We went to the vault at the Royal Saskatchewan Museum to view collections of beading housed in their permanent collection. I knew we would see amazing beadwork in the Mary Weekes and Nottingham collections particularly because of the research I had been doing for the "Land and Beaded Identity" essay that I later published in 2017. That day we opened boxes and drawers filled with beadwork, and I remember watching your eyes lighting up as we looked closely at this diverse group of work created by mostly Cree, Saulteaux, and Dakota women from the early twentieth century. I have wondered if that visit has helped to shape your own beading practice?

AM: I absolutely remember that because it was one of the first times I was able to see ancestral beadwork up close. Being in the vault and seeing the details of the colours and how the artists were laying down their beads was so important and interesting to me in terms of researching design. My relationship to beadwork at that time was seeing it used in contemporary regalia, and so I had this idea that beadwork was technically perfect. Seeing older beadwork was helpful to me as a beginner beader, because older beadwork is perfect and beautiful in such a different sense.

JA: A series of events led me to realize that I couldn't speak to beadwork in a real way, and I didn't understand the complexities of beadwork. So, around 2006, I audited Cree artist Sheila Orr's Indigenous Art class at the First Nations University [FNUniv]. She taught me the running stitch, which I couldn't do, and then she taught me two-needle, which was life-changing. Two Needle Forever!

Your mentor and artist extraordinaire, Jeffrey Gibson, mentioned to you that he could tell that you were learning as you were making art in your practice. Can you speak to that?

AM: This has been at the forefront of my mind since the conversation happened, and to give some context, I recently had a studio visit with Choctaw-Cherokee artist Jeffrey Gibson. We've been conversing back and forth for a couple of years now. He's been really generous by speaking with me about my practice, and he recently brought up this reality that when I first started sharing my art, it was evident that I was at the beginning of my beadwork practice and that I have been visibly getting more

FIGURE 2.1. Audie Murray, *maskihkîy* (2020), tea bag, glass beads, 5 x 5 x 10 cm. Photo courtesy of Dave Dyment.

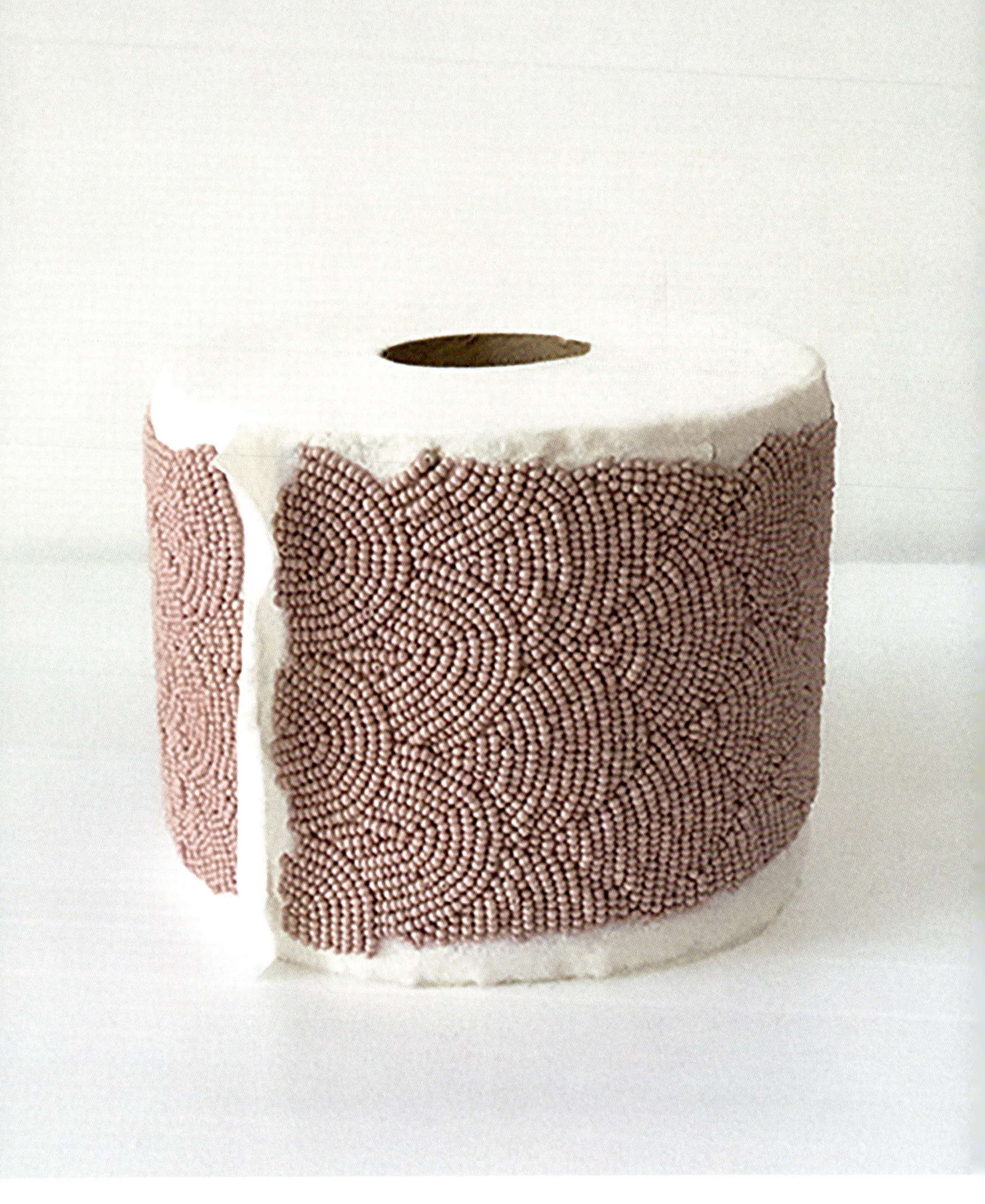

FIGURE 2.2. Audie Murray, *T.P.* (2018), toilet paper, seed beads, 10 x 10 x 10 cm. Private collection. Photo courtesy of Fazakas Gallery, Vancouver, British Columbia.

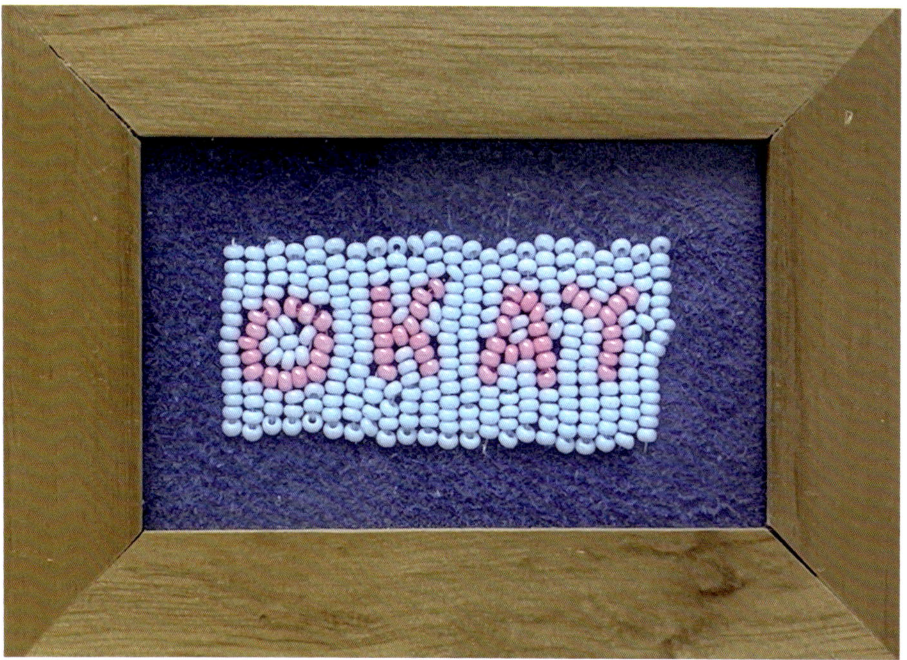

FIGURE 2.3. Katherine Boyer, *Okay* (2012), glass beads, felt backing, 2.5 x 5 cm. Photo courtesy of Judy Anderson.

refined with my technical skills. It might have been an upsetting thing to hear that for some people, but for me, it was just a simple truth.

When I started working with beads, it was so much fun, and I was really drawn to the process. I enjoyed trying to understand what beads represented for me and my relationship with them. As I had continued to put hours into beadwork, of course, I got technically better. As I progress with my beadwork, my relationship with them keeps changing. Something I've been thinking through is at what point does getting too technically skilled with a material render it less interesting to work with? On the flip side, it's really fun to push myself into trying to bead well on inconsistent materials like plastics or rolls of toilet paper.

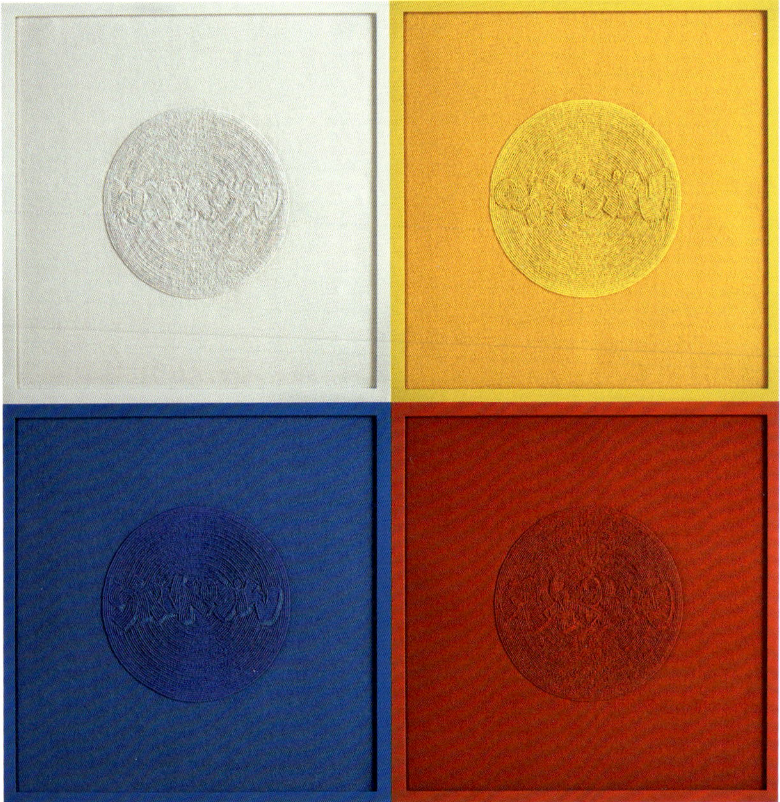

FIGURE 2.4. Judy Anderson in collaboration with Cruz Anderson, *There is life in there (North)*, *There is life in there (East)*, *There is life in there (South)*, *There is life in there (West)* (2018–19), Italian beads on stroud cloth, 43 x 43 cm. Collection of TD Bank. Photo courtesy of Anthony McLean.

JA: I think imperfections give a beadwork personality. Although I love and desire beautifully flat beadwork, wiggles or bulges sometimes make the work stronger because you can see the person in the work.

Katherine Boyer gifted me one of her first beadworks. I love it; it's crooked, it's beautiful, and I know that it was made for me with love [Figure 2.3]. It sits in a specific spot in my office so I can see it at all times. It says "okay" because we used to say "okay" a lot when we worked together. We would have these conversations where we would only say "okay," and we knew exactly what each other was thinking and saying. We also checked in with each other to make sure we were "okay." This piece reminds me of those times.

AM: That reminds me of this time I gave a friend a beaded patch of a rose, and the beads were so packed in there. It wasn't super bumpy, and I was really proud of that, but I gave those beads no space to breathe. I had gifted it to a talented bead worker and artist. I was thinking about that this morning and laughing to myself. So, it's reaffirming to hear you say that you cherish Katherine's early work and its "imperfections."

JA: Can you speak to learning beadwork in university?

AM: It's interesting to reflect on how I learned how to do a culturally important thing in an institutional space. I have memories of trying to bead because my mom had done some beading, and she's been picking it back up these last few years. Back then, I wasn't interested in it, and I also was not interested in wearing beadwork. I wanted to fit in as much as I could with White culture. Wearing anything that was an overt cultural marker felt embarrassing because it wasn't considered cool and would invite weird racist comments. Of course, I do not think that way now, but I didn't come to a place of appreciating culture until I was in university doing my education degree. All of the students were also Indigenous, so it was really helpful to be in that setting. It allowed for the unpacking of uncomfortable internalized racism and then held space for us to start understanding and loving ourselves and our cultures. Beadwork is something that appeared in my life because of those classes.

JA: Audie did a presentation to the students in my Indigenous art class. At one point, she said, "I didn't learn at home. I learned in university." Without skipping a beat, one student said, "Yeah, me too!" The whole room erupted in laughter because that's where everybody in that room learned to bead.

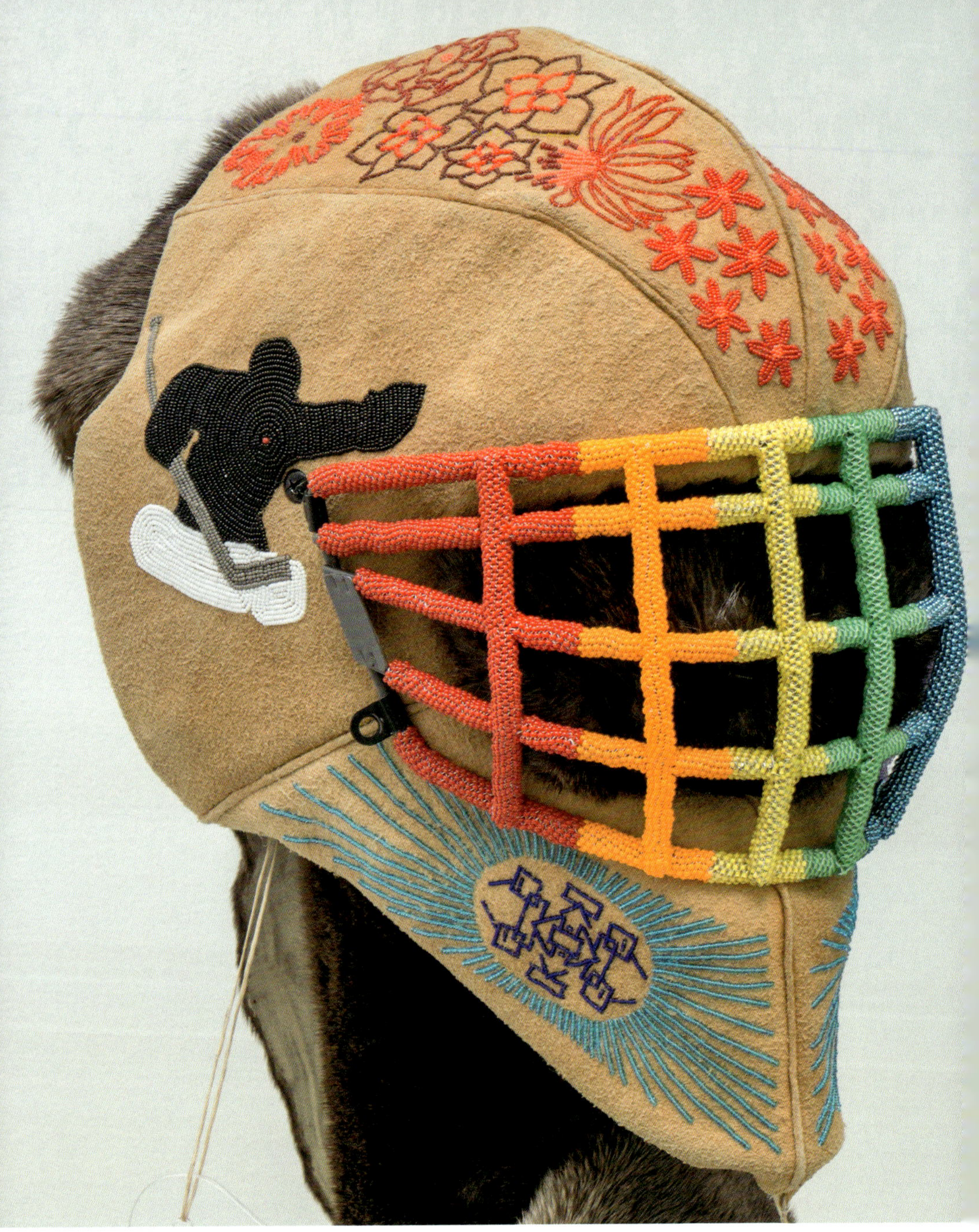

FIGURE 2.5. Judy Anderson, *This one brings me the most pride* (2016), glass beads, moose hide, goalie helmet, acrylic, otter pelt, 45.7 x 30.5 x 38 cm. Photo courtesy of Andrew Barcham.

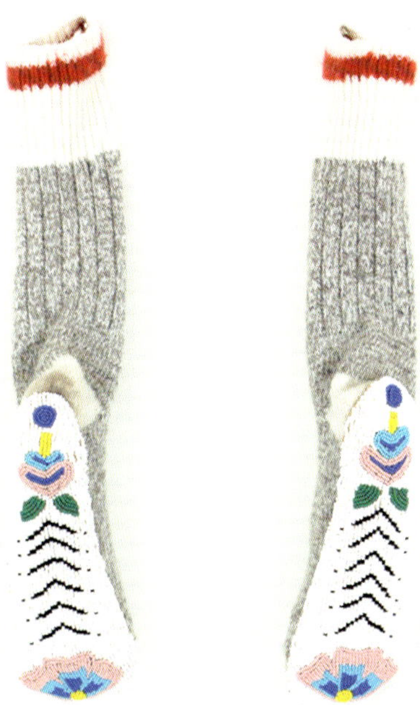

FIGURE 2.6. Audie Murray, *a pair of socks: chi fii* (2018), glass beads, tanned hide, wool socks, 30 x 41 cm. Collection of TD Bank. Photo courtesy of Macaulay & Co. Fine Art.

This was a profound moment because it confirmed the importance of having a space where Indigenous people can learn if they've been separated from their culture.

AM: What is your relationship to beads?

JA: My relationship is . . . I don't know . . . I didn't claim beads, beads claimed me. I didn't plan to bead beyond wanting to do something epic like Ruth, but they snuck in anyway. That was it! They had me. Whenever I am near beads, I have to be with them, touch them, and whenever I'm in a bead store, I can't walk out empty-handed. My relationship with beads is a love relationship.

AM: When I first started picking up beadwork, and then when I revisited beadwork within my art practice, were times in my life when I wasn't necessarily feeling my best. Beadwork was something I could always come back to, and I think it was the repetitive motion and the ability to do it anywhere that was helpful. My relationship with beadwork is that it feels like a supportive friend.

I want to mention that when I started beading, it didn't come with a lot of teachings, and one of the teachings that I often hear, mostly on social media, is that we're not supposed to bead when we're not in a good place or if we're not thinking good thoughts, and I totally break that rule. Beadwork has helped me get through some tough times, and they have been there through some good times too.

JA: I'm going to respond to the teaching about not coming to the beads angry. I'm going to get a lot of haters by saying this, but I think that's a colonial and Christian thought.

We have T-shirts that say "beading is medicine," and people constantly say "beading is medicine." If beading is medicine, we have to let the medicine do the work. You can't do all the work before coming to the medicine, or you may set up a wall between whatever is happening within you that needs the medicine and the actual medicine. If we want the beads to be the medicine, we need to accept that people may come with negative thoughts, feelings, and words.

I have no problems with people swearing around the beads or being angry when they walk in, because when people are too angry, or too sweary, or too whatever around the beads, the beads will let

FIGURE 2.7. Judy Anderson, *And from her parts of me emerged . . .* (2016), size 13 charlotte cut beads, cotton fabric, coyote pelt, rocks, acrylic, handmade paper, 30.5 x 18.75 x 12.7 cm. Copyright: Used by permission of McClelland & Stewart, a division of Penguin Random House Canada Limited; original photo of Maria Campbell by Dan Gordon. Collection of Indigenous Art Center, Indigenous and Northern Affairs Canada. Photo courtesy of Andrew Barcham.

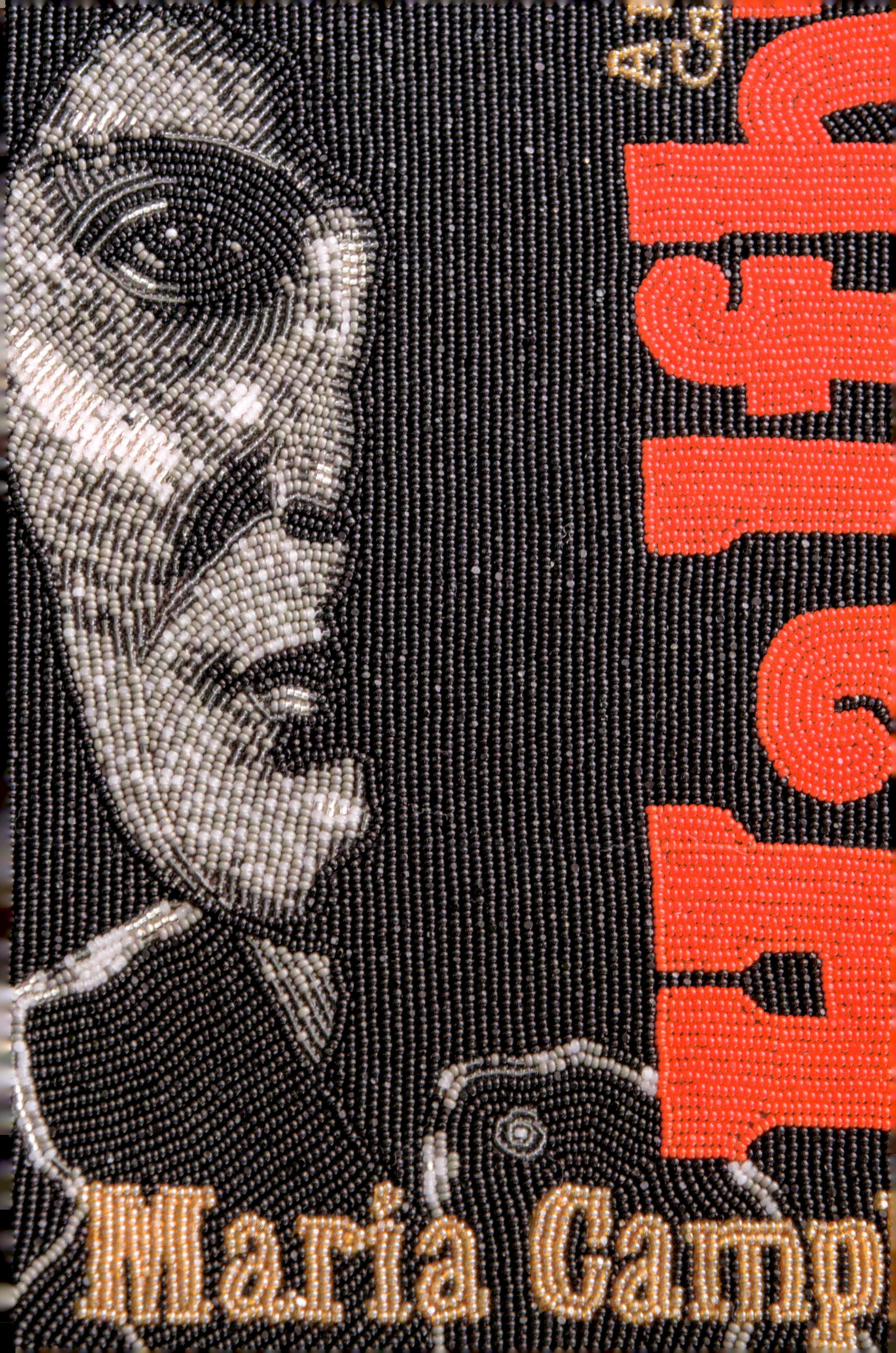
Maria Camp

them know they should walk away. I've been taught this by coming to the beads angry and quickly realizing that the beadwork I intended to do would not happen. The beads told me I needed to go away, be respectful, and come back later. But if I came to the beads with negative feelings and I could bead—that friendship, love, and medicine came through with every stitch. I've also witnessed this happening countless times with students.

That's my teaching.

AM: Thank you for putting those words to those thoughts. I've never heard it laid out in that way, and everything you're saying is true.

CR: I totally agree also, Judy. So many people have said not to pick up the beading until you're in the right mindset for them, or to smudge first so that you know you've really got to come to this from a good place. I like how you turn this around, and I appreciate you saying that the act of beading puts you into that good place! I think the beads put you into a good space because they are our relations and their presence helps us think about the present rather than what has been haunting us over the course of the day. It always makes me feel better, even though I still can't always thread my needle [laughter].

AM: Once you keep developing that relationship with your beads, the beads won't let you continue to work if you're in a bad mindset.

What does your metaphorical kitchen table look like, if you have one?

JA: It took me a while to understand my metaphorical kitchen table because I was stuck on the notion that the kitchen table was where family passed down Traditional Knowledge. This was not my experience, and I feared that this idea left out those of us who did not learn from our families. To top it off, as I worked my way home, many Indigenous people questioned whether I was a "real" Indian because I may not have behaved or acted in a way they deemed Indian. And when your people question you, it has an incredibly negative effect on your thoughts. That is the power of colonization, and we know it has been successful

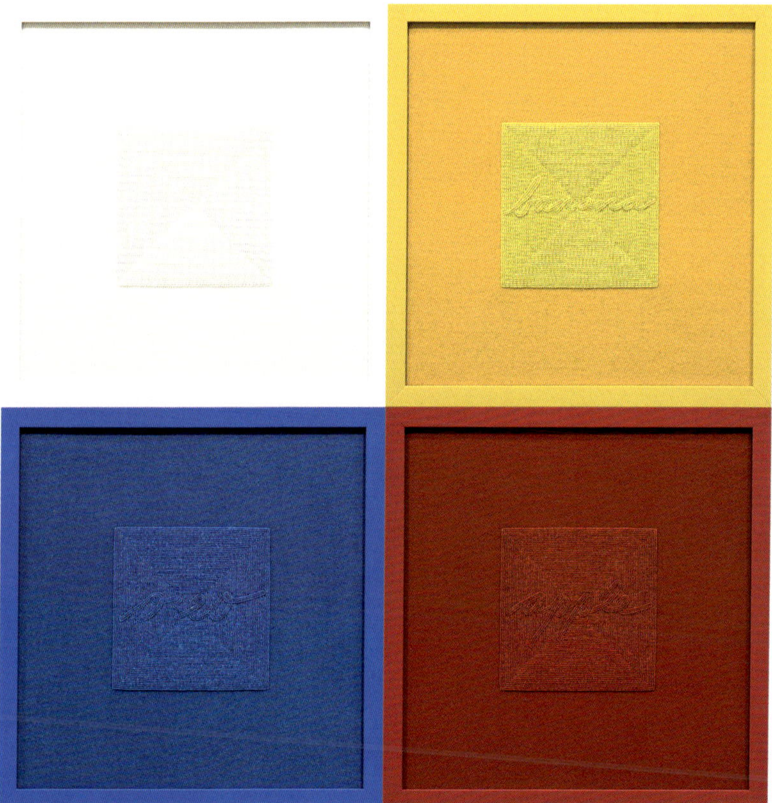

FIGURE 2.8. Judy Anderson, *A Square is Not a Circle (North), A Square is Not a Circle (East), A Square is Not a Circle (South), A Square is Not a Circle (West)* (2020), size 12 French reproduction white heart beads, size 11 Czech beads, size 12 antique Italian beads on stroud cloth, 43 x 43 cm. Collection of Canada Council Art Bank. Photo courtesy of Carey Shaw.

when we question each other and ourselves. Please note that I am not speaking about questioning people who are wrongfully claiming Indigenous ancestry.

In a symposium, I heard Kanien'kehaka (Mohawk) artist Jackson 2Bears say, "The Elders have always said that traditionally we have always been contemporary people." So when thinking about the kitchen table, not as a static definition but one that is evolving or changing, I started

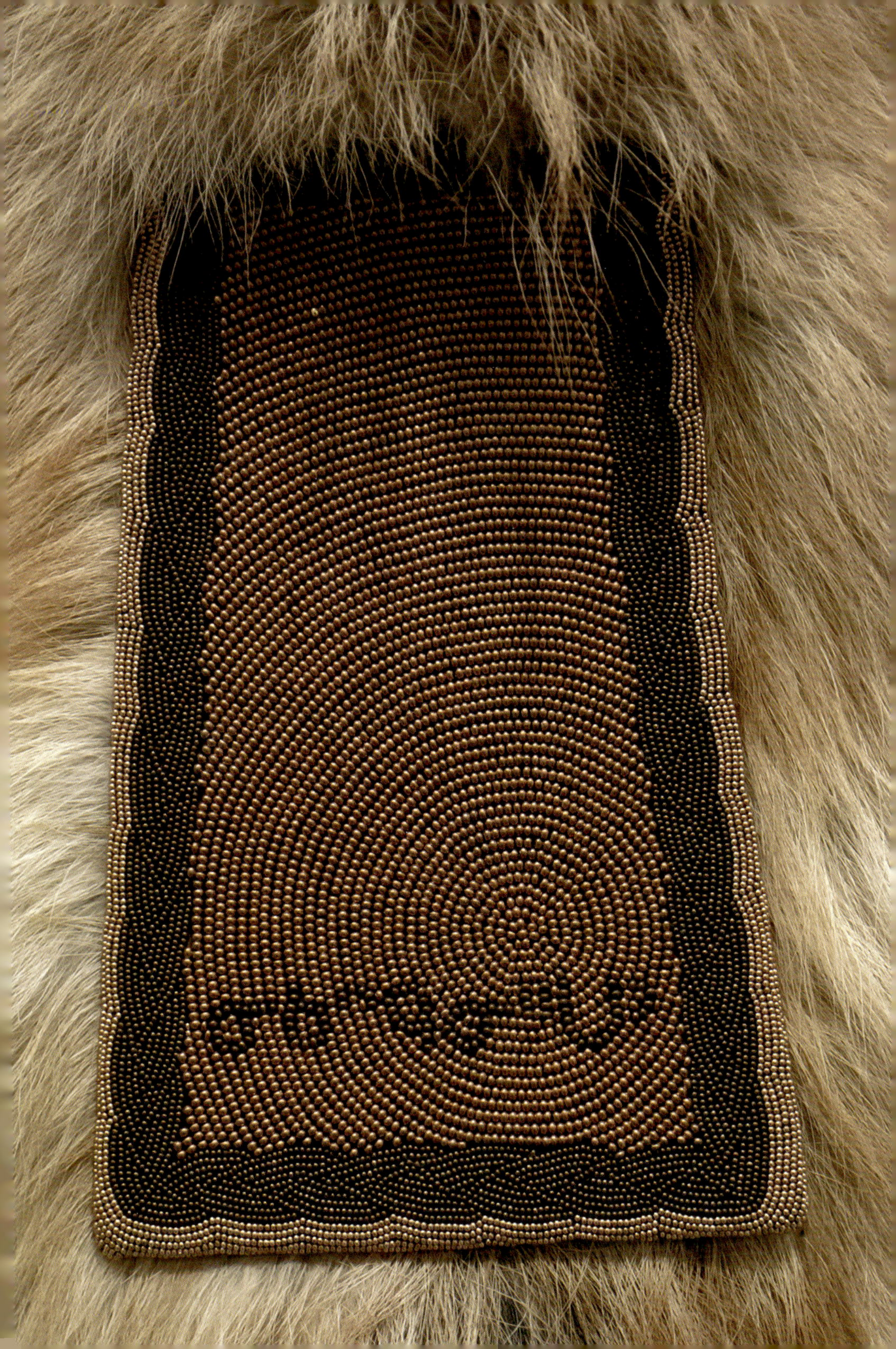

to see that the work I was doing in the university was a kitchen table. I have taught a lot of people to bead and quill, but I need to acknowledge that just because I stand in front of the room doesn't mean I am always the teacher. I have taken on the role of student in many instances. Early on, a student taught me the applique stitch and that backgrounds do not have to be a solid flat colour. A student recently taught me how to attach a jingle, and another showed me how to make moccasins. By approaching the kitchen table this way, we all become pseudo aunties, kokums, cousins etc.

AM: I know that you've reflected on those thoughts quite a bit and hearing you speak about it is helpful. When I think of the kitchen table and community, I think of how the kitchen table is where you get all the good information. So when I'm reflecting on the times where I've been in that sort of community setting, I realize how it's been foundational for me in many ways. Another way that I've come to understand community is by being at the table with Ancestors and working with objects that my relations would have worked with. Maybe they've left that work for twenty or a hundred years, and I'm just picking it up. It's like I'm working at a metaphorical kitchen table with a long and non-linear timeline that anyone can join at any point.

JA: That's beautiful, and it makes me think of designs. I was visiting with a student at FNUniv, and I told him that I didn't have any designs, but I had dreamt one. He said, "That means that's your design. You have a design, and you should work with that design." This experience is how I understand what you say about the Ancestors coming to the table. Thank you.

AM: Some people replicate designs, and I've only done that if it's from a family member. I'm fortunate to have bead workers on my maternal and

FIGURE 2.9. Judy Anderson, *I feel this way all the time* (2020), detail, size 13 and 15 copper plated beads, coyote fur, approximately 50 x 167 cm. Photo courtesy of Carey Shaw.

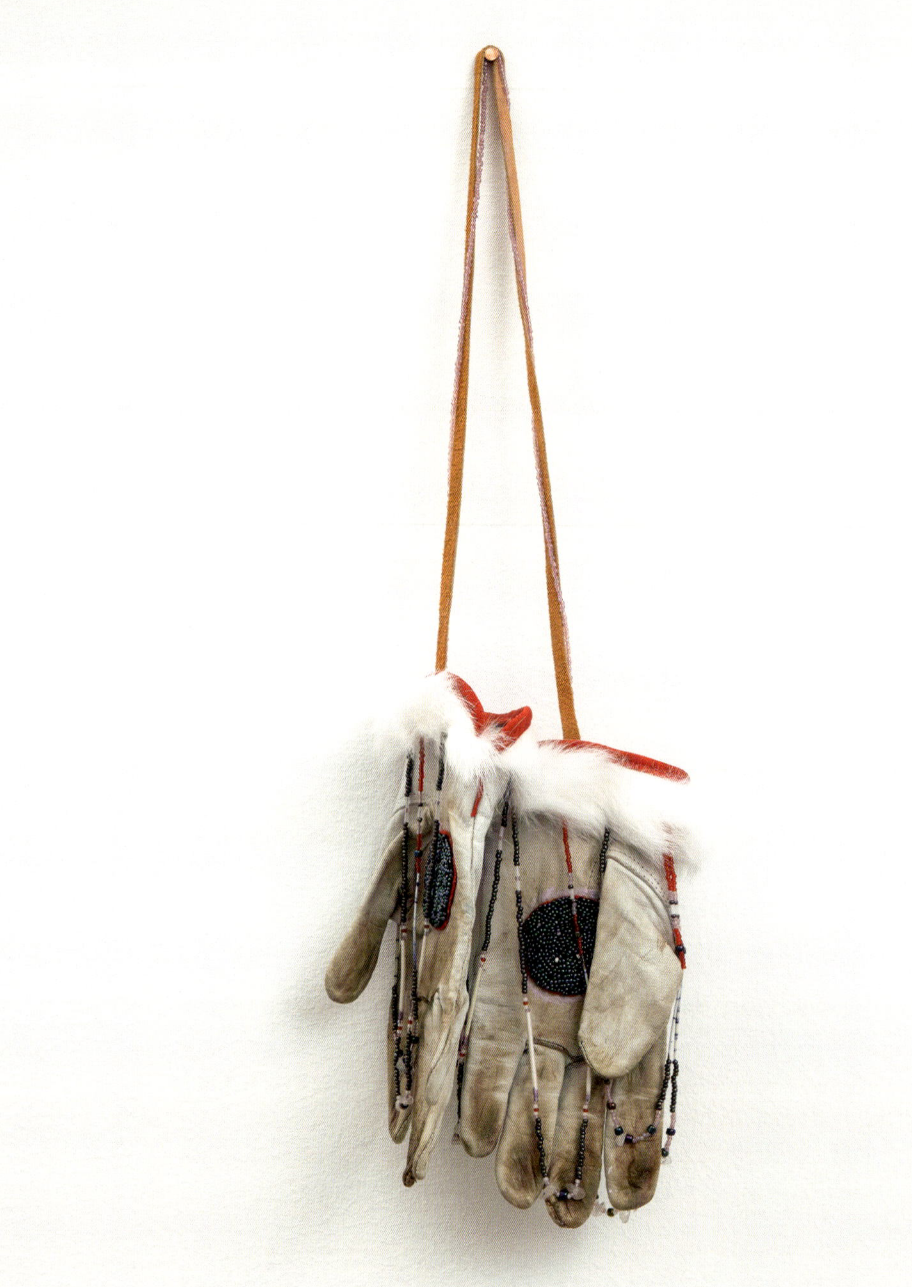

FIGURE 2.10. Audie Murray, *Celestial Gloves* (2021), worn work gloves, porcupine quills, glass beads, acrylic paint, rabbit fur, tanned hide, 60 x 35 cm. Collection of Forge Project. Photo by Sean Fenzl, courtesy of Nanaimo Art Gallery.

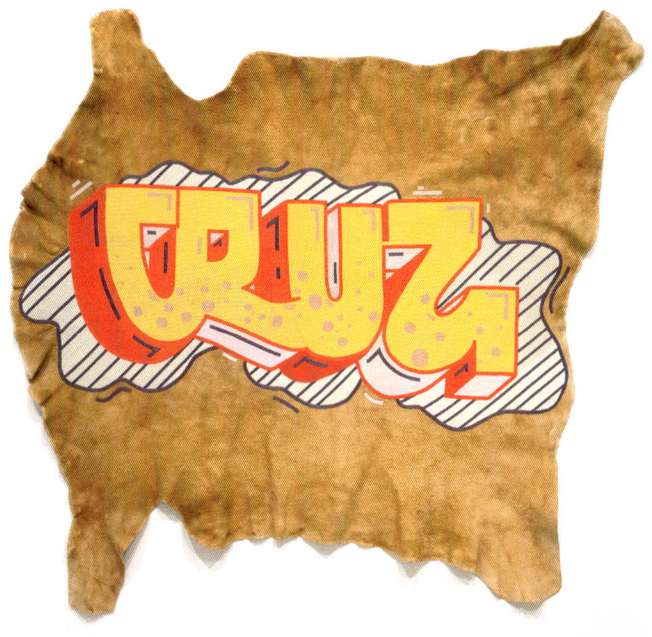

FIGURE 2.11. Judy Anderson, *Exploit Robe (Going Pro)* (2022), size 10 Czech beads, traditionally tanned moose hide, 182.88 x 203.2 cm. Photo courtesy of Don Hall.

paternal side, but those are designs that I've come to know recently by seeking them out. I feel thankful to have that access, but I also recognize that not everyone does, so I think it's possible to look at a wider language of ancestral design as a source of inspiration as long as you are not appropriating.

JA: I decided not to research designs in archives or museums because I don't want to be unintentionally influenced by someone's design. From what I understand, in the past, there was an unspoken but understood "copyright" on designs. So, I wait for a dream. I think this is one of the reasons why I work with letters.

JA: Can you just speak to how your work may or may not be minimalist?

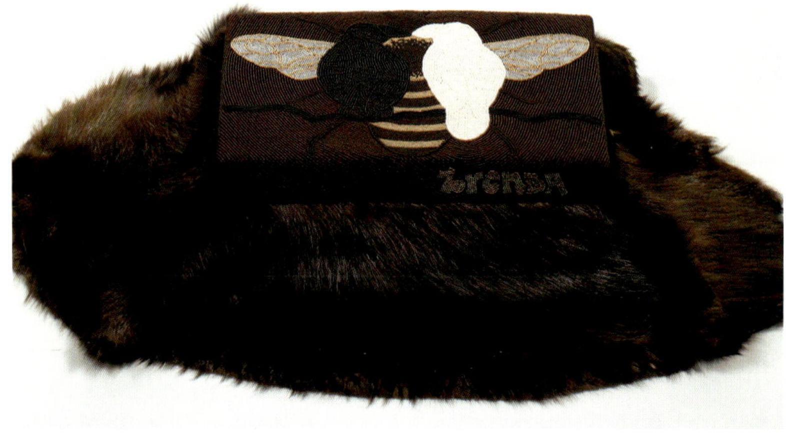

FIGURE 2.12. Judy Anderson, *Fuck ya, besties . . .* (2019), beads, beaver skin, 68.58 x 40.6 x 17.78 cm. Photo courtesy of Mike Patten.

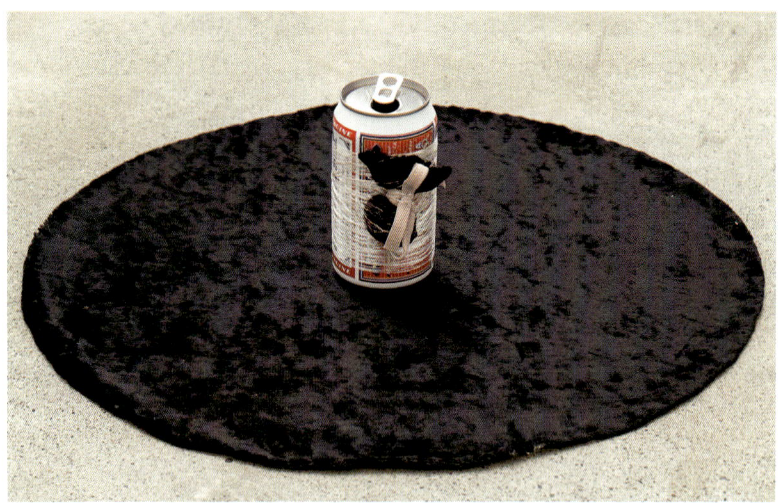

FIGURE 2.13. Audie Murray, *Bud, Tobacco & Spider* (2021), vintage Budweiser beer can, silver thread, tobacco bundle, black velvet, 47 x 13 x 47 cm. Photo by Sean Fenzl, courtesy of Nanaimo Art Gallery.

AM: Many of my pieces feel simultaneously minimal and like a lot at once. I think this is because, visually, I am trying not to pack everything into one work. *Celestial Gloves* is an example of this. There are subtle details, and the gloves themselves have life in them; therefore, I feel like they can energetically hold the space of an entire wall, even if it looks like a minimal installation.

JA: Nice! When I thought of this question, I was specifically thinking about *Bud, Tobacco & Spider* and how you installed it. The space, itself, seemed empty, but I know *Bud, Tobacco & Spider* to be powerful. If it could be the size of what is actually in the piece, it would fill the entire room. It could be an entire exhibition, that piece.

AM: I'm curious about your relationship with beadwork in terms of scale.

JA: In thinking about work specifically, the size suits the concept in the piece. For *Exploit Robe (Going Pro),* I wanted it to be big because it is a type of graffiti that generally would be big, bigger than a hide. For *Every time I think of you I cry,* this piece speaks to the grief I felt and the amount of tears that I cried over my brother who was scooped. While this piece is large (6'6" x 9'), I made this piece as big as I could go in the time frame I had. However, if I were going to make this piece where it lived up to the title, it would be the entire gallery. Not just the gallery where the work showed, I mean the entire MacKenzie Art Gallery, because I could fill that space with my tears.

AM: As you were talking, I reflected on how that question was lame of me to ask. As an artist, questions about scale and time can be boring. When I look at your work, Judy, I feel that as an artist and as a person, you have so much love to give that your work has to manifest as a big piece. I see how that love comes through with the labour of making and sourcing materials. Something that strikes me about your practice is how important all of those choices are within your process, and I think that's really powerful. I've also noticed when you're making your work, the intention is not about commercial gain; rather, the importance is to put all of that energy into one piece that feels exactly right.

JA: You made me sound so beautiful and amazing as a human being! Even so, I'm always wondering if somebody will collect this.

AM: Well, gee, me too. I hope your pieces get collected soon. I hope someone will collect mine, too.

JA: I'm reminded of you talking about decentring decolonization. While my work is about decolonizing, I don't centre decolonization. I believe that decolonizing is at the core of all of our work. For example, when we're honouring and loving, we're decolonizing, or when we learn to love each other and ourselves, it's decolonizing.

Thank you for picking up on those beautiful things because I think that's what you're doing in your work, too. If you don't mind, could you briefly tell Carmen about *Bud, Tobacco & Spider*?

AM: The work is inspired by an experience I had one summer when I went to Meadow Lake, Saskatchewan, to visit these gloves that my great-great-grandma beaded. I went to the graveyard to visit her, too. I did not plan to do that, but I went anyways and gifted her some beads. Since I was there, I had to say hi to everyone. So I went to my grandma's grave, and I had a tobacco bundle in my pocket that I had been carrying around for an unknown reason and amount of time. I put that on her grave, and we happened to have some Budweiser in the back of my truck, so I poured out a beer for kohkum, and a spider crawled out. I was with my partner, and his mind was blown, but I was desperately trying to play it cool. As you know, I've been doing work with spiders, and they've come to be important.

CR: Thank you for sharing that story, it is powerful.

3.

PARALLEL LINES MOVE ALONG TOGETHER: A BEADED LINE THAT CONNECTS ME TO YOU

KATHERINE BOYER AND DAYNA DANGER

ORIENTATION

In a gesture to honour the work and creative/research journey of Dayna Danger, Katherine Boyer wanted to design, make, and ultimately gift a vest. Our goal through this conversation was to expand on pre-established connections, generate new dialogues related to beading and kinship, and develop a design in a collaborative, mutually consensual manner. The following is the edited conversation recorded at the end of September 2021.

KATHERINE BOYER: So, I am currently working on a vest—I have been doing skies for a little while now, which has a lot of significance for me. It's this type of knowledge that is underappreciated, and I think it has entirely to do with the future . . . if we understood better what the sky was telling us then we could see what is coming, in a weather-based sense, but there is something else to that.

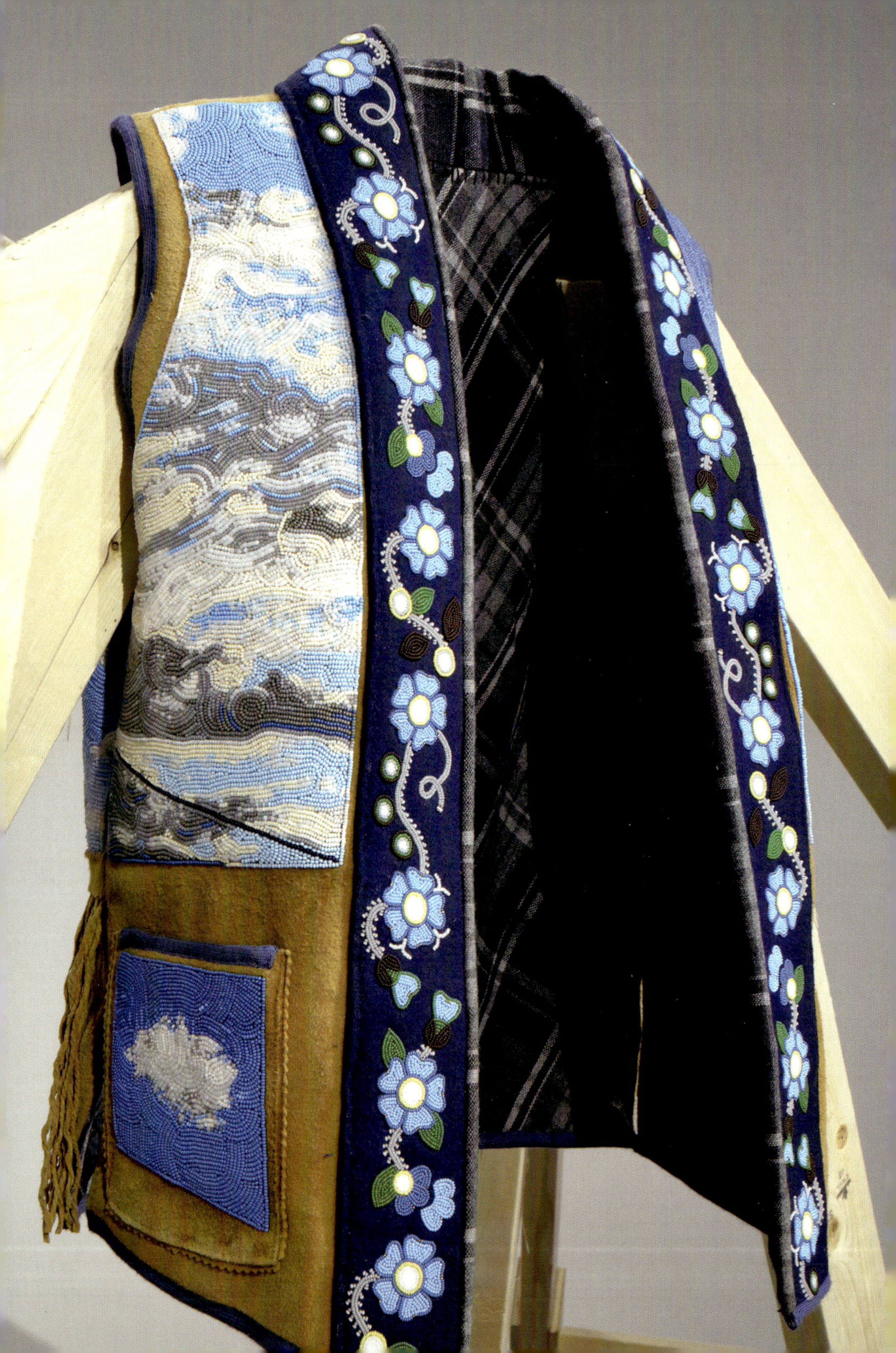

DAYNA DANGER: That makes me think of the Star People and the constellations, those connections, knowing how to navigate space when you look up to the sky even if it's at night or in the day, it was all indicators of how . . .

KB: Yeah, how to orient yourself,[1] which was another big part of my thought process. The sun tells you where you are and where you're going. In terms of orientation, that's a big cornerstone to an LGBTQIA2S+ experience is trying to [orient] yourself and understand the world as you experience it and how the world sees you . . . does that resonate with you?

DD: That is ringing so true for me because I am talking about that erasure, that rupture, that severing from those teachings and those connections, especially from being in the city that has kind of numbed me to knowing. When I go home, I can feel it right away, I feel the sky, I feel its presence right away, when you come back to the place where you feel so small and insignificant, there is all of this space above me. What I like about what you're talking about is the wind. I remember—even my great-great-grandfather would always talk about the [incoming] *keewatin*, the Northern Wind, then he would know to get out of the fish camp so he could go on to the next task, which was probably tend the farm at this time of season. Even when we were talking about the directions, there are certain things that you know. A wind will always have a certain way . . . somebody was telling me, when you light a fire or match, if you are always pointing your back towards a certain direction, it will always block the wind because it always comes a certain way. Just knowing this, it just seems obvious . . . but people don't always think about the presence of the wind, and I love what Jas M. Morgan writes in "The Prairie Wind Is Gay Af": "The prairie wind is gay af. The prairie wind propels the queer body forward in a way shared among queer kin who perpetually followed those sparkling lights on the landscape: that queer lust for the city, that home in the horizon, and that desire for queer possibility."[2]

FIGURE 3.1. Katherine Boyer, *The Sky Vest* (2022), seed beads, moosehide, stroud cloth, 2x4s. Photo courtesy of Don Hall.

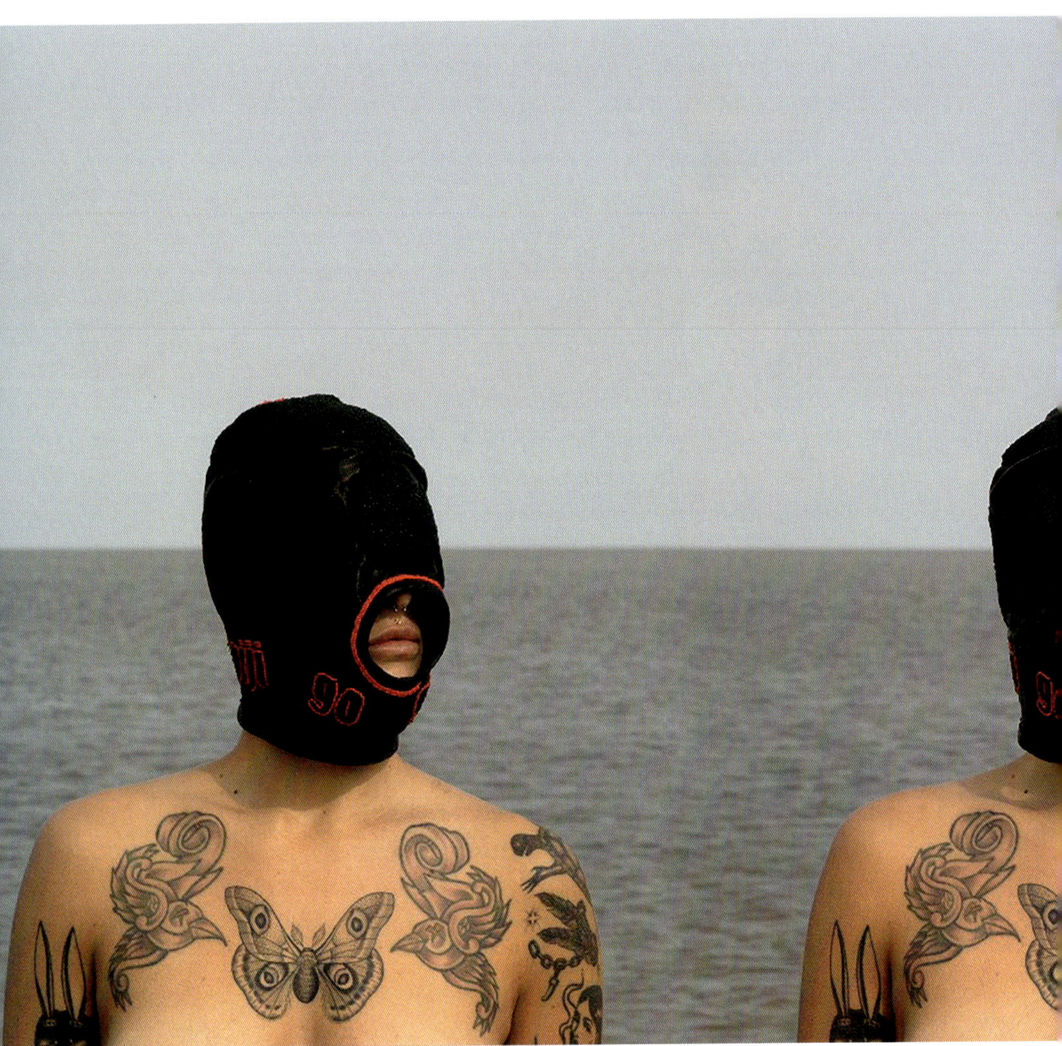

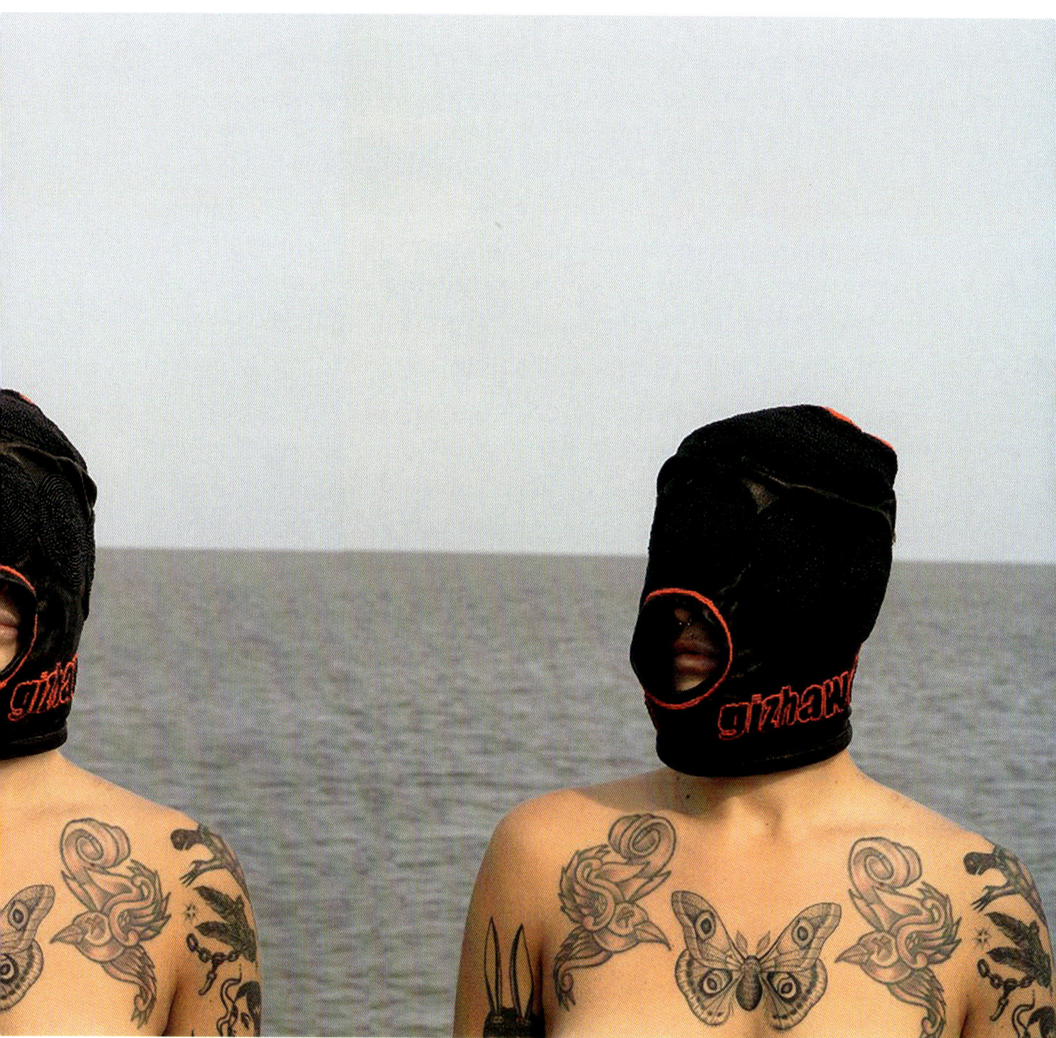

FIGURE 3.2. Dayna Danger, *Aapiji go gizhawenimin, Adrienne* (2021), digital print on aluminum. Photo courtesy of the artist.

SPIDER RECIPROCITY

DD: I think these ideas of reciprocity for Two-Spirit people are huge, especially for us that are Métis, I find that a lot of our queerness is so easily erased. There is the dichotomy of the Métis man and woman and already you're seen as subhuman because [the term] "Halfbreed," the language around it, the dirtiness of being mixed, I think of Amy Malbeuf's work: they were "a little touched with the prairie wolf";[3] this derogatory idea of bestiality that is attached to us that is also a projection of sexuality because they know how powerful we are, because we own that shit.

KB: I just attended an online conversation with Kai Pyle [held by the Mamawi Aachimotaak Project] called "Métis, Queer, Trans and Two-Spirit Histories."[4] It was great to hear some historical accounts of Métis-specific experiences . . . these people were defiant and so noteworthy that there are public accounts of them. Several [accounts] were from explorer journals, so the stories definitely have that settler gaze . . .

DD: Even though those accounts are from a gaze that doesn't understand us, that sees us as different, I have to recognize that that is their perspective, and they are witnessing, and you have to take it with a grain of salt because . . . we were just so part of our communities it just *was*, we just *were* happening.

KB: What I [am eventually] hoping to see is [historical] work by the queer or Two-Spirit hand, that is just what I desperately want to find—that is a big want.

DD: It is. But at the same time, it's not, those are some of the things we are trying to remember. . . . I remember having this moment of being really validated that my family doesn't have any of our beadwork patterns either. . . . If we talk about working through Spirit and that [type of] remembering with a need to get something out, I just go with that and see what that becomes.

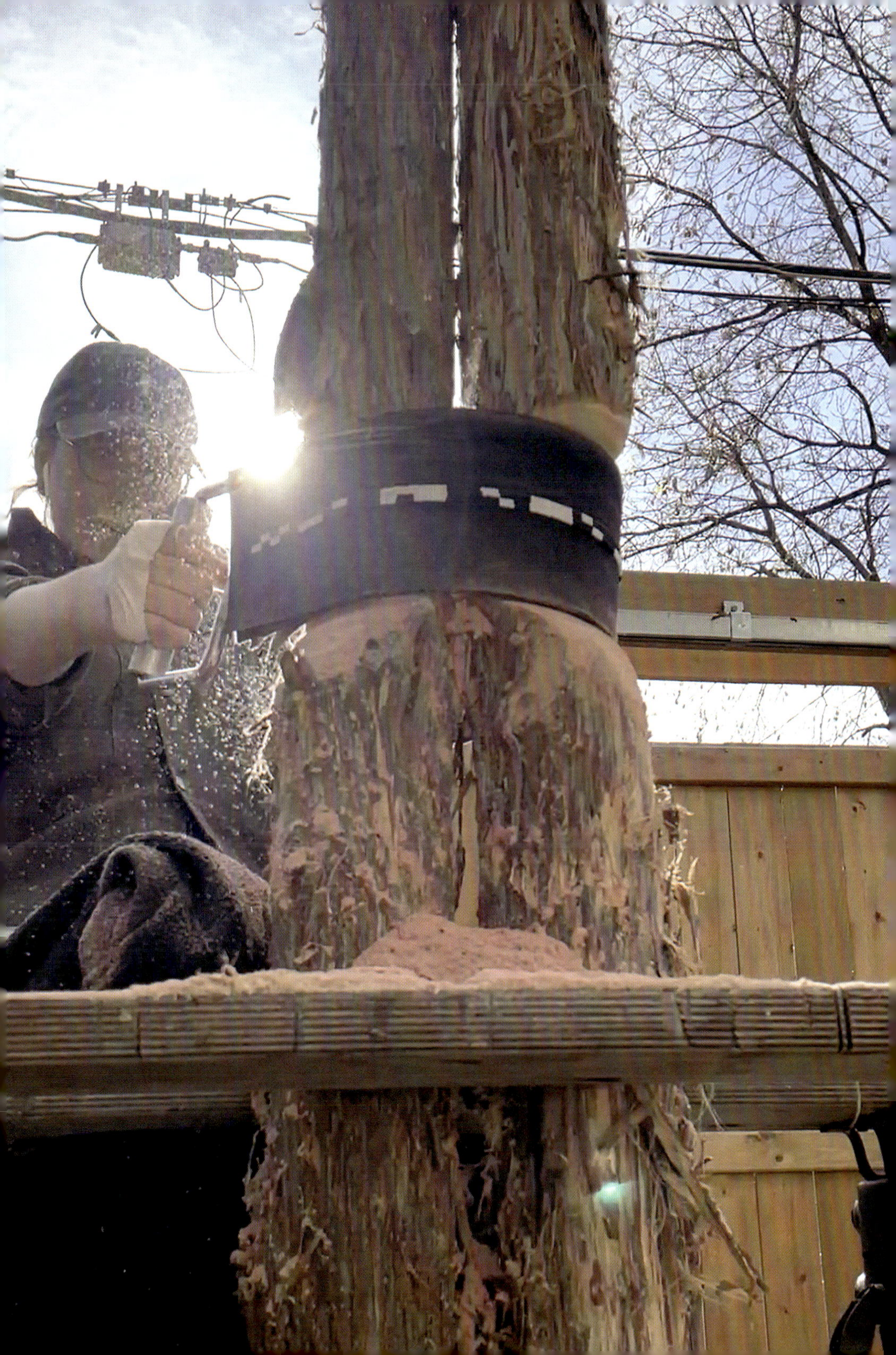

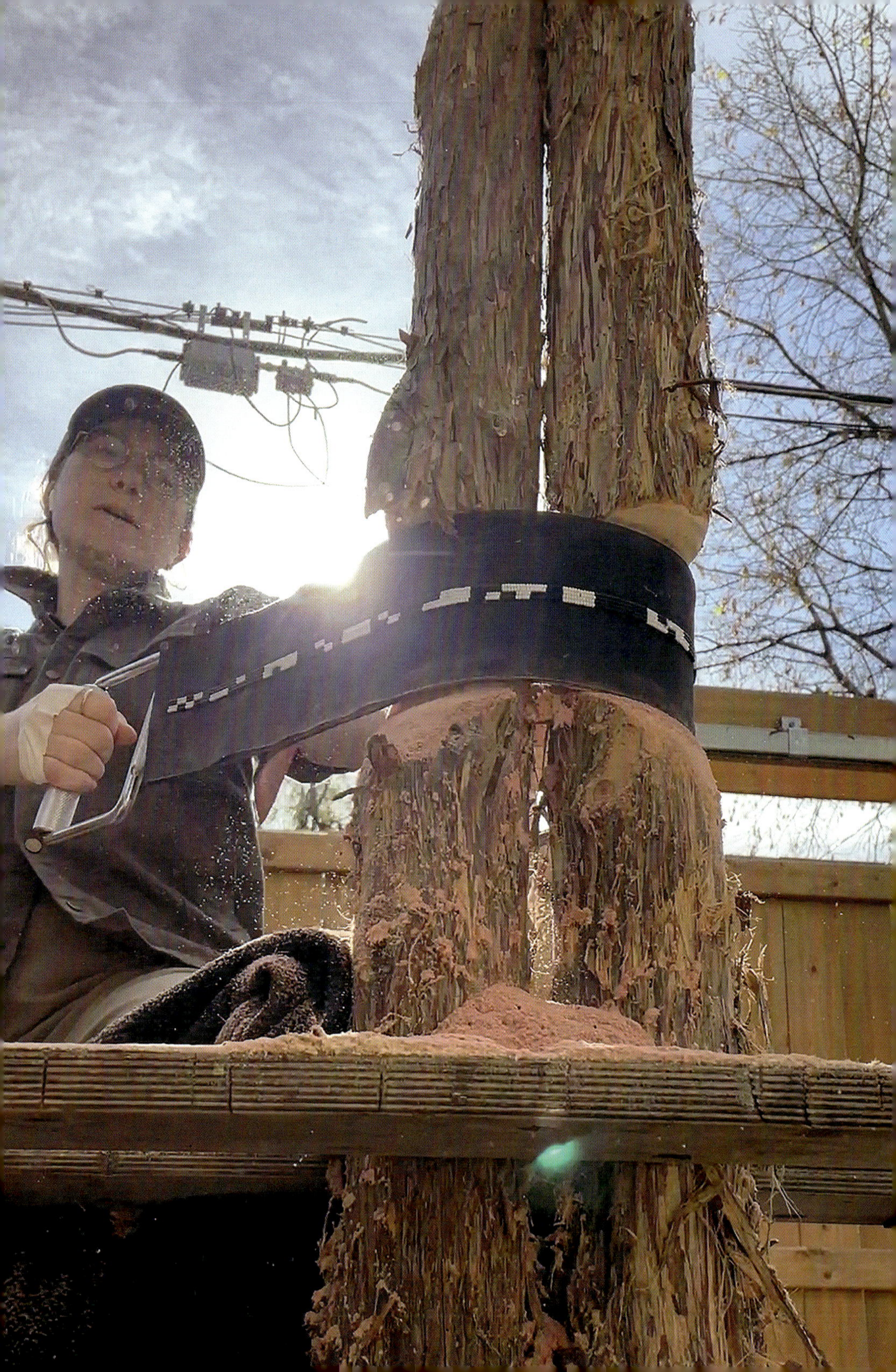

KB: Yeah, I don't think any idea of visual culture is ever fixed. And I have always let that be a relief for the pressure to do things in a certain way. Because there is no precedent to what we are trying to do today as Métis artists. What I am very grateful to be doing right now is . . . to honour what you do for the Indigenous queer Two-Spirit community, that's really what I want to be doing here [with this collaboration and gift]. Especially as you go into this PhD mode [in 2022, Dayna began their PhD studies at Concordia University], that's major research, writing, and idea building.

DD: You know when somebody first shows you how to look for sage and then all of a sudden you keep on seeing sage everywhere. When you put those intentions out there, they start to come back to you. If you're going to ask for something, there's reciprocity, you know we have those *asema*, those tobacco teachings of putting stuff down [on the land] and asking for help and just starting to look around and listen and feel. So many spiders have been coming to me, which is really interesting because I was talking to my mom about it and she said, "They're the connectors, they connect all the different constellations, and you bring people together, that's something that you do."

EXTEND, GIVE, RECEIVE

DD: Maybe part of the process is talking about how we are looking to build our visual cultural language; when that has been severed and disrupted, how do we remember? Spider reciprocity is connecting kin together, and [it is] those lines of connection that we have to each other that builds this larger web. I feel that spider reciprocity is a Two-Spirit teaching because we rely so heavily on making kin with a range of people and across long distances. . . . Art has been the connecting factor to how I find other Two-Spirit community.

FIGURE 3.3A AND B. Katherine Boyer, *blurthebinary* (2021), video stills. Video stills courtesy of the artist.

KB: One of the things that I think of, which connects art making and lived experiences . . . [is something that was presented by] Hazel Meyer,[5] an artist who has done . . . research in queer world-making and [led me to] this idea of constructing a world when you are faced with one that does not accept you . . . that, to me, is why I do anything. What are your thoughts on that?

DD: I definitely feel that's something I [rely on]—my imagination and my mind were what I used because this world reflects nothing back to me. When I feel so alone, I create a world where I can exist, because it feels possible. Somebody built this world, so who's to say that I can't simultaneously build another reality within this reality. A reality where we exist free of projection, where you can be empowered or objectified, where you get to choose, where you get to have agency in your presentation and in who you are in your being, and it isn't questioned.

KB: Hazel Meyer and Cait McKinney have a project where they used pegboard [visually citing content from Chicago's Leather Archives and Museum],[6] it was about tools and hardware and utility.

DD: I think about tools a lot, we are a people of tools . . . thinking about the tools that come out of us and enable us to have these queer-ass experiences. It isn't about the phallus, it isn't even centred on genitals; to think of that is to think of it in a cisnormative way . . . I like that I can choose, that I have agency, that I can give pleasure in so many different ways with so many different types of tools. I also don't want to be limited by my own body and what pleasure can look like . . . I think these belongings have a very specific spiritual [essence] too, as if I don't feel a connection with my strap-on, of course I do. It's not just a piece of silicone attached to my body, it's an extension of me, my reciprocity, my love, my trust for that person and my desire and the pleasure to just exist and to give that pleasure as well.

KB: I don't know if you know this, but when Franchesca Hebert-Spence curated us [with Camille Georgeson-Usher and assinajaq] both into the exhibition *May the Land Remember You As You Walk Upon Its Surface,*[7] one of the things she asked of me was to finish a piece that was in progress, *Carry the Horizon With You.*[7] Fran described this urge to see our [Katherine's and Dayna's] works function together, mine as a physical barrier or boundary within the space and specifically protecting what was going to be your contribution, which was a recycled bike tire flogger with a peyote beaded handle. Seeing our work together as a healthy balance of the tools that we have at hand to give, receive, respect and define boundaries. That is a really key thing, our art is an extension of ourselves. I think those things are the cornerstone of [the process of making] a vest, or a pouch, or another beaded object [for someone], these gifts are also part of our community experience, and share those exact same qualities, as an intimate experience.

MATERIALS

DD: The masks are the first piece of the puzzle that started the use of ethical materials. For me it's really important that if I don't take the life of that animal in those traditional ways, I feel like I need to source it out or buy directly [from Indigenous hunters/trappers]. I was working to get access to whatever [type of leather was available] and then this idea of better understanding the work that goes into those belongings, the prayers, the whole process along the way, needs to be recognized and honoured.

KB: The moose hide that I want to use is from Robertson's Trading Post [La Ronge, Saskatchewan]. . . . I also wanted to talk about designs and bead colours—I've got matte colours in everything except for green. The orange is *very* orange. I've got some interesting options for red. I've got matte but they are also a little bit transparent and then a darker tone.

DD: I am leaning towards the lighter one, but what do you think?

KB: The lighter one is a bit closer to what I think of as tobacco tie red.

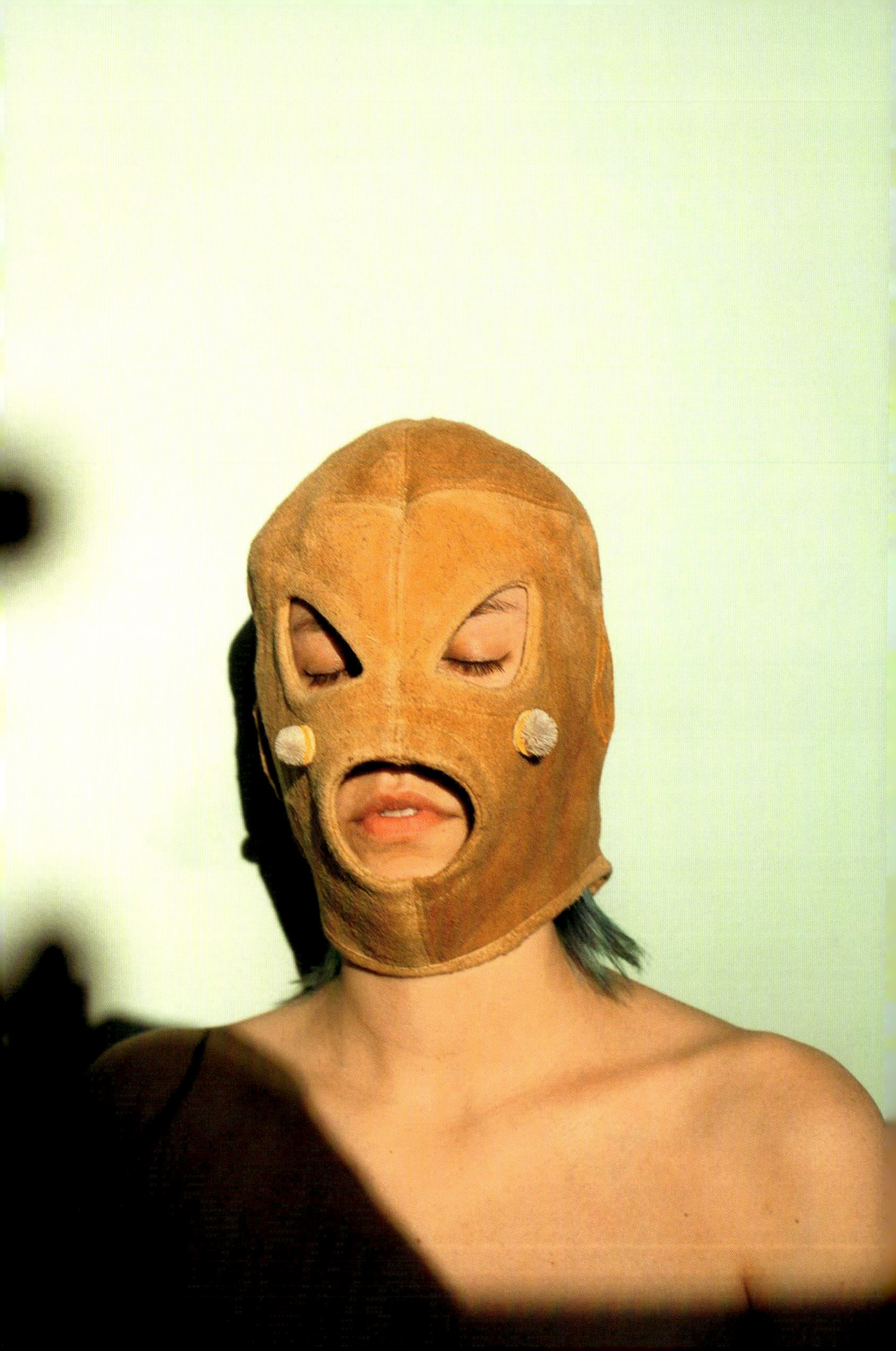

DD: I like that, and I like the clear, I've been getting more into clear lately.

KB: Okay! Now I wanted to show you these, these are black-light-activated beads, what do you think?

DD: Yes, I like them!

KB: Okay, because I have zero other applicable use for them. [laughter]

DD: You mean you don't use bright fluorescents ever? [laughter]

KB: No, funny enough, blues, blues, and blues are my colours, and not having a blue in the mix is such a strange feeling, but I like it because it's giving me a really good change.

DD: Way out of your comfort zone too! That will be interesting to see how you move through that because I know that our key colours, like for me to not work with orange . . . or black . . . would be so weird.

KB: I love a challenge.

DD: I'm not opposed to other colours coming in, for example if you incorporated an antler, there would be the typical white, brown.

KB: Imagery is the other thing we should discuss—antlers?

DD: Antlers show up so much in my work and, along with my hide tanning journey, I would love to see more brains [used in traditional tanning]. Because the brains are so important for this process to remain sustainable. And then the other thing is a moose leg but cut off or dismembered. You know me, I like to lean into the horror and the desire around that . . . That is something I really lean into, becoming familiar with mortality and the process as we go back into the earth and honouring that, because that's one of the pieces: how does that life go back into the land? The land processes that death and we become the land, that is the whole cycle.

FIGURE 3.4. Dayna Danger, *Kinship Masks* (2019), digital print.

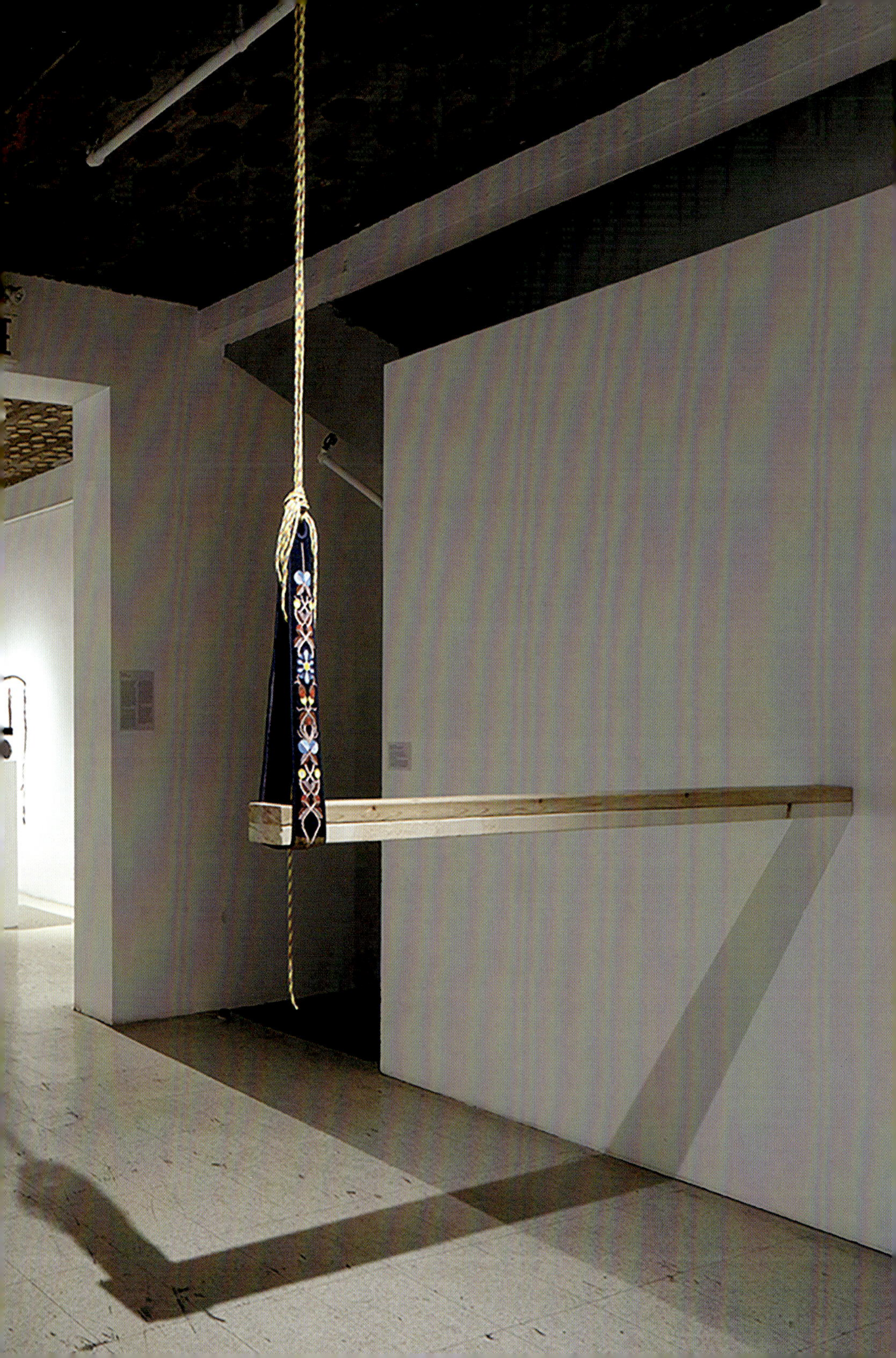

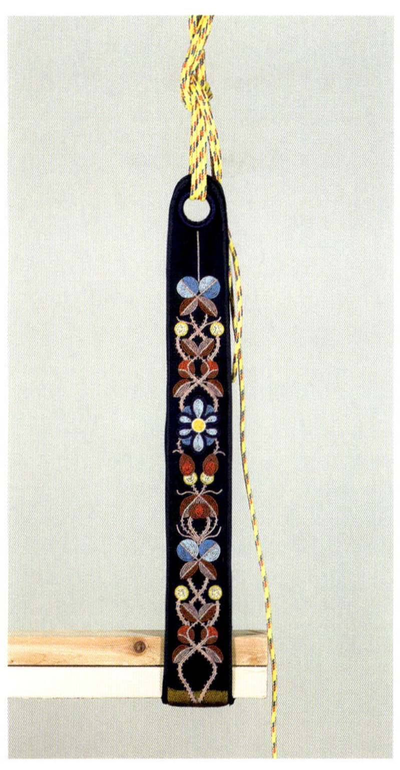

FIGURE 3.5A AND B. Katherine Boyer, *Carry the Horizon With You* (2019), seed beads, stroud cloth, cedar, fir, 2x4s. Photo courtesy of La Biennale d'art contemporain autochtone (BACA).

DD: And as a part of our Two-Spirit epistemologies, as a teaching and learning tool to understand, it's so much more than just the masks. It's this whole ethical process that you have with the animal beings, with the land, with the individuals you are making this for, there is the teaching of consent the whole way through. Even now, I am consenting to the colours that I like. These are the yesses, are there any no's? Not for me, we could have a safe word though. [laughter]

KB: In terms of bags, there is often something that is usually sound related . . . like tiny cones, or even beads [on fringe], those are sound activators. I'm wanting to put thimbles on mine. What do you think of bullet casings?

DD: Okay, hear me out, I have this bullet belt that I got in Vancouver a while ago, and now I don't know what to do with it because I'm no longer in this punk scene. So maybe we refurbish it!

KB: Yes, let's repurpose that as the fringe! One place that you can carry weight more comfortably is below the shoulders, we could put those there.

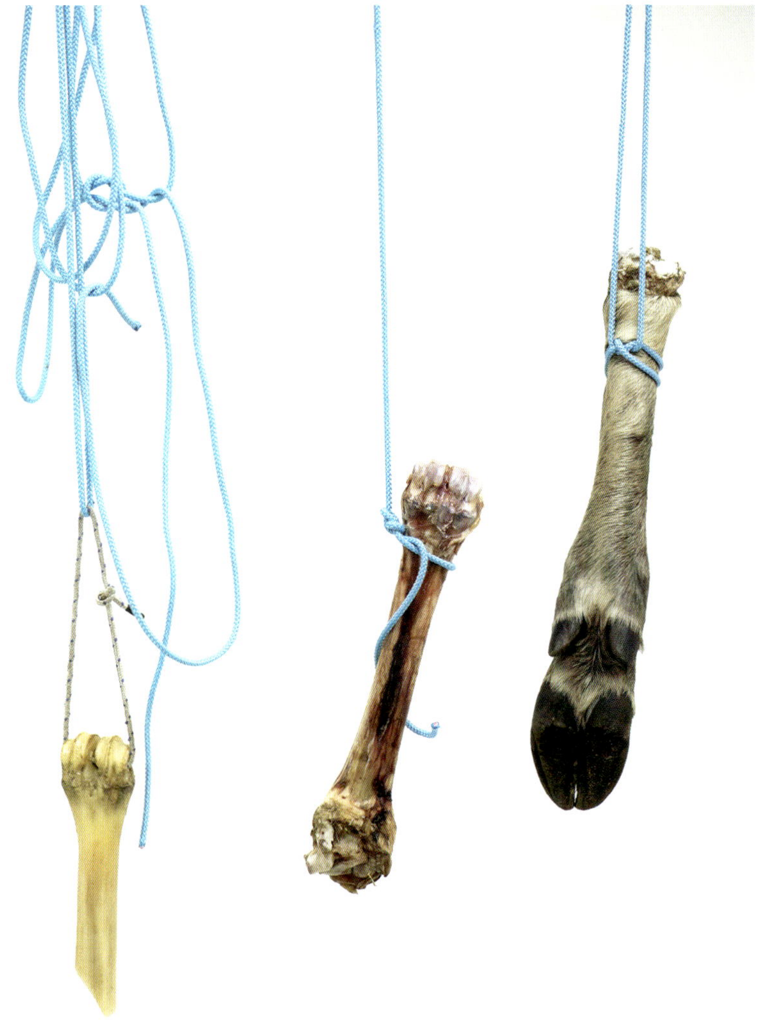

FIGURE 3.6. Dayna Danger, *Weight of Inheritance* (2022), digital print on aluminum. Photo courtesy of the artist.

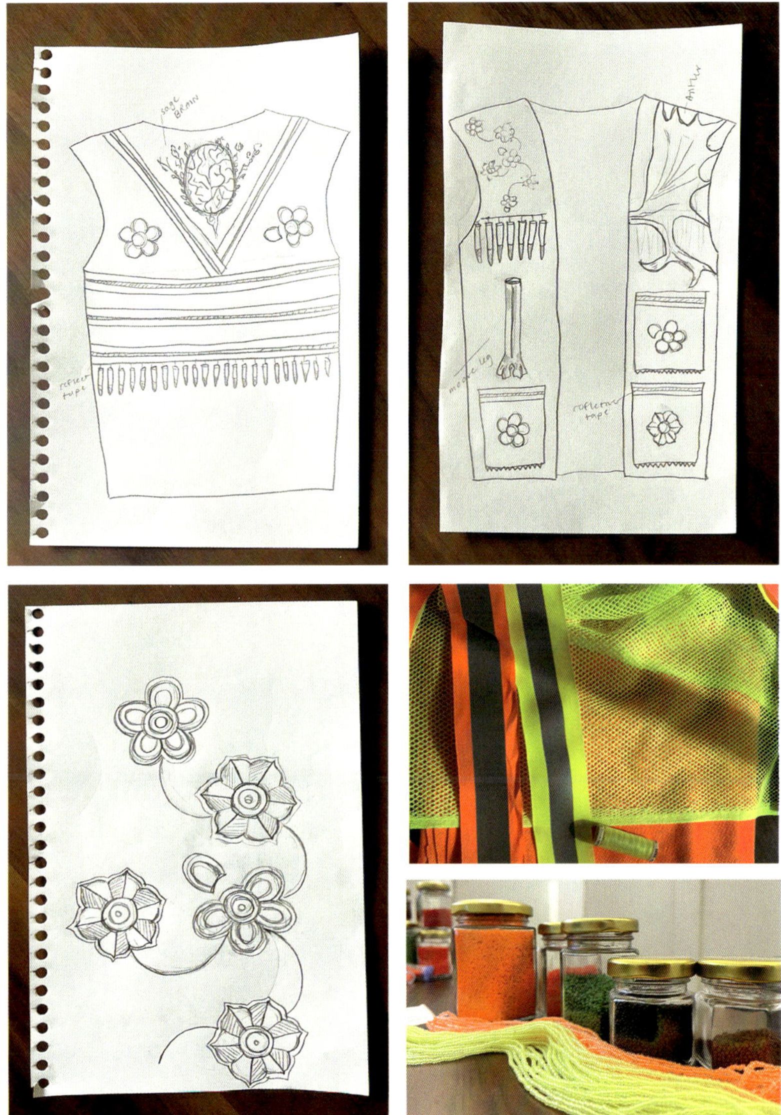

FIGURE 3.7A, B, C, D, AND E. Process images of materials and sketches for vest. Photo courtesy of Katherine Boyer.

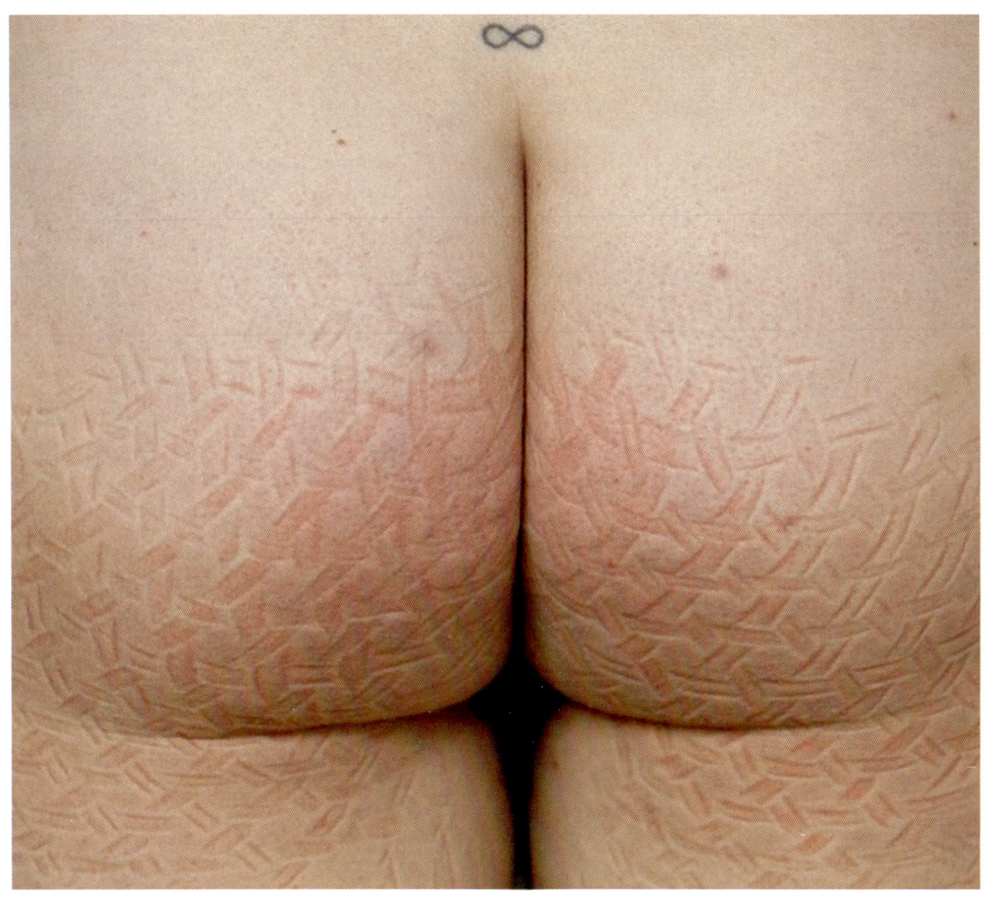

FIGURE 3.8. Dayna Danger, *Métis AF* (2019), Digital print. Photo courtesy of the artist.

DD: I would be interested in some florals, I know on the vest it's usually the mirror . . . you can play around with colour and shape, use your liberty.

KB: I am keen to not do a straightforward mirroring, because that essence of symmetry means something. And I don't want to impose upon what your experience is . . . but something tells me that symmetry is maybe not your experience. [laughter]

DD: Okay, so this is what I learnt from Jeneen [Frei-Njootli], this Gwichin hack that they talk about. But it's a secret. So that's where the work *Métis AF* came from, from my ass being on this wicker basket and the mark making. So yeah, asymmetry is all good for me . . . I'm also wary about things that talk about balance because you're talking about it through the gaze of a binary, and I don't believe in the binary.

KB: The thing that I have observed, this common five-petalled flower, this has now become extremely widespread and accessible as a flower. To me it's a universal in some way that can carry a lot of different meanings that are more individual when it comes to colour and surroundings. I'm inclined to use that, but are there other plants [that are] part of your teachings?

DD: For sure . . . sage, and the tobacco flower . . . those are two big medicines for me.

NOTES

1 Sara Ahmed, *Queer Phenomenology: Orientations, Objects, Others* (Durham: Duke University Press, 2006).

2 Jas M. Morgan, "The Prairie Wind Is Gay AF," in *nîtisânak* (Montreal: Mytonymy Press, 2019), 46–47.

3 Art Gallery of Southwestern Manitoba website, *tensions* exhibition, https://agsm.ca/tensions-amy-malbeuf.

4 Kai Pyle, "Métis, Queer, Trans and Two-Spirit Histories," virtual presentation for the Mamawi Aachimotaak Project (23 September 2021), https://www.facebook.com/themamawiproject/.

5 Hazel Meyer, "Rubber, Leather, Wood" (*A Handmade Assembly*, Struts Gallery & Faucet Media Arts Centre, Sackville NB, 2017).

6 Amy Fung, "Gay Liberation, Sex Dungeons, Gossip, and What We Want in Art: Writer Amy Fung joins artists Hazel Meyer and Cait McKinney for a deep lez bro down about a project at the Canadian Lesbian and Gay Archives," *Canadian Art* (13 September 2016), https://canadianart.ca/features/hazel-meyer-cait-mckinney/.

7 Winnipeg Craft Council, Winnipeg, 2020.

4.

THE POWER OF GATHERING: REVISITING THE SEEDS OF ZIIGIMINESHIN

FRANCHESCA HEBERT-SPENCE
AND CARMEN ROBERTSON

On 20 October 2021, via Zoom, Carmen Robertson and Franchesca Hebert-Spence discussed the Beading Symposium: Ziigimineshin Winnipeg 2020, and how it was organized. Ziigimineshin Winnipeg 2020 was a gathering held 6 to 9 February 2020 that focused on contemporary engagements with beadwork and beading circles. Ziigimineshin's precursor, Beading Symposium: Manidoominensagemin Toronto (2019), was organized by Lisa Myers and Anna Richard at the Textile Museum of Canada and has been documented through essays such as "Beads Need Threads."[1] Ziigimineshin was a gathering that featured speakers, events, and programming, and was a multi-institutional collaboration with support from Mentoring Artists for Women's Arts, the Manitoba Museum, Urban Shaman, the University of Winnipeg, the Manitoba Craft Council (MCC), and the Winnipeg Art Gallery. The organizing team members were Katherine Boyer (Representative for Presenters), Albyn Carias (Gathering Helper, MCC), Rachel Erikson (Education

Coordinator, Manitoba Museum), Maureen Mathews (curator of Ethnography, Manitoba Museum), Daina Warren (Director of Urban Shaman), and Franchesca Hebert-Spence (Gathering Coordinator, independent curator).

Ziigimineshin consisted of twelve presentations, five collection visits, evening programming on all four nights, three exhibitions, and a curatorial talk. The Manitoba Museum (MM) was contracted to provide two primary gathering spaces: the theatre where presentations were held and Alloway Hall, which was referred to as the Community Hall during the event. The Community Hall was divided to hold both the dining area and the community beading tables. There was also a market area that carved out a space for folks to sell the goods they made as a way to recognize beadwork as a commercial activity. The community beading and market area was open to the public and live-streamed the talks being held in the theatre.

CARMEN ROBERTSON: Fran, it is December 8, 2021, and I'm thrilled to find time to have a conversation with you about the beading gathering Ziigimineshin: Winnipeg 2020, the amazing symposium that you organized that February. I have to tell you that I thought it was brave to organize a Winnipeg event in February, but now it seems like brilliant timing given what happened with the COVID-19 pandemic soon after. Can you give me a sense of what motivated you to bring together this gathering?

FRANCHESCA HEBERT-SPENCE: Ziigimineshin happened specifically because of the fact that institutions—and by institutions, I mean universities, art galleries, museums, and granting and funding bodies—had a growing interest in Indigenous customary making processes such as beadwork. I observed the romanticization of "crafting" but not the heart of what I felt made beadwork unique, important, powerful. These institutions began including beadwork in shows—like using moccasins

FIGURE 4.1. Katherine Boyer (L) and Judy Anderson at Ziigimineshin, Winnipeg, MB, February 2020. Photo courtesy of Albyn Carias.

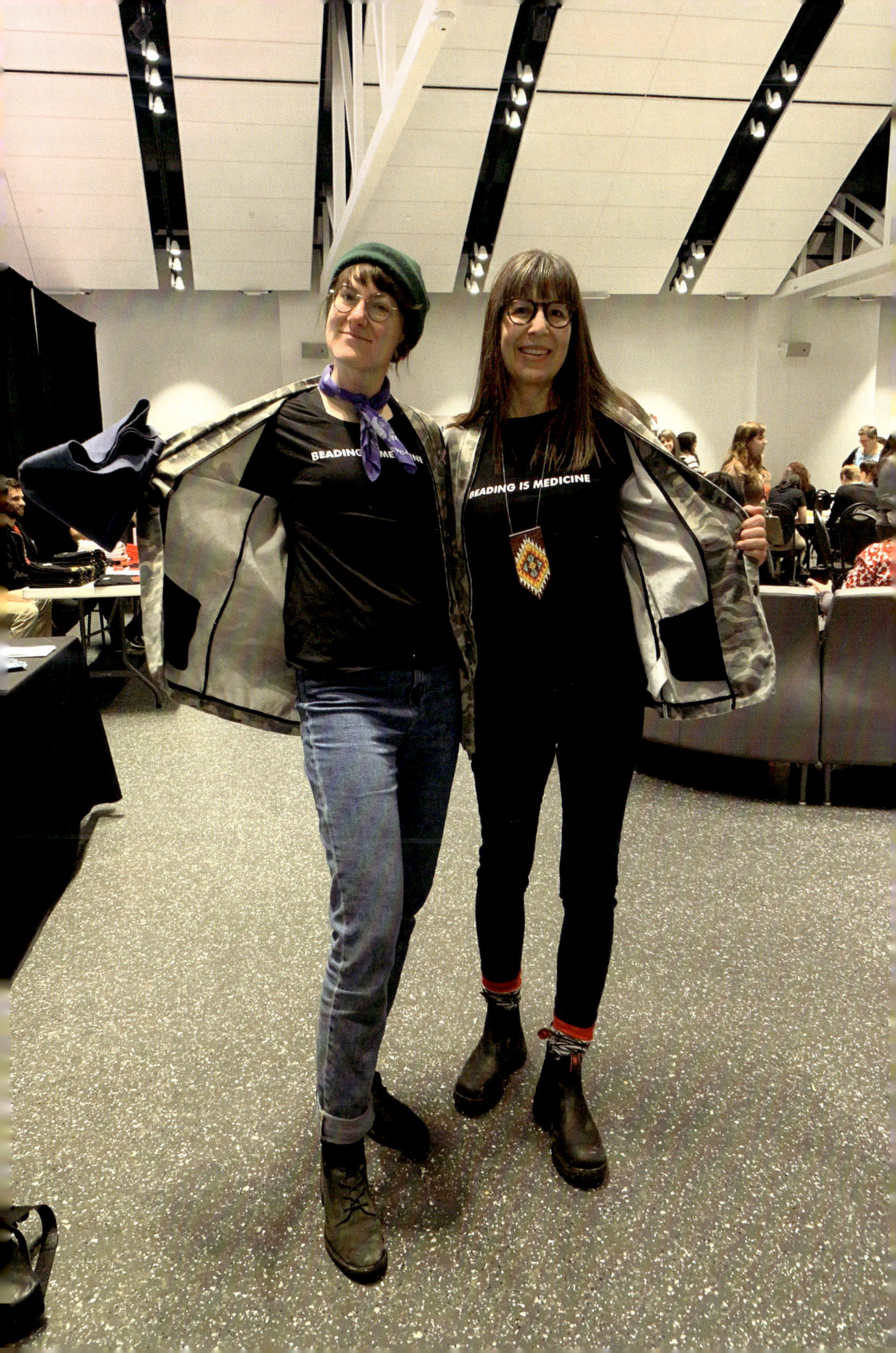
BEADING IS MEDICINE

to illustrate Group of Seven paintings of snowy landscapes—along with programming, like beading workshops that cost twenty to fifty dollars a pop. In contrast to this essentialization, or the use of beadwork as a shorthand for Indigenous traditional making processes, a gathering like Ziigimineshin was motivated as an event that would give beadwork and beadworkers space and a voice.

CR: Ziigimineshin accomplishes your goals to shift this discourse. The reorientation away from a programming "add-on" to an event that not only honours process and the real power of beading combined with deep expressions of reciprocity was refreshing. Also, it was so much fun to get together [Figure 4.1]!

Can you expand on how your vision for the event came about?

FH-S: In Cathy Mattes's essay "'Until We Bead Again'—The BU Beading Babes and Embodying Lateral Love and Generous Reciprocity" [Chapter 6], Mattes discusses in depth the recent proliferation of beading circles following *Walking With Our Sisters* and Nadia Myer's *Indian Act* (2002), and the fact of the matter is I was largely motivated as a student and young person who saw and experienced the results of how these spaces can generate discourse, a sense of belonging, and *fullness*.

One of the moments when I realized there was a need for *something*, like a beading symposium, was in a classroom setting. I made the grand statement, "beading is love," in a paper and after it was marked it had a note beside those words that said, "citation?" It was an important moment where I realized I didn't know how to cite embodied knowledge—embodied through my experience of participating in the beading circle, the Beading Babes with Cathy Mattes at Brandon University for five years. When we need to look for these citations, or put these ideas forward, it feels like we're working backwards to justify what we need to do.

That moment was a beginning for [my] better understanding of the formal spaces that we move through as Indigenous folks, be it academia or the professionalization of art, culture, and production; I realized that gathering can be a space to generate those "citational" moments. Ziigimineshin was an opportunity to organize a gathering of individuals who love to bead, who love to talk about beading, who love to be around beadwork and to celebrate that. To give that action of celebration the value, the attention, the care, the time, and the support that it deserves.

The first time I talked about the symposium was to Lisa Myers at an Indian restaurant in Brandon. It was the first project I had been offered as a fully fledged graduated curator from my master's program and I showed up at this restaurant *so* excited, having pitched my first exhibition. Lisa asked what it was about and my response was, "It's a beading exhibition!" Lisa said, "Oh, I'm doing a beading exhibition too!" I was like, "Okay, so this is the iffy part—I want to do a symposium! I'm not sure—it'll be a lot of work. It's my first exhibition. I should calm down." Then Lisa said, "I'm also wanting to do a symposium!" There was no moment of, "Oh, you're doing it, I shouldn't do it," or "I'm doing this." It had always been collaborative, and it was exciting! To have the same urgency I felt, to be affirmed by someone whom I have so much respect for, and to walk in stride together. I've told that story in talks and in the opening of Ziigimineshin because Lisa's generosity in that moment, and the intergenerational exchange, is something that I hold close and dear. Lisa's response is what gave me the confidence to go ahead with Ziigimineshin because I was seriously doubting myself in that moment.

CR: Can you talk a little bit about how you organized this event? This was not like any symposium I've ever attended, and I mean that in the best way! All participants were cared for in respectful ways. Can you talk about Indigenous hosting methodologies that you drew upon to design and set up this symposium?

FH-S: I had read this paper written by Lorraine Mayer called "A Return to Reciprocity" (2007) as part of our readings in my undergrad. Its intended purpose was to lead our class into a discourse about feminism and Indigenous women[2] and the thesis of the text lays out how Eurocentric feminism fails Indigenous communities. One section in this text is about a symposium held in 1989 called The National Symposium on Aboriginal Women of Canada: Past, Present and Future.[3] Mayer uses the symposium to illustrate the critiques of a Eurocentric feminist approach, but also how that's tightly intertwined within a colonial, White supremacist institutional approach. Participants were disgruntled by the format of presentations, described as talking heads, and academic papers, and there were not enough opportunities for discussion and information sharing. Highlighted in "Return to Reciprocity" was the disjuncture of what it means to organize a symposium for Indigenous women about Indigenous women and how much of an impact a colonial format has. Basically, the formatting didn't reflect the values of what the participants were talking about or why they gathered.

And so, these are the ideas and challenges that were instilled in me throughout my undergrad at IshKaabatens Waasa Gaa Inaabateg [Department of Visual Art] at [the University of] Brandon through hosting events like *Walking With Our Sisters*, coordinated with the Native Studies Department. Since graduating, I was able to participate in events like Listen Witness Transmit held in Wanuskewin [Heritage Museum, Saskatoon, Saskatchewan], which was organized by Nikki Little and Becca Taylor, both of whom use these methods of hosting and being in service in their practices and day-to-day life. I also participated in The Future is Indigenous, the third annual Initiative for Indigenous Futures organized by Julie Nagam concurrently with *Insurgence/ Resurgence,* a giant exhibition co-curated by Julie and Jaime Isaac. These two examples, although quite different from one another, were really, really momentous events that were funded and supported by institutions after the release of the Truth and Reconciliation recommendations in 2016. As the funding has increased, the size of these events, the frequency of events has increased, and also the financial freedom (if the partner institution holding the grants sees fit) to adjust these models and integrate protocols that are important to us. So within these events we see hosting epistemologies taking place—things that can be as simple and straightforward as food, for example.

[Laughs] I can't count the number of times I showed up, as a poor undergrad, to conferences, surviving on the complimentary tea and bread. I also can't count the number of times more established folks would kindly take me out for a meal. It was always accompanied with the phrase "I remember when I was a student at these . . ." That's what the difference between standard practice is and hosting. There are very clear epistemologies of hosting, so the question is, how do we integrate and adopt these principles that are embodied knowledge and resistance? I've thought a lot about this since reading Leanne Simpson's book *A Short History of the Blockade* (2021). One of the stories she talks about [is] teaching her child beaver how to build a dam and the internal dialogue of whether it's enough, will that young beaver carry that lesson forward.[4] What's described isn't a formal dam-building class, it isn't a formal exchange, it's just the act of building in the presence of this young beaver who doesn't look up from their phone [laughs]. I felt that story really resonated with the way that I was taught at Brandon University, not just in the classroom but at the beading table. It wasn't about telling me what to do or when I was doing something wrong, it was about showing and having that activity present. I was responsible for pouring tea, the number of times I got distracted and forgot to refill people's cups was real. That, in and of itself, is my reference to guest/host epistemologies. It doesn't come from being an expert but from wanting to do better and holding myself accountable to that learning process.

The hardest part, I found, enacting methodologies based off of these hosting epistemologies, is to resist the concern about a bottom line. The commercial, capitalist, and corporate aspects are seeping into the discussion because we have to report to granting bodies and we are partnering with Euro-Western institutions with their own agendas. The labour of organizing these gatherings is co-opted by institutions, for social currency, to present themselves as being different in order to look better when nothing changes internally or policy-wise. Negotiating these dynamics has a high risk of competing interests, and essentially, those interests can overshadow the true purposes of gatherings such as

Ziigimineshin as spaces that are meant for Indigenous audiences and Indigenous subject matter for Indigenous cultural sovereignty. It's my hope that conversations like this can create a precedent when we're asked to compromise and are put in positions having to justify what our processes are—regardless of how our local community knowledge differs. We can maintain, protect, and justify practices that are in contrast to mentalities of a bottom line, measurable outcomes, and social currency.

CR: Excellent. You activated really important concepts and actions. And because assimilationist practices within colonial institutions often seem to co-opt and/or override the enactment of Indigenous methods, your ideas and the ideas you drew from Indigenous scholars and curators also relate to a sharing of knowledge and community. Can you talk about how Ziigimineshin reflected beading table values specifically?

FH-S: The beading table values that I learned with the Beading Babes, off the top of my head, involved considerations of time, challenging ideas of expertise in institutions, and what community-centred accessibility looks like.

I'll rewind a little bit. In Brandon, there were two tables that ran on Tuesdays. There was the beading table for students at Brandon University through the Indigenous Peoples Centre [IPC], and then there was the beading table for Brandon community members in the evening [also at the IPC], which is the table we call the Beading Babes. And so, working as Cathy's assistant, and also just as a person who likes chatting with people, I would go to both.

CR: That's a lot of beading, a lot of visiting, and a lot of time.

FH-S: Yes! The meeting table during the day with other students was invaluable because I built a community with Indigenous students outside of my department. So there's value in breaking down and creating an open space for non-hierarchical departmental-separated conversations and, essentially, a space where you could build community. And if it wasn't for the beading space I also don't know if I would have had the courage to go out to search for those relationships. I had so many opportunities to be more open to vulnerability and to listening and building that trust slowly.

That concept of time carried over to Ziigimineshin's format. Leading up to Ziigimineshin there was a large discussion around mental health and burnout within my circles—something that I was dealing with personally. The half-hour break in between each talk not only allowed for time to process what you listened to but to grab coffee and maybe some food. You also would have some time to open yourself up to other folks and visit, to ask "oh, what did you think about that talk?" There are opportunities for vulnerability and quiet, with time and space in between. It also gave the Ziigimineshin team time to work on technical problems between talks because no PowerPoint *ever* works perfectly.

CR: [laughs]

FH-S: So, thinking about the evening community beading table, the Beading Babes, I was super privileged to spend time with Barb Blind, Deborah Tacan, Kimmi Charlton, Leah Thorne Phillips, Christine Tokohopie, Eleanor Daniels, Debbie Huntinghawk, and Verna DeMontigny. They are community members who have done a lot within Brandon and the surrounding area. Folks do work in schools, in the Brandon Bear Clan Patrol, in healthcare, social work, "good morning" posts on Facebook, and just through *being*. For example, Verna is a Michif speaker who translates texts for galleries across Canada and has been generous in naming people's projects, but that's only a fraction of her contributions to the community. And so, knowledge doesn't only come from institutional affirmation. It was really, really important to recognize that the people who were present at Ziigimineshin hold as much knowledge as the people who were invited on stage, and folks onstage weren't there purely because of qualification gained through institutional spaces.

Spending time at the beading table didn't solely affect the method but also a lot of the content presented at Ziigimineshin. The stories

I'm telling clearly outline how my time with the Babes helped me re-engage with community—the Indigenous community in Brandon, the Indigenous academic community, and a larger Indigenous arts community—after growing up in CFS [Child and Family Services]. The talks in Ziigimineshin resonated with that community-building aspect. They followed these themes of connecting through beadwork [Jennine Krauchi, "Connecting with Our Ancestors"; Judy Anderson, Katherine Boyer, Ruth Cuthand, and Carmen Robertson, "Knowledge Transmission: When the Lines are Broken"; Margaret Nazon, "McKenzie Delta Beadwork"], connecting through beading tables [Brandon Beading Babes, "Beading through Generations"; Lisa Myers, "Beads need Threads"] and larger community pushes [Nalakwsis, "#Beadthisinyourstyle Challenge"; Amber Sandy, "Memory, Meaning-Making and Collections Project: bringing Elders together with museum collections"].

The practice of taking care stemmed from the community table too. One student was always in charge of going and picking up Beading Babes; it was my responsibility to make sure the beads were sorted and cared for too. Cathy made it clear [that] it isn't about people getting to you, and then you do the exchange, it's about making sure that people can get there, and that was such a big lesson. With that lesson in mind, it was important to do a big push to invite students from programs across Canada, to make sure they knew this event was happening. We also extended the offer to write support letters for students and community members who wanted to come. This involved writing letters to Band councils, to craft organizations, arts organizations, and university departments explaining why the event was important, why that person needed to be there and, in the process, getting to know these folks, which was really lovely. Also important was making sure everything was as financially accessible [as it could be]. It can also be expressed in coordinating

FIGURE 4.2. Alexandra Nahwegahbow and community members at Ziigimineshin, Winnipeg, Manitoba, February 2020. Photo courtesy of Albyn Carias.

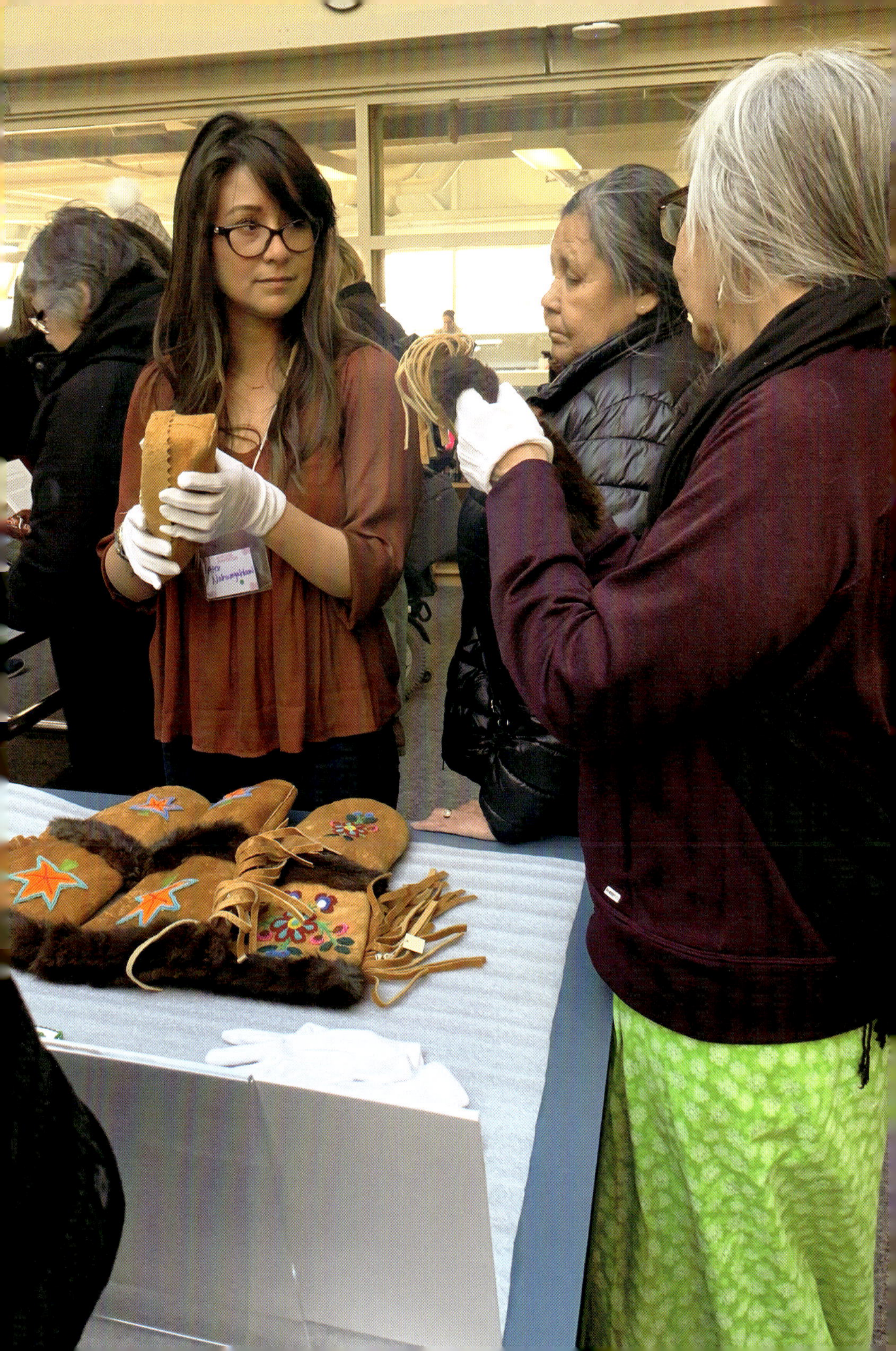

little actions like sending out a weather report every morning. It's not enough to put on an event, you have to get people there, and you have to anticipate the barriers of people being there.

CR: Thank you for explaining your process and the background to planning the gathering. I want to acknowledge that it was palpably different to feel cared for physically, emotionally, and spiritually. You know that almost never happens, right? From my perspective it was a wonderful opportunity to connect with not only friends, colleagues, and students who were there but also to meet new people. Such a supportive community! To finally meet the Beading Babes was a highlight because, a year prior to Ziigimineshin, Cathy Mattes had shared her experience with the Beading Babes in another context. Cathy, Ruth Cuthand, Katherine Boyer, Judy Anderson, and I organized a beading panel in Quebec City at the national Universities Art Association of Canada [UAAC] conference to talk about beading. It was different from the other academic panels presented at the conference. For one, we were all beading at the table while giving our presentations. Cathy shared her experiences at Brandon University, but I didn't really get a good sense of the Beading Babes given the limited time she had for her presentation. The problem with academic panels is the tight timelines that force us to rush through our scholarly discussions!

To meet the group and learn more about their beading experiences during their presentation with Cathy at Ziigimineshin in a setting that made space for personal stories was a breath of fresh air. The opportunity you had to take part in the loving relationships created around the beading tables in Brandon was clearly important to your design process for Ziigimineshin. From what I understand, you succeeded in replicating those experiences and that sense of community in Winnipeg. [pauses]

There were so many powerful moments such as this embedded into the design of Ziigimineshin. Concepts of care and gathering in all aspects of the Winnipeg symposium leave me asking, what's the future?

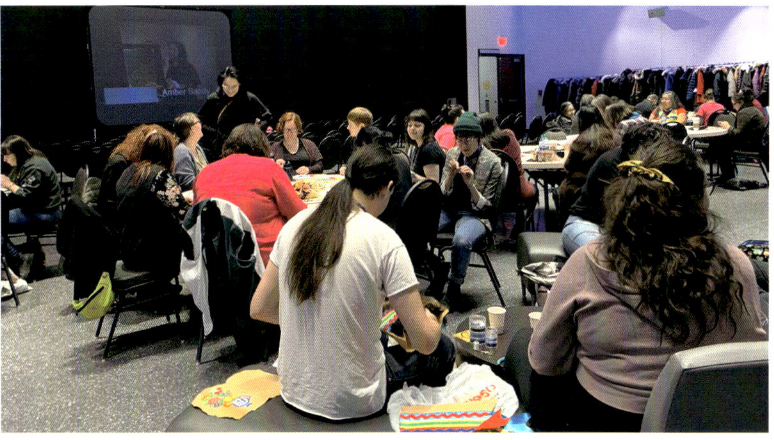

FIGURE 4.3. Beading tables at Ziigimineshin Community Hall, February 2020. Photo courtesy of Albyn Carias.

FH-S: The future of the symposium [laughs]—Lisa and I have talked about it in the past and it really isn't a proprietary event, so I think working within an art—I think, working with institutions, and inheriting some of that pseudo-academic space as curators, we function both as curators and as academics with an idea of intellectual property or territory. That type of thinking really just doesn't have a place in the way that we see the beading symposium moving forward.

This has to do with how we want to see more and more iterations of the beading symposium, to be able to support each other. Lisa helped with the grant application and would pick up the phone whenever I called, [and would ask her] "this is what I'm thinking about. . . . Does this sound like a good idea to move forward?" Lisa spent a decent amount of time talking me through what she was thinking about when she organized Toronto, and so there's this iteration of exchange and intent that's happening. There are future symposiums and conversations happening, I've begun an entire dissertation in guest/host protocols through Carleton University with you as my supervisor on that, and

Ziigimineshin has led to discussions about organizing an Indigenous Craft Council to support this work.

CR: Right, sharing is key.

FH-S: And that's the future of the beading symposium. Every year someone's going to take it on in some form and they'll reach out to somebody who's done it. I'm happy to hand over all the notes and tell them where the grants come from, and it'll just keep being handed around like a bundle, and it'll eventually come back.

CR: Thank you for that. After I moved to Ontario from the Prairies, I became more aware of how different protocols are shaped by different territories. For me, what you did in Winnipeg seemed to reflect Flatland ways of knowing. I felt very at home there even though I'm not from Manitoba!

Do you feel this way about Ziigimineshin? The homeland of the Métis, Cree, Anishinaabeg, Saulteaux, Dakota, and Dene, do these ways of knowing make for something different in the gathering than in Tkaronto, traditional territory of the Mississaugas of the Credit, the Anishinaabeg, the Chippewa, the Haudenosaunee, and the Wendat Peoples, where the symposium you organized with Lisa Myers was held?

FH-S: A lot of what I've talked about is really about space. When you think about imagery around the Prairies, and about cold winter nights, it makes sense that those would translate to Prairies practices. Space and time is a big thing when you think about that. . . . Essentially, each iteration reflects not only the beading culture that's specific to the community it's held in, and is really community-based, but also reflects the knowledge and the perspectives of the individuals who are organizing it. Lisa's symposium[5] focused a lot on making and makers and bringing in artists and talking about making processes and techniques. Lisa's background is multi-disciplinary; a folk-rockstar, chef, curator, writer, an artist, a super involved community member, and activist. It was fun and intimate, and in some ways felt like a residency retreat without the pressure of coming out with an artwork. I felt the joy of making that Lisa embodies.

For Ziigimineshin, the Winnipeg team was made up of makers, community members and individuals who have all participated in beading tables. Rachel Erickson and Maureen Mathews were both museum staff who had been part of beading tables. Albyn Carias is also a member of the Beading Babes; Katherine Boyer is [a] multi-disciplinary artist known for her beadwork, and Daina Warren is a curator. Having a team with those experiences of beading affected how Ziigimineshin was organized. I'm really, really looking forward to seeing how similar projects unfold. There are other iterations or other spaces throughout the country that want to host, and [they are] coordinating who's doing what and when and just doing it in an open dialogue.

When I was preparing for [this] conversation about Ziigimineshin, and the question of what was unique and how, I thought of this story as an example. It's become pretty standard to begin events with land acknowledgements, and for events that relate to Indigenous content, there's drumming that welcomes guests. For Ziigimineshin I had asked members of the Beading Babes to come and sing because we have drummers in the Babes. It was on the schedule, in a neat little box as you do, saying, "Thursday: 10 am, Land acknowledgement and welcome in Community Hall." Following that we would then move downstairs to begin the talks. After the Babes finished drumming, Barb Blind, a Beading Babe and Elder from Brandon, turned to the audience and asked if anybody else wanted to offer a song. This was a beautiful gesture and very much wasn't programmed. That moment of teaching, where Barb demonstrates what I should be doing—and didn't know enough to do—is full of reciprocity; it embodied reciprocity to open up a space in the event for guests to bring their own knowledge and practices, acknowledging how far some folks had travelled; there was reciprocity in the guests taking up the offer; and lastly, the reciprocity of the attendees—a predominantly Indigenous audience—who understood and showed the same amount of respect for those who offered their songs.

This entire network of exchange, I think, is really what made me realize that it wasn't something that I could own. This was an event that proliferated on unplanned moments and moments that couldn't be programmed. In the Prairies, I was taught about reflexive frameworks and the fundamental difference between Euro-Western colonial events and Indigenous pedagogy. So, whether or not the symposium reflects Prairie beading culture is definitely a question: the exchanges that happened stemmed from the focus, investment, and recognition of what the local knowledge and local relationships were. I think that's a [prairie beading] cultural expression but it's the *framework* that offers a cultural expression that will be further enriched by communities anywhere. It'll manifest differently in different spaces, and that's what's exciting. That is the potential for the future.

NOTES

1 Lisa Myers, "Beads Need Threads," in *Becoming Our Future: Global Indigenous Curatorial Practice*, eds. Julie Nagam, Carly Lane, and Megan Tamati-Quennell (Winnipeg: ARP Books, 2021), 193–204.

2 Lorraine F. Mayer, "A Return to Reciprocity," *Hyatia* 22, no. 3 (Summer, 2007): 22–42.

3 University of Lethbridge, 18–21 October 1989.

4 Leanne Simpson, *A Short History of the Blockade: Giant Beavers, Diplomacy, and Regeneration in Nishnaabewin* (Edmonton: University of Alberta Press, 2021).

5 Beading Symposium: Manidoominensagemin Toronto, 2019.

5.

BEADS IN THE BLOOD —CURATING RUTH CUTHAND'S ART

FELICIA GAY AND CARMEN ROBERTSON

Felicia Gay and Carmen Robertson met online in late 2022 to discuss Felicia's work on Ruth Cuthand's exhibition, *Beads in the blood: Ruth Cuthand, a Survey*. The following is the edited transcript of their conversation, which took place via Zoom.

CARMEN ROBERTSON: Felicia, I'm excited to talk about your curatorial project, *Beads in the blood: Ruth Cuthand, a Survey*, mounted at the Kenderdine Gallery at University of Saskatchewan in 2021. I'm interested in learning about your curatorial process and the outcome of the amazing exhibition that not many people got to see because of COVID-19. If you could start by talking a little bit about the way you create or put together a show, and what that means in relation to working with an artist like Ruth.

FELICIA GAY: Thank you for this opportunity to allow me to talk about my curatorial process and my relationship with Ruth and how the show came about. I'm very strongly connected to my community in northern Saskatchewan and Cumberland House. My background on my mother's side is Swampy Cree and my father's side is Scottish. I have a mixed heritage but was raised by my mother's parents because I'm the oldest child. Half my life was spent with my grandparents and half was spent with my mom, so that is my worldview. I think when you're young you don't really realize how your upbringing affects your worldview. You don't really think about it or critique it. It was during graduate studies that I started to really look at my curatorial practice, and I started to realize that a lot of my practice, the way I work, is *because* of my Swampy Cree background. Since starting my studies, I've been building up this vocabulary [situated in academia] for the work I did, which I learned experientially. [The process] I'm thinking about is what I thought made sense to me [as I experimented as a curator]. Because I primarily work with Indigenous artists, [my process and worldview] just melded with other Indigenous artists. A lot of the facets of my worldview connect [or are relatable to] other Indigenous artists, in terms of relationships [or relationship building].

I wanted to share my curatorial statement for *Beads in the blood*:

> From 22 January to 10 April 2021, *Beads in the blood: Ruth Cuthand, a Survey* was displayed at the Kenderdine and College Art Galleries at the University of Saskatchewan in Saskatoon. The opportunity to work as a curator over many years, practicing from a lens that is specific to Swampy Cree ways of knowing, has revealed to me a curatorial praxis [or custom] based on relationship. With this lens, traditional aspects of power and hierarchy are happily displaced, and friendship, mentorship, and acts of care are centred. Fostering collaborative approaches to curatorial work means that relationships between artists and curators cannot be built on performative gestures of care but instead built over many years where respect and trust can be mutually gained.

Ruth and I met during my undergraduate studies; she was my art history instructor. I switched to art history from archaeology because of Ruth. We formed a friendship, first with me as a student—this was seventeen years ago. Our relationship grew, and [later I had the opportunity] to curate her in different exhibitions. She was always generous; she is such a mentor and mentors Indigenous women strategically. I'm grateful to her for that.

CR: Well, I want to say that I think we're all grateful to her for that as well, because the fact that she really inspired you to shift out of archaeology or anthropology and into curatorial is important for all of us.

FG: Ruth has created this cause and effect [stemming] from her own practice, and it's really beautiful. When I was given the opportunity to do this survey of Ruth's work, I really wanted it to be something different, something special, something that was built on trust and collaboration.

When she was an artist-in-residence at Wanuskewin, outside of Saskatoon, around 2017, Ruth was producing beadwork for different projects while I worked as a curator there. One time I mentioned to her, "Hey, I had this weird dream about you. I dreamt you were in the valley [at Wanuskewin], planting these beaded crocuses." I shared that I was watching her from afar, she didn't know I was there, but she was walking and planting crocuses. When I told her about it, Ruth said, "Well, let's do it!" So, she created beaded crocuses, and we went out and planted them and we documented it. It was just like in the dream. They're still out there somewhere. This was our first collaborative project. After that I wondered, what else can we do with this?

CR: I love the image of her beaded crocuses on the prairies. Imagining Ruth's crocuses in the coulees at Wanuskewin, poking through the snow, makes me smile.

FG: Stories like this led to *Beads in the blood*. I was approached sometime after Ruth's artist-in-residency at Wanuskewin by Leah Taylor, a fantastic curator who works at the Kenderdine Art Gallery (and College

Galleries) at the University of Saskatchewan. She knew of our relationship, and Leah really wanted to put together a survey show for Ruth. That is how this came about. Unfortunately, the project occurred during the height of COVID when the institution was closed [to the public]. The project didn't receive a lot of public attention since the gallery was closed [except by appointment] so we are hoping that there'll be other iterations of this project down the road.

CR: Yes, and we were so happy when you agreed to have a conversation about this show because none of us got to see it either. The little bit that is online is just insufficient to honour both you and Ruth.

FG: There are multiple projects within *Beads in the blood,* and they are all connected to story as well as [to] how beads are considered animate. They are called migis (beads), and in Swampy Cree and Plains Cree epistemologies, stories and beads are animate.

CR: Yes, that's one thing that you've really captured in this show, the notion of migis as this animate being within the room, within the work. I think that's an important way of shifting curatorial process about beads so that there's an understanding of the powerful role beads play in galleries.

FG: I've said it time and again, and I usually try to mention it in interpretive labels or panels for my shows so the public can be reminded that [Indigenous] languages are not based on feminine and masculine concepts, they're based on animate and inanimate ones. We understand materiality so differently, and you know, it is such a neat way to look at things!

Story is a very important facet to Ruth's practice. One of the things I had to think through with this project was, how can I implicate or talk about story in a collaborative way in this exhibition? The first thing we did was to talk [with one another] and share stories, and this may sound simple, but it wasn't. The thing about stories is sometimes they're given as gifts, or sometimes it's just your own personal recollections. Ruth told me a story about growing up in southern Alberta in Cardston. She talked about the remnants of a burial practice she remembered seeing as a child

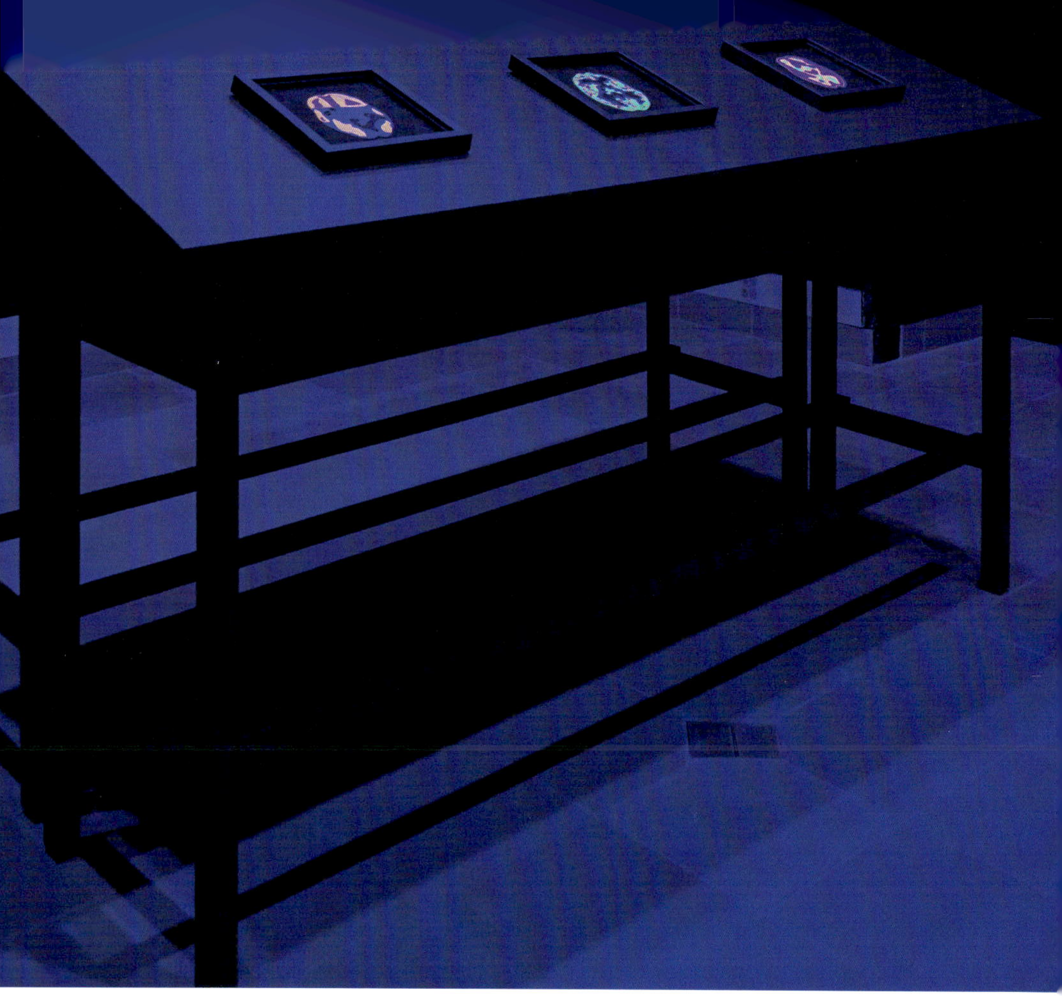

FIGURE 5.1. Ruth Cuthand, *Beaded Brain Scans*, from *Beads in the blood: Ruth Cuthand, a Survey* (2021). At College Art Galleries, University of Saskatchewan, Saskatoon. Photo courtesy of Carey Shaw. See also Figure 1.1.

with her father, a practice that had been adapted by the Kainai who no longer [after colonization] could use traditional scaffolding for bodies as they had done prior to contact. So, one thing that really stood out to her was seeing a metal bed frame used as a contemporary form of scaffolding (once a traditional practice). A body, long gone, *had* been laid out on this bed. She remembers seeing the bed frame and blue beads that had fallen to the ground, fallen off the clothing, lying there in the shape of a woman's cape. She remembers just the outline of the cape in beads and most of the beads were blue. What Ruth thought about [later in her life] was that this was a woman's mark on the land. Ruth collaborated with Theo Cuthand, who is a well-known filmmaker [and her child]. Inspired by Ruth's memories of seeing this solitary structure, the film depicts someone throwing beads out onto the land, which abstractly connects to the story. For the *Beads and the blood* show, Ruth wanted a reinterpretation of the story. So, she did that with an installation, which was simply a metal bed frame and beads beneath it on the gallery floor. A lot of the work Ruth has done these past years has raised the concept of disease and its relation to Indigenous people. Beads and blood could be about germs and bacteria that enter your blood, it's an image with layers of meaning.

CR: Seeing these images from the installation shots from the show adds to their power, and especially given that it was mounted during the COVID pandemic [Figure 5.1]. There's a sense of cyclical reality present. Past, present, future all seem to meld together through this.

FG: Yes, this is something we need to take [as] advice from our stories, because they are fluid. I think this is one of the main things that made me sad about this exhibition, because you cannot see the story online or experience these stories the way they were meant to be [experienced]. One of the exciting things about this show was that I got to show off

FIGURE 5.2A. Ruth Cuthand, detail of *Boil Water Advisory #1* (2016), glass beads, resin, found glassware, 30.5 x 30.5 x 30.5 cm. Collection of Saskatchewan Arts Board, College Art Galleries, University of Saskatchewan, Saskatoon. Photo courtesy of Carey Shaw.

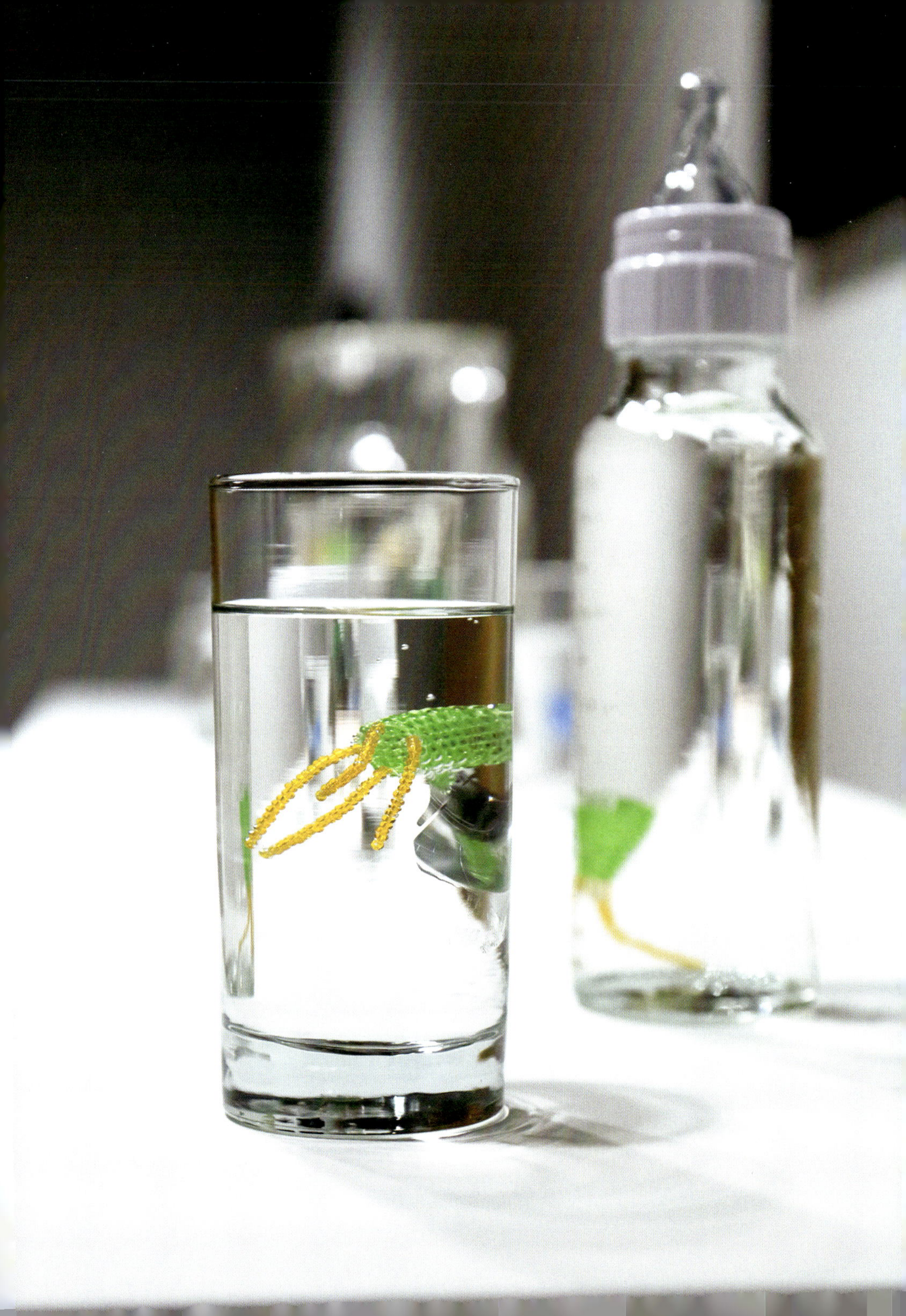

some of Ruth's new work. People may know of her *Trading* series, especially in Saskatchewan. Her new series features [beaded] brain scans and it's the first time they've been shown publicly. The brain scans are MRI machines images [of mental health issues like PTSD or neurodivergent scans of the brain such as ADHD] and then beaded with glow-in-the-dark beads. The work talks openly about mental health issues. What we did to display these works was to use blue light [Figure 5.1].

I think one thing to point out about the importance of these works is that there seems to be a taboo within our [Indigenous] communities [about openly talking about mental health], and I'm not sure why that is. Ruth wants people to realize that it's not your fault that your brain is working in a different way. The beaded scans show that. Utilizing beads to show what's animate and what isn't animate in your brain is a beautiful way to describe these issues.

CR: When Ruth told me she planned to create a body of work that would capture what's happening in our brains using glow-in-the-dark beads, I couldn't imagine it having such power. I really love that you were able to capitalize on the dramatic energy of the glowing beads by using blue light.

FG: Ruth's beaded work in resin is another area I really wanted to showcase. A domestic sphere with the concept of repulsion and beauty [is the same aspect] that audiences also encountered with the beaded diseases. I wanted viewers to think about being on the rez and sitting at the kitchen table with your family and having these [contaminated] drinks, instead of displaying them in a sterile way [on gallery shelves or plinths].

The table and chairs allude to a domestic sphere, and I was also thinking about Cathy Mattes, a fellow curator who has done this wonderful research around the concept of the kitchen table. She talks about the kitchen table as a site of revolution, resistance, and community. The kitchen table is all those things, and so I really hope people understand that.

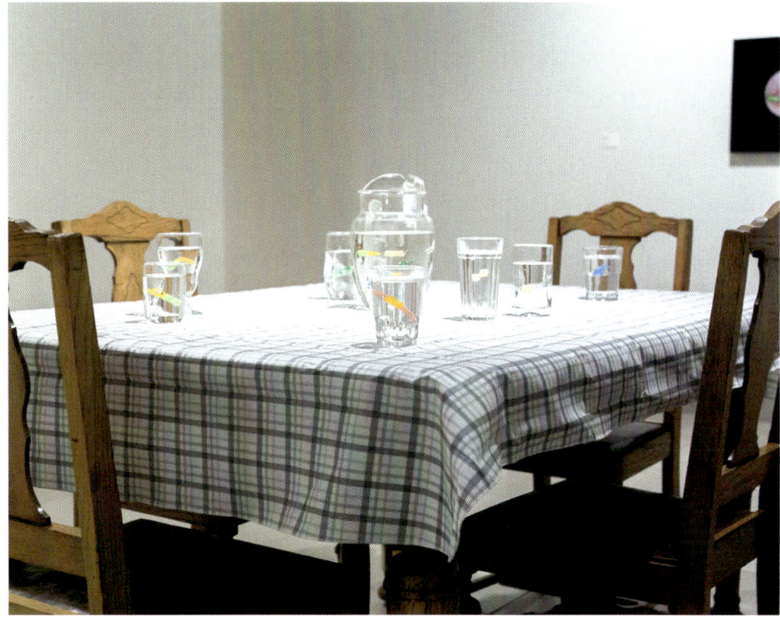

FIGURE 5.2B. Ruth Cuthand, *Boil Water Advisory #1* (2016), glass beads, resin, found glassware, 30.5 x 30.5 x 30.5 cm. Collection of Saskatchewan Arts Board, College Art Galleries, University of Saskatchewan, Saskatoon. Photo courtesy of Carey Shaw.

CR: I think, especially on the prairies, the idea of sitting around the table resonates with audiences. It's so important in Indigenous communities, and of course Cathy's research highlights that in ways specific to Métis communities. A jug of water and the glasses sitting on the table signal how fundamental the tainted water is to lives [Figure 5.2A and B]. You know, there's a beauty and a warmth, and then there's the—as you say, with Ruth's work—the repulsion.

FG: I really love how she uses beauty to talk about something very ugly. Usually, people like to look away from ugly topics [or difficult knowledge], and this really tricks the viewer into thinking about issues, whether they like to or not. I think that's such a great strategy.

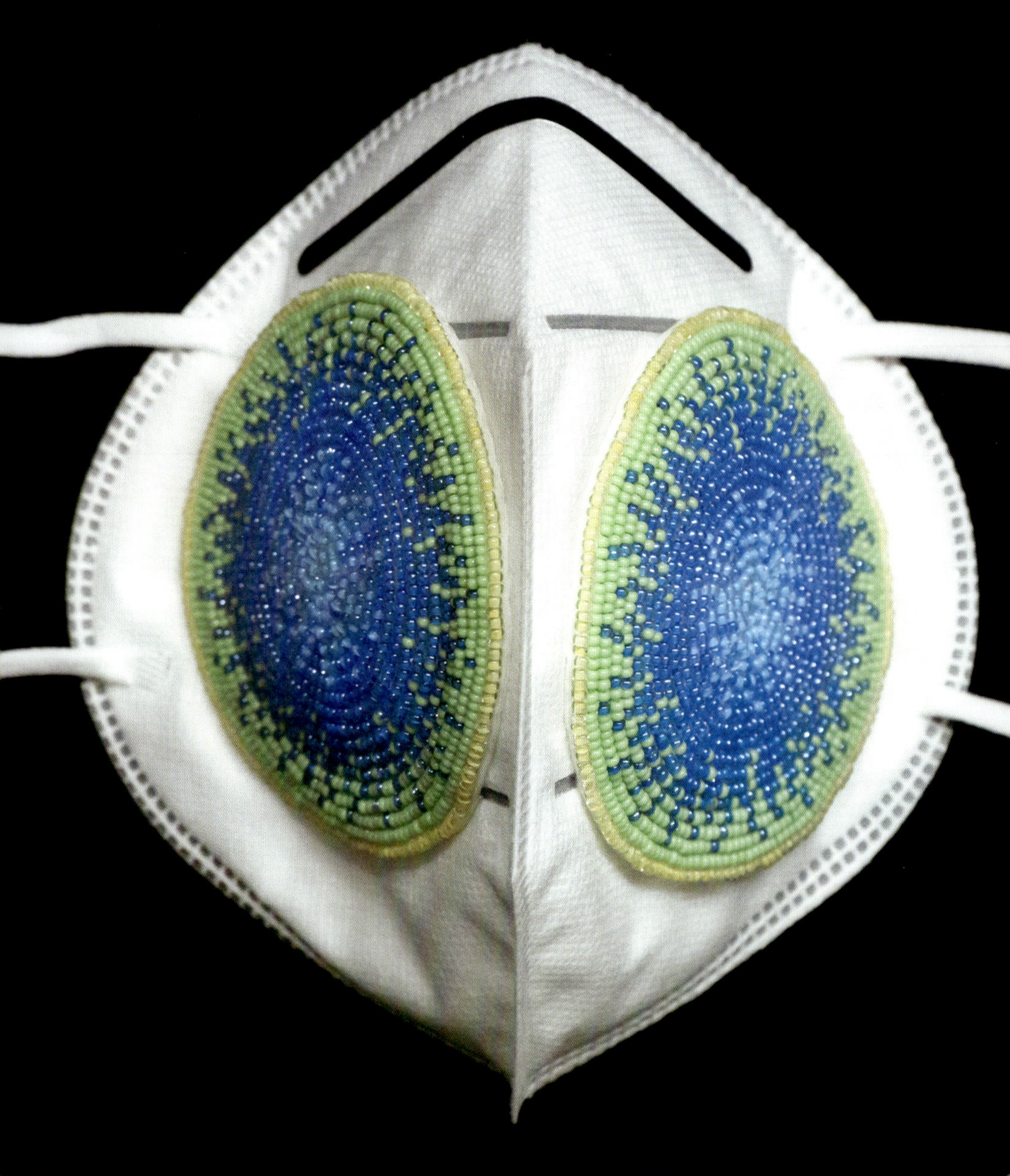

FIGURE 5.3. Ruth Cuthand, *Surviving: COVID-19 mask* (2020), glass beads, mask, thread, backing, 12 x 12 inches. At College Art Galleries, University of Saskatchewan, Saskatoon. Collection of the artist. Photo courtesy of Carey Shaw.

CR: Absolutely.

FG: Ruth's COVID masks, too [Figure 5.3]. Those are quite new as well. She was, I think, one of the first artists who utilized the N-95 masks and inspired other artists. Her practice keeps evolving and growing, but it's always foundational to what she has always been doing.

CR: This exhibition is very much connected through Ruth to the Plains territory. But its themes resonate throughout Turtle Island. It seems to me that you were able to translate Ruth's powerful visual stories into your curatorial vision. Did you find that curating this exhibition for Ruth has shifted or changed or, you know, reinvigorated aspects of your own personal curatorial process?

FG: I think what's probably the most difficult aspect of this type of show is that you have to really foster your relationship with that person, and it has to be built on respect and trust, and you're not always going to find that, and you're not always going to have access to that, so when it comes along, you need to be grateful about it.

I have this relationship with Ruth, but [this type of relationship between artist and curator] is not always going to come my way. With Ruth, she's not only been someone I've curated [for or worked with], she is also someone who mentors me.

CR: Felicia, thank you for sharing your ideas. I think that's a wonderful place to stop, for now.

PART II:
ESSAYS

6.

"UNTIL WE BEAD AGAIN"—THE BU BEADING BABES AND EMBODYING LATERAL LOVE AND GENEROUS RECIPROCITY

CATHY MATTES WITH FRANCHESCA HEBERT-SPENCE, DEBBIE HUNTINGHAWK, ALBYN CARIAS, CHRISTINE TOKOHOPIE, JUSTINE HUTCHESON, JENNA BRISSON, KEVIN MCKENZIE, BARB BLIND, ELEANOR DANIELS, KIMMI CHARLTON, AND JESSIE JANNUSKA

"BEADING WAS MY WAY HOME." —FRANCHESCA HEBERT-SPENCE (SAGKEENG FIRST NATION)

It was in collecting hands to create gifts for Brandon University Indigenous graduates that collective hearts instigated the BU Beading Babes (the Babes). With generous reciprocity steeped in lateral love, we soaked ourselves into the campus concrete. Brandon University (BU) didn't envision or create us, though as an academic institution with pressures to decolonize, Indigenize, and reconcile, it has certainly benefited from our existence and presence. Instead, we instinctually and organically sewed ourselves into relation, and made our way around, within, and beyond the university walls, with beads as our guides.

"IT WAS MY DRUM THAT LED ME TO BU, AND IN 2013 I STARTED UNIVERSITY." —DEBBIE HUNTINGHAWK (ANISHINAABE)

The BU Beading Babes was activated in 2013 during the tenure of Peter Morin (Tahltan) and me (Michif) at Brandon University when we were invited to join a cohort of students and community members to make beaded keychains for Indigenous graduates. We were provided with materials and space in the Indigenous Peoples Centre (IPC) at the end of the winter term. The IPC is dedicated to ensuring Indigenous student success through advising, cultural teachings, study groups, art workshops, potlucks, and medicine picking. It is a home away from home for many students who move to Brandon to attend BU. Although the Babes was not an official initiative of IPC, the Centre was supportive, and the group quickly became a staple in the IPC.

When Peter Morin and I were first asked to help make grad gifts in 2013, it became an opportunity for us to connect with students and community and promote our department. IshKaabatens Waasa Gaa Inaabateg—Department of Visual Arts (IWGIDVA) is one of the only visual arts departments in Canada that has a Knowledge Keeper in residence, carries a spirit name, and provides an accredited degree program in Indigenous art. Since its inception in 2003, it has offered courses in Indigenous art history, design, and customary techniques, and an annual guest artist lecture series featuring many Indigenous artists. It is one of the only programs in Canada where students can major or minor in Indigenous visual culture, and beading has been a key artform taught by Indigenous artmakers.[1]

That initial invitation was an opportunity to encourage Indigenous visual art students to learn to bead outside of a classroom and find community in the IPC. Despite its being a safe and welcoming space, some of our students were timid about entering the space. The relationship created

FIGURE 6.1. Sample of graduate gifts made by members of the Brandon University Beading Babes, 7 May 2019. Photo credit: Cathy Mattes. Permission was granted by all contributing members of the BU Beading Babes for the use of these images.

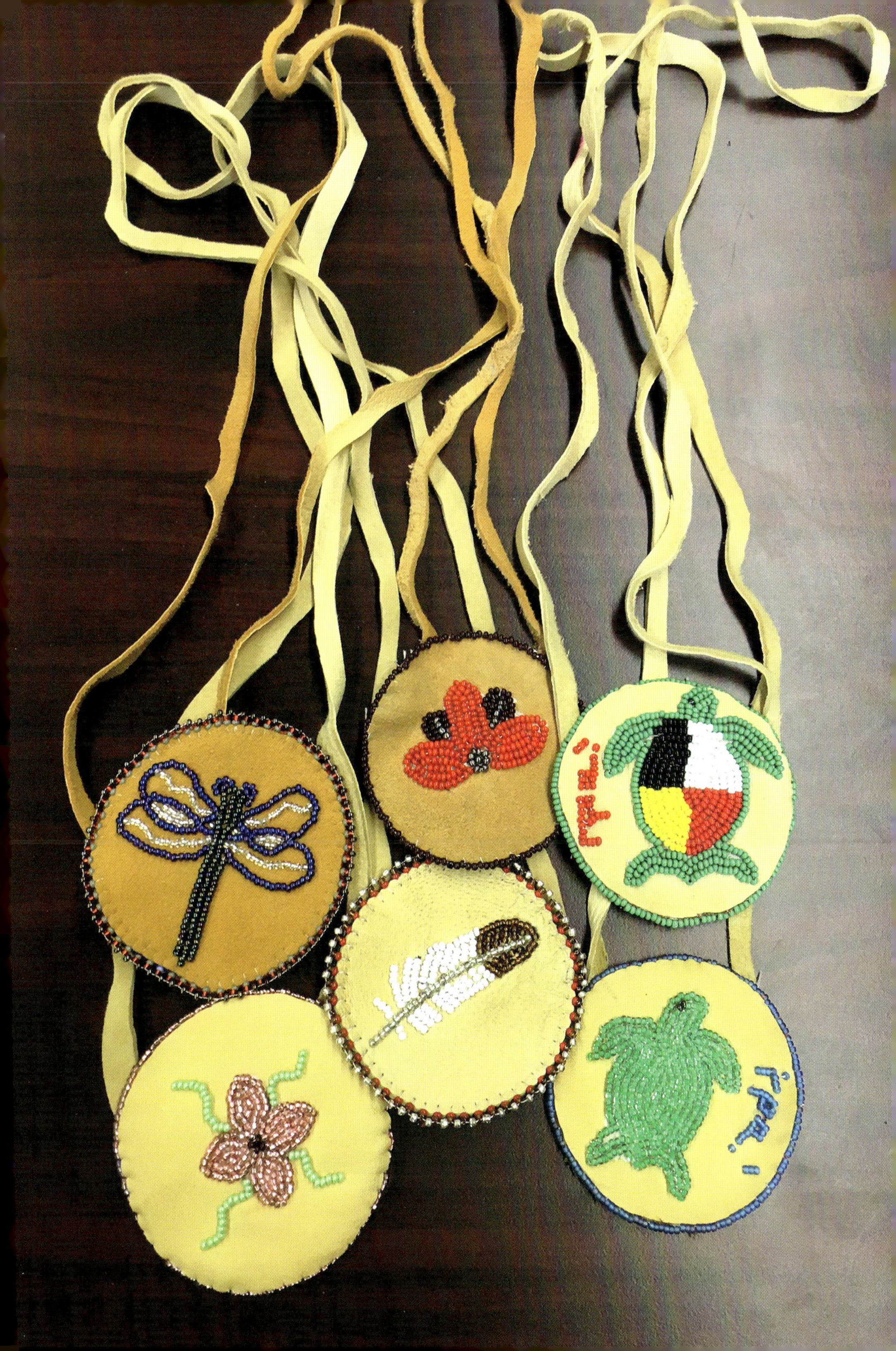

between IPC and IWGIDVA via the Babes remedied this, and a shift happened where our students saw the IPC as a place that culturally cradled, nurtured, and cultivated them.

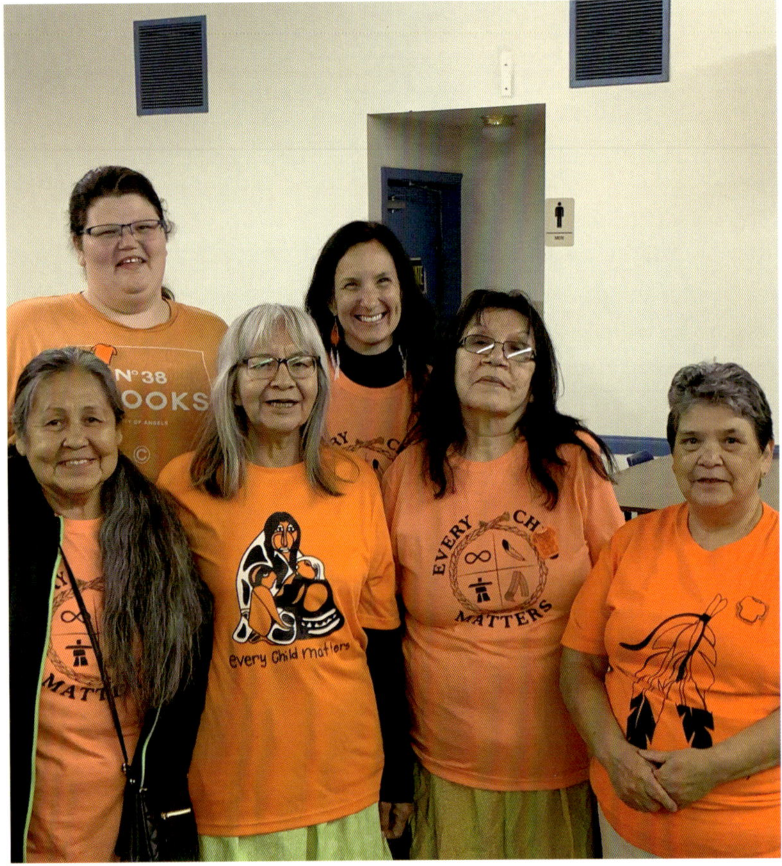

FIGURE 6.2. Some members of the BU Beading Babes at a community gathering for Truth and Reconciliation Day, 30 September 2019, Brandon MB. From Bottom Left: Christine Tokohopie, Justine Hutcheson, Barb Blind, Cathy Mattes, Eleanor Daniels, Verna DeMontigny. Photo credit: Cathy Mattes.

"I FELL IN LOVE WITH IT. NOT JUST THE BEADING BUT THE PEOPLE I MET THERE."
—ALBYN CARIAS (EL SALVADOR)

When *Walking With Our Sisters* (*WWOS*), a commemorative art project in honour of Missing and Murdered Women and Girls, was touring across Turtle Island, Peter and I noticed there were students and local community members who were teaching themselves to bead with online tutorials. Their desire and resourcefulness to contribute a pair of beaded moccasin vamps to the project led us to offer weekly beading sessions in IPC during the scheduled free period throughout the fall and winter terms. Shortly afterwards, in 2016, Brandon University hosted *WWOS*, organized by a cohort of Indigenous Knowledge Keepers, community leaders, and students. One part of the *WWOS* programming was weekly "bead-ins," opportunities for local people to come together and bead. These sessions were hosted at the Art Gallery of Southwestern Manitoba and were very well-attended. When they ended, participants shared their wish for the beading sessions to continue. Peter and I responded by adding another session at BU, held in the evening for community members to join students in gathering to bead and visit. Since the closing of *WWOS* in Brandon in 2016, Tuesdays in the IPC have included two BU Beading Babes sessions—one during the free period in the afternoon, and one later in the evening.

"THEY WERE STRICT IN A LOT OF WAYS. THEY TAUGHT ME HOW TO PUT BEADS AWAY, PRAY BEFORE YOU BEAD, IF YOU DROP BEADS, PICK THEM UP . . . WHEN I WAS YOUNG, I WAS MOSTLY ON THE FLOOR PICKING UP BEADS."
—CHRISTINE TOKOHOPIE (NAKOTA)

From the start, first-time beaders begin by separating small bags of mixed beads on felt with a needle. This helps them to get used to the scale, colours, shades, and shapes of the beads, and to develop patience. We ask experienced bead artists to help those new to beading and to be as encouraging as possible with them. Select IWGIDVA students assist in the weekly beading sessions, where they learn to teach workshops, immerse themselves in Indigenous knowledge transmission, and develop their own visual language while bringing their Indigenous hearts home. In the spirit of generous reciprocity and spreading lateral love, they learn how to host newcomers to the space, offering tea and food, and making sure they feel comfortable and are enjoying themselves. During these sessions participants collectively bead with good hearts, share stories and knowledge, and as Christine was taught to do in her youth, we pick up beads whenever they fall onto the floor.

"WHEN I CAME BACK TO SCHOOL, AND I CAME BACK TO THESE LADIES, WE LAUGHED SO HARD. THEY HELPED ME REMEMBER WHAT IT WAS LIKE TO LAUGH LIKE THAT. THEY REALLY REMINDED ME HOW BEAUTIFUL LIFE IS AND HOW BEAUTIFUL PEOPLE ARE, AND HOW MUCH LOVE YOU CAN HAVE BY BEING YOURSELF."
—JUSTINE HUTCHESON (CREE/MÉTIS)

The Tuesday gatherings are child-friendly, and the IPC provides bead supplies and tea. We meet all year round, instead of basing our time together on the university calendar. Students often come gather where we bead to listen to our conversations and watch us work. The rhythm of our collective breath sometimes helps them get through their days and weeks and we have been told by students that we are a reminder of home. There is also a Facebook message group, where members share photos of their beading projects, ask for guidance on techniques, and provide positive feedback and encouragement to one another. The messenger group includes current and former students and community members who may have spent limited time with the Babes, or have been there from the start. Whether in person at the IPC or online, the Babes provide a space of solace, knowledge transmission, and friendship. With that has come continuous encouragement, humility, and humour . . . the Babes always bring the laughter.

"I BROUGHT MY SON AND WHEN I GOT THERE, I REALIZED THAT THIS IS WHAT I WAS MISSING THE WHOLE TIME."
—JENNA BRISSON (MOOSE FACTORY)

While continuing to make beaded gifts for graduating students, the group's focus expanded to learning how to make a wide variety of items—moccasins, gauntlets, earrings, medicine pouches, lanyards, pen cases, Remembrance Day poppies, and orange T-shirt pins in honour of residential school survivors and those who never came home. We began to demonstrate beading at the local Career Symposium, Brandon's Truth and Reconciliation Week, Louis Riel Day events, and BU's annual Long Night Against Procrastination event. With this new exposure, we started getting requests to sell our beaded wares. Moving from solely gifting grad students to selling items for profit was a tricky process, as some Babes were unsure about making money from their beadwork. So we started by holding Remembrance Day poppies sales. And a portion of the proceeds went to the local Army and Navy, some to replenish our supplies, and the rest to the bead artists. We then began selling beaded orange shirt pins upon request and split profits between individual bead workers and the group. Selling these items became a way to spread the Babes' beaded love outside of the IPC, while helping them financially.

"I JOINED THE BEADING BABES TO GET MORE EXPERIENCE AND TO HAVE KINSHIP, WHICH I NEVER HAD BEFORE. AS MUCH AS I WAS DOING MY OWN THING IN THE CONTEMPORARY ART WORLD, I FELT FURTHER ISOLATED FROM MY COMMUNITY. BUT NOW I BELONG TO A COMMUNITY, AND I GET SO MUCH KNOWLEDGE AND PLEASURE FROM HANGING OUT WITH THE GROUP . . . FIRE IS NOW COMING FROM MY FINGERTIPS WHEN I BEAD."
—KEVIN MCKENZIE (COWESSESS FIRST NATION)

In 2017, the BU Beading Babes' reach extended beyond the IPC and demonstrations at events. When I was the visual editor of the *Canadian*

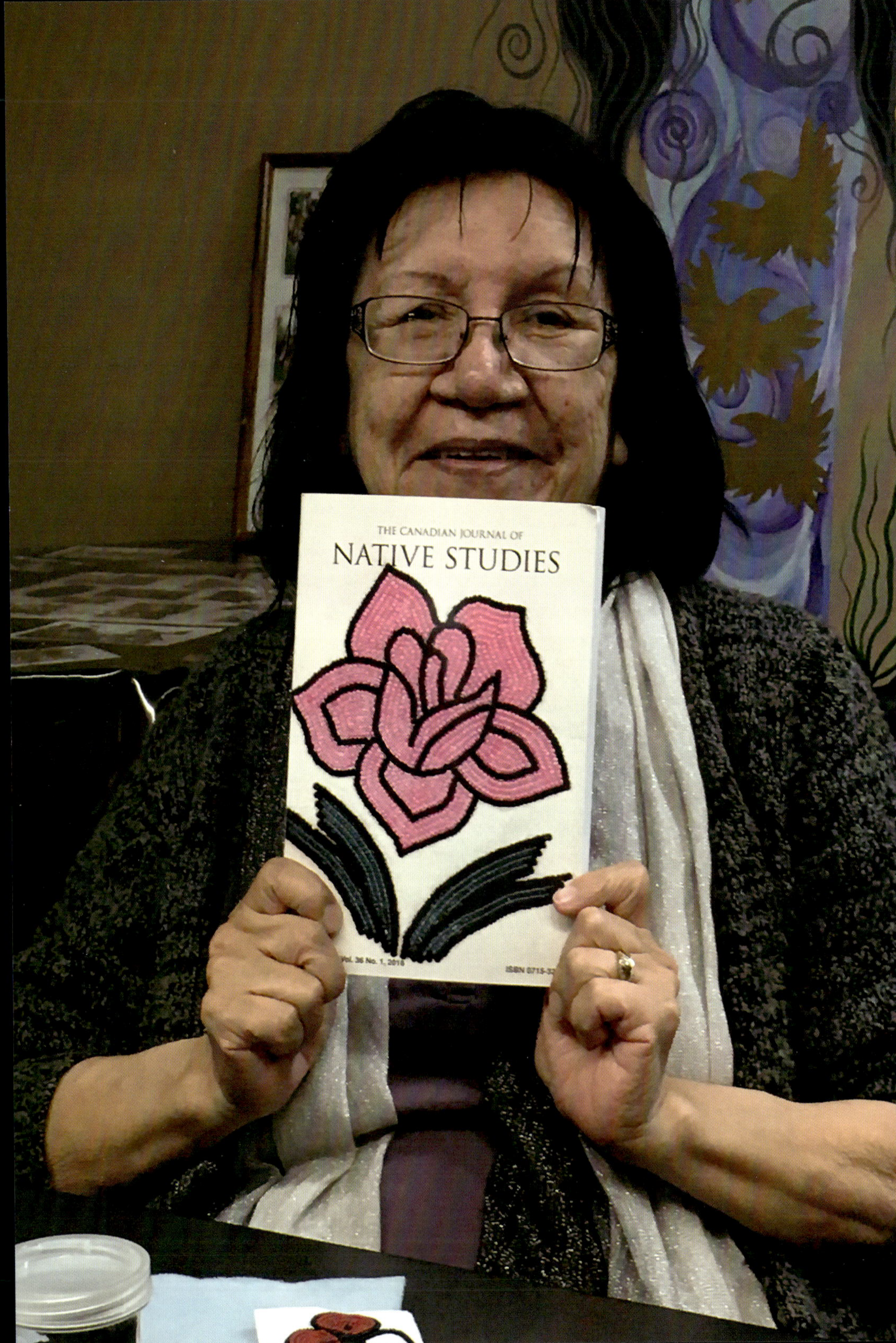
THE CANADIAN JOURNAL OF
NATIVE STUDIES

Journal of Native Studies, I asked Eleanor Daniels (South Indian Lake) if I could feature the first beadwork she ever shared with me, a tightly sewn bright pink rose on a white hide background. Eleanor spent her youth beading with her mother, and her technique and designs are impeccable. Featuring the stunning work on the cover of an academic journal signalled the seeping of the Babes into the academy and the deepening of our relationality, which prioritized local Knowledge Keepers' artistic contributions.

Courtesy of IWGIDVA, visiting artists provide workshops in the IPC and visit with the Babes, a highlight for guest artists like Amy Malbeuf, Dayna Danger, and Judy Anderson. In return, the Babes come to their public talks and art shows and encourage students to do the same. Some of the Babes also became cultural conduits for IWGIDVA bachelor of fine arts (BFA) honour students like Cameron Flamand (Métis), Fran Hebert-Spence, Jessie Jannuska (Dakota, Ojibway, Settler), and Albyn Carias. Barb Blind (George Gordon First Nation), Debbie Huntinghawk, Deborah T. Tacan (Cree/Métis), and Verna DeMontigny (Michif) all invested in the students' art exhibitions through sharing stories, providing art critiques, and introducing them to ceremony, language, and customary art practices. And when Kevin McKenzie, an established mixed media artist and studio professor, joined IWGIDVA in 2019, it became more obvious that it was the Babes who were our teachers, and those of us in official teaching roles were on the receiving end with our students.

When he was first hired as a studio professor, I asked Kevin to shadow me when I taught an Indigenous studio techniques course so he could learn customary art practices, including beading. As the Knowledge Keeper in Residence for the department, Barb Blind, a long-time Babe, attended the course to learn these art practices and provide guidance and support to the students, Kevin, and me. Because he would eventually teach beading and help lead the BU Beading Babes, I felt Kevin needed to perfect his technique

FIGURE 6.3. Eleanor Daniels with her beadwork on the cover of the *Canadian Journal of Native Studies*, 16 November 2016. Photo credit: Cathy Mattes.

and learn how to assess beadwork. I invited Eleanor Daniels and Christine Tokohopie to visit the class and provide critiques to the students and Kevin on their beadwork. Before their first visit, I encouraged them both to "be a bit tough" on Kevin with their evaluation of his beading. Instead, Christine and Eleanor gifted Kevin nothing but encouragement and accolades. They recognized that as an established artist, Kevin would figure things out on his own and didn't need strongly delivered critiques. They clearly knew what I didn't at the time: all Kevin required for his artistic and cultural development was lateral love and praise. As cultural conduits, they taught Kevin and me how to teach customary practices in a good way and not to always adhere to conventional Western art practices. The presence of Barb, Eleanor, and Christine set a different tone for my students, who learned how to actively listen, engage with the quietness, and recognize the importance of providing care in learning moments.

"THE BU BABES ARE NOW FAMOUS, EVERYONE WANTS TO BE A BABE." —BARB BLIND (GEORGE GORDON FIRST NATION)

In 2020, artists, curators, scholars, and community members from across Turtle Island experienced the BU Beading Babes first-hand at Beading Symposium: Ziigimineshin Winnipeg 2020. It was held at the Manitoba Museum, in partnership with a variety of local arts organizations. This was a big deal to the Babes not only because it was in Manitoba but because it was organized by our very own Fran Hebert-Spence. We knew that her participation with the Babes over the years somehow played a role in her organizing this event as part of her curatorial and academic practices. We were proud of her and wanted to be a part of the gathering.

Student Justine Hutcheson worked with other Babes to propose a roundtable session that would mirror our weekly gatherings: beading

FIGURE 6.4. Collaborative Beaded Turtle Shell art piece (in progress), 7 February 2020. Photo credit: Cathy Mattes.

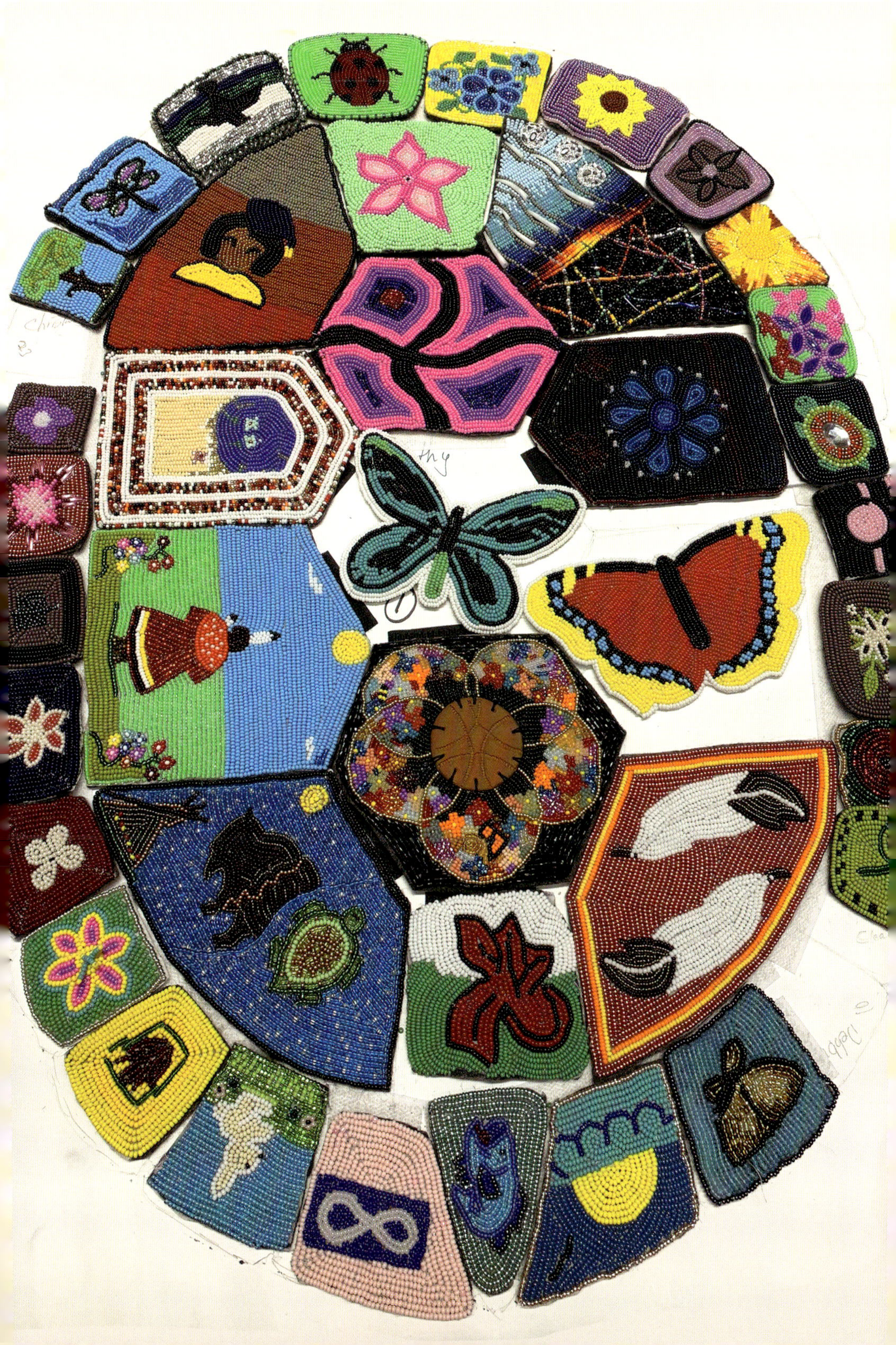

around a table, drinking tea, and chatting. Over the months before the symposium, Justine organized a collaborative beading project that would guide the Babes in how they would introduce themselves during the roundtable and answer the question she would pose: "What does beading mean to you?" Recognizing the importance of how Turtle Island (North America) was built on the turtle's back, she collected thirteen large beaded pieces and twenty-eight smaller ones to represent the turtle's shell and convey how we bead ourselves into relation. In addition to the group's regular attendees, community members who sometimes joined the Babes and current and former students (some who had left Brandon) contributed beaded turtle shell patches.

During the roundtable, the Babes who represented the group revealed what beading meant to them and what it was like to be a Babe.[2] Everyone shared their heartfelt response to Justine's question, then described the turtle patch they contributed and what it meant. Most had never been to a symposium or spoken publicly until that moment, and they all captivated the audience. One Babe in particular, Eleanor Daniels, was even approached by television media afterwards and interviewed for news programs. That may have been the moment that led to Barb's joke that the Babes are famous!

Once I left Brandon University to teach at the University of Winnipeg, I was encouraged to organize a beading circle with students and the Babes at my new workplace, as word had spread about the Babes' impact on students. When I shared with my students that I would try to organize a workshop with the group, some of them became elated. They asked how they could help host the Babes, how many people could attend the workshop, and shared stories of meeting or witnessing the group at the symposium. The Babes' presence there was strongly felt by many, and it was then that Barb's joke took meaning; not because the Babes are actually famous but because the love grown in the heart of the group was admired, and in some cases yearned for, by those who had attended the symposium. The Babes are now recognized, in part, because we show the impact of prioritizing relationships and art over university structures and systems. And sometimes it is as if the university doesn't exist for us when we sit together to bead, drink tea, and hysterically laugh out loud, warming the hearts of those around us.

"UNTIL WE BEAD AGAIN." —KIMMI CHARLTON (INUK, HAY RIVER)

At the end of every in-person session, or the end of a conversation on Facebook Messenger, Kimmi Charlton will often say, "until we bead again." Then everyone else present in person or virtually extends the same words. This saying, that is now part of our social language, carries weight for various reasons: the "we" in the statement can include the 200-plus people who have participated with the Babes over the years, and "we" can mean visiting artists, students, and community regulars. At the height of the COVID-19 pandemic, these words gave hope that we would soon bead together in person and make it through such difficult times. Saying "until we bead again" is a gesture of appreciation for having spent time together with our beads. These words recognize the impact of the BU Beading Babes and our connectivity, and they remind us that when we pack up our beads and clean our teacups, we will always bead again, if not in person, then in spirit.

NOTES

1 Before 2003, when it became an accredited degree program, IWGIDVA was the Visual Arts Program, first instigated in the late 1970s and early 1980s by artists Arthur Amiotte and Colleen Cutschall.

2 Representatives on the roundtable were Jessie Jannuska, Debbie Huntinghawk, Christine Topohokie, Eleanor Daniels, Albyn Carias, Kevin McKenzie, Jenna Brisson, Barb Blind, and Justine Hutcheson.

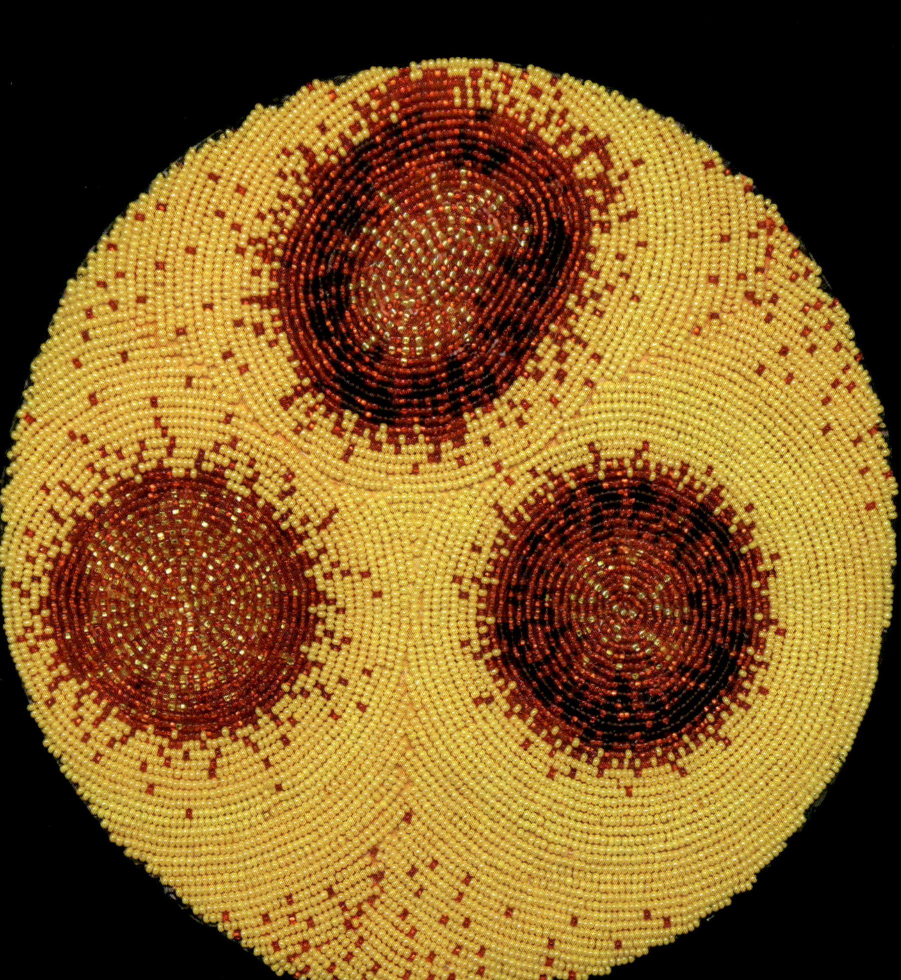

7.

VISITING KIN: INDIGENOUS FLATLAND BEADING AESTHETICS

CARMEN ROBERTSON

"STORY LIVES WITHIN THE BEAD MIKIS (MEEGIS), IN OUR BODIES, IN OUR BLOOD."
—FELICIA GAY, 2021[1]

Visiting became a difficult practice during COVID and even today it sometimes feels like a difficult undertaking. Yet, we know that visiting fills a room with new ideas, supportive directions, old and new stories that can lead to tears but also to lots of laughs. Sitting around a kitchen table, a staple of beading on the Flatlands, brings relational interconnections to mind, extending understandings of relations far beyond human interaction.

Knowing beads as active agents—as kin we visit with—opens fresh ways to contemplate beadwork for many who encounter it in the gallery for the first time. Setting aside associations with finished objects, the process of sharing knowledge through the communal ceremony of making and visiting

FIGURE. 7.1. Detail of beads from Ruth Cuthand's *Covid Disease* (2021), *Surviving COVID-19* series, *Beads in the blood: Ruth Cuthand, a Survey.* College Art Galleries, University of Saskatchewan, Saskatoon, Saskatchewan. Photo courtesy of Carey Shaw. See also Figure 0.3A and B.

shifts beads from things to beings. The epigraph to this chapter by Swampy Cree curator Felicia Gay captures the interconnected ways that beads are kin and hold our stories (that is also the focus of the discussion between Felicia Gay and Carmen Robertson in Conversation 5 of this book). "Cuthand believes the bead is alive, because the bead is alive, it is a story keeper."[2] Sharing stories is what beading is all about. Cuthand's representation of *Covid Disease* (Figure 7.1), with its glowing yellow orb with red spots, which throbs with life force and celebrates the process of visiting with kin, prompts viewers to ponder shared old and new stories.

Today, the parameters around ways of seeing and understanding art are expansive. Yet, in galleries and museums, the eye is still trained mostly on art objects—finished products. Objectifying art through a Western lens values stasis and possession. Objects are things that can be hung on a wall, kept in a vault, admired for their beauty and/or sublimity, and bought and sold as an investment. This way of knowing art remains nearly universal. However, such appreciation is steeped in Western philosophical traditions and, as such, tends to shut down understandings of art made by Indigenous Peoples that centres expansive ways of knowing rooted in relationality. Concepts that intersect with kinship ties, where stories are shared and interrelationships are as monumental as the prairie sky, situate beading within a very different milieu that forces viewers to see and know beadwork differently.

Intervening in the confining webbing that entangles understandings of Indigenous beadwork from the Canadian Prairies in mainstream art institutions stand artists who maintain active beading practices with deep ancestral connections to nêhiyawêwin stories of the prairie homelands. By situating these beaded artworks within an Indigenous aesthetic frame steeped in both ancient stories and new stories that hold teachings to shape future generations, I visit with these works and the group of artists who make them.[3] These featured artists are not alone in creating beaded works that are now more readily welcomed into gallery exhibitions and institutional art collections; rather, they are an integral part of a rich artistic movement helping to shift ways of seeing in galleries. This analysis considers recent examples of Indigenous beadwork from the Prairies within a discourse of

Indigenous ways of knowing, which upends current archival collection practices, challenges linear temporal structures, and posits shifting understandings of beaded works through story as part of a decolonizing discourse.

As part of a web of interrelated kin, glass beads keep and share stories in sentient ways similar to how shells and seeds have done in cultures around the world for millennia. Beadwork, including the works highlighted in this book, carries forward ancestral stories. Sherry Farrell Racette reminds us that most of the beadwork collected by museums was accessioned in their vaults with little regard for the maker or the community from whence it came, which leads to a lot of labels that say anonymous or unknown.[4] Yet, these same vast numbers of beaded artworks in museum collections that are locked away in vault drawers hold stories waiting to be shared with their relations. Tahltan artist Peter Morin invites us to experience the power in the artwork of Ancestor artists, by holding and feeling the beading that has come before us.[5] Beads and beaders from the past and present grow communities and collaborations for the next generations, despite barriers imposed by institutions. Beading, then, ensures that the new stories beaded today contain the threads of earlier ones and inspire stories yet to be told.

Flatland beading reflects kinship patterns formed in this Prairie territory that are naturalized and sometimes difficult to pick out for those who are not part of a given community. Still, histories, stories, and kinship ties shape beaded understanding within Prairie Indigenous ways of knowing. The rich beading traditions encountered here are unique to the Flatlands. Fusing land and sky, labour and promise, Ancestors and spirits, movement and sovereignty, *Meet You Across the Medicine Line* (2021) (Figure 7.2) by Métis artist Katherine Boyer connects to ancient and contemporary stories through the beads she sews. The horizontal 2 x 4 wood members conjure the imposition of colonial grids on the land even as they demonstrate a meeting place of land and sky. The role of colonization cannot be ignored; the imposed Medicine Line (the Canada/U.S. border) partially shapes Boyer's sculptural work.

The storied meaning of *Meet You Across the Medicine Line* is infused with so much more than colonial signifiers. The work reveals the complexities of Indigenous aesthetics, multi-temporal locations, and Métis visual

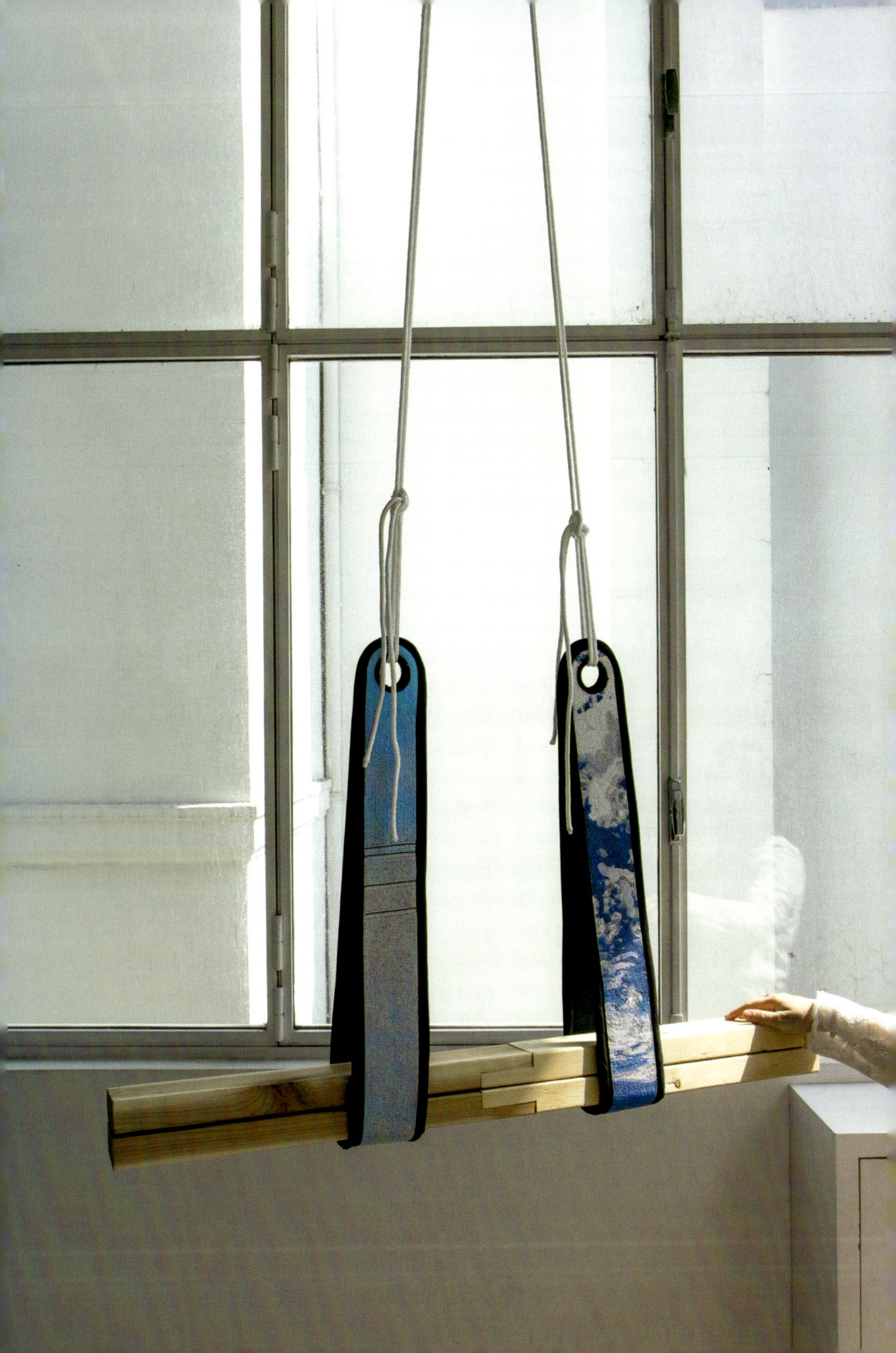

storying of Indigenous Peoples who routinely moved throughout the Prairies following the buffalo, tending garden plots, and later, because of the colonial imposition of national borders, crossed the Medicine Line to seek haven and create homes. As a fluid place of union, of visiting, Boyer's careful use of beads, cord, and construction-grade wood shape and reshape concepts of visiting, of home, of cultural spaces, and of aesthetic traditions in beading on the Flatlands today. The horizon is always evident on the prairie land, stretching out ahead where earth and sky meet, where stories of creation connect with twenty-first-century stories of resilience that meld complex Cree and Métis understandings of land and place with identity.

Boyer's vast body of beadwork situates Métis ways of knowing at the heart of every stitch she makes. "To bead is to visit," says Boyer, and her work shares family, Ancestors, and homeland with viewers. Indigenous Peoples throughout parts of Alberta, Saskatchewan, and Manitoba—Nêhiyawak, Anishinaabe, Saulteaux, Lakota, Dakota, and Nakota peoples in concert with Métis people—hold similar stories as well as those unique to their cultures. They serve as intersections and interactions that shape us and help to shape our future generations.[6] Utility and functionality are part of this complex Métis aesthetic, according to the artist, that also resonates with her experience of "queering" and queer worldmaking in a heteronormative settler nation.[7] Boyer made trips to the hardware store and the bead store to construct her horizon line as an imagined site for an internalized sense of home built into *Meet You Across the Medicine Line*. She demonstrates the recognition of difficult labour that comes with responsibly caring for the land and working on and with the land.

VISITING

Métis scholar Brenda Macdougall similarly writes of wakohtowin as the practices of kinship, where individuals are known in relation to their family, community, environment, the sacred world, and outsiders.[8]

FIGURE 7.2. Katherine Boyer, *Meet You Across the Medicine Line* (2021), seed beads, stroud cloth, terry cloth, cedar, fir, 25 x 41 in. Collection of the artist.

Despite the range of obstacles wrought by colonization, Macdougall demonstrates in her exhaustive study of kinship connections in the Île-à-la-Crosse region of Saskatchewan how Métis communities embody this concept.[9] In the foreword to this book, she beautifully posits how wahkotowin is linked to kiyokewin—visiting—that activates sharing as it asks us to take time with one another. The laborious process of beading makes similar demands. Sharing knowledge through stories, through visiting, provides a powerful embodiment of multi-generational bodies of knowledge. The complexities around kinship particular to cultural communities of the Flatland are contained in beads. Métis Elder Maria Campbell beautifully captures this sensibility:

> There is a word in my language that speaks to these issues: "wahkotowin." Today it is translated to mean kinship, relationship, and family as in human family. But at one time, from our place it meant the whole of creation. And our teaching taught us that all of creation is related and interconnected to all things within it.
>
> Wahkotowin means honouring and respecting those relationships. They are our stories, songs, ceremonies, and dances that taught us from birth to death our responsibilities and reciprocal obligations to each other. Human to human, human to plants, human to animals, to the water, and especially to the earth. And in turn all of creation had responsibilities and reciprocal obligations to us.[10]

Mitákuye oyás'iŋ is an Oceti Sakowin (Seven Council Fires of the peoples who speak Dakota, Lakota, and Nakota) phrase that resonates conceptually with the rich and complex associations of wakohtowin. Often misunderstood and misused as connecting only human relations, mitákuye oyás'iŋ similarly reflects a deeper worldview of interconnectedness or oneness with all living beings. Lakota historian Nick Estes reminds us that all knowledge is produced through relationships.[11] Dakota scholar Kim TallBear adds that, as with many other cultural story traditions, Dakota stories "feature relationships in which human and nonhuman persons, and nonhuman persons between themselves, harass and trick one another; save one another from injury or death; prey on, kill, and sometimes eat one another; or collaborate with one another. Our stories avoid the hierarchical nature-culture and animal-human split that has enabled domineering human management, naming, controlling, and 'saving' of nature."[12] Beaders and beading from the diverse nations of this territory reverberate specific and sometimes interconnected stories, designs, and colours. For the Oceti Sakowin, the gift of quillwork was brought to this land by White Calf Woman.[13] And while glass beads came to Turtle Island as trade items that somewhat replaced the sacred quillwork, they quickly became more than that.

Glass beads are not part of the land in the same ways porcupine quills are. They come from places like Venice and the Czech Republic, and they once operated as trade goods.[14] Yet, they quickly came to serve as kin with whom we have forged relationships. Oglala Lakota curator Emil Her Many Horses echoes this idea in an exhibition of Plains, Plateau, and Great Basin dresses at the National Museum of the American Indian, explaining how Indigenous women have always found innovative ways to adapt and adopt new materials like beads and stroud into their sewing and beading.[15] Understanding beads as more than trade items introduced in the nineteenth century to Indigenous women on the Plains is not something new. Farrell Racette describes a process of "Indigenization" that occurred in the Métis homelands, where women integrated and synthesized glass beads into their knowledge system.[16] "Through the small actions of our needles, and the careful stitches we make," says Farrell Racette, "we create and recreate our world."[17] The integration of new technologies into extant Indigenous Flatland cultural practices demonstrates a fluidity based in story and sharing. Similarly, beading generates collective energies, feelings, and relationships that activate beads to hold our embodied stories and sovereign power.

BEADS/AUNTIES

Artists and aunties Judy Anderson, Katherine Boyer, Ruth Cuthand, Dayna Danger, Marcy Friesen, and Audie Murray, whose beading and conversations come together in this book, serve as the focus of this discussion. Like their fellow beaders on the Flatlands—past, present, and future—their work collectively and individually helps visualize what it means to *know* beads as kin and to appreciate beads within an Indigenous aesthetic that varies from maker to maker and from culture to culture, while containing interconnected threads. Each of these artists understands the significance of intergenerational knowledge transmission present in their unique storied ways of beading art and lives lived today on Treaty 3, 4, and 6 territories.

Beaded stories tend to be complex and nuanced, sad, happy, and sometimes painful. When I walked into the MacKenzie Art Gallery in summer 2021, I was reminded of how beads can support us and help us to heal when we are faced with the losses that have come from colonial policies. Judy Anderson's rich body of work unfailingly honours the people in her life. And while she lamented at times about the hours and hours she had spent beading over the fall and winter prior to creating *Every time I think of you I cry* (Figure 7.3A), seeing the work installed at the gallery gave me a new understanding of how beads viscerally help to connect families that have been pulled apart.

Standing face-to-face with this monumental work, I was unprepared for its impact on me. It is both heavy and light. An embodiment of the many strands of threads that make up the story of the '60s Scoop as much as the specific story of Judy's family, the beads contain complications that intersect with experiences of many Indigenous families. Woven into this traumatic narrative is a promising discourse of love that speaks to resiliency and strength. A row of porcupine quills that runs the length of the floor below the hanging piece reminds us of the deeply rooted intergenerational

FIGURE 7.3A. Judy Anderson, *Every time I think of you I cry* (2021), size 8 Miyuki seed beads, porcupine quills, white deer hide, 9' x 7'. Photo courtesy of Don Hall.

FIGURE 7.3B. Detail of *Every time I think of you I cry* (2021), size 8 Miyuki seed beads, porcupine quills, white deer hide, 9' x 7'. Photo courtesy of Gerald Saul.

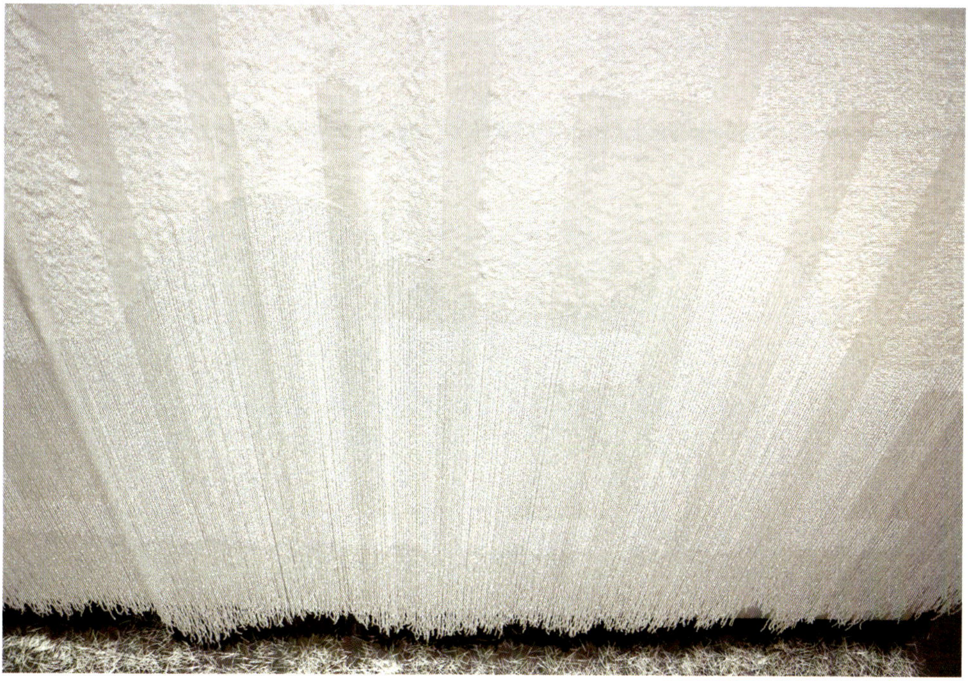

strength that is part of the story held by these beads. The use of quills reaches back long before the arrival of glass beads.

Judy explained *Every time I think of you I cry* to me this way:

> my intention was to honour my brother and our relationship. So, while this piece is about grief, it is also about connection. I have silently grieved my brother since the time he was scooped when we were both very young. After he was scooped I was not fortunate enough to ever see or meet him again; however, around the time of his death, my grief deepened and finally manifested itself into tears. This experience speaks to a connection that goes beyond the physical body to the spiritual, a genetic level—this is a connection that fits within Cree ways of knowing, one that we do not need to talk about or question; it just is. His spirit was instrumental in developing the idea for this piece. As I worked on this piece my family came together at different times throughout the process to help. Even though he's gone, my brother brought everyone together to mourn and celebrate his existence. He reminded me that grief is not carried alone, an idea that affirms our Cree beliefs in the importance and centrality of familial relationships as rooted in sharing with, and supporting, one another. Having this piece show at the MacKenzie, for the first time, was significant because my brother was scooped in Regina. While he died in eastern Canada, with a different family, his story and his spirit still belong to the prairies, as do ours.[18]

The white-on-white effect of the beads (Figure 7.3B) appears like a shroud or a whitewashing that separated Eugene from his family. The beads in this work also hold fast the complicated narratives that Indigenous Peoples traverse because of colonial circumstances. Anderson's process of care and love in beading this work ensured Eugene's place in a large and loving family that not only mourns him but honours him.

Michif artist Audie Murray's beadwork stitches us to our stories, Ancestors, and land through found and repurposed materials. As with the work of Boyer and Anderson, Murray's process of beading brings generations of family together and while their stories are different, her practice pulls together threads of story that relate to family and place in ways that challenge us to consider beading beyond conventional forms. Murray reminds us that story lives in the remaking and reusing of materials such as used socks, rolls of toilet paper, and tea bags (see Figure 2.1 and 2.2). Sewing beads into her art gives new life and story to them and she's shared this poem as a point of departure to understanding her process:

> as I create, the intention is not about how the labor will look
> the intention is to be open,
> to receive lessons,
> to listen
> every bead is a mentor
> if you can learn to truly accept
> you can find answers in dreams,
> you can hear them from the earth
> your hands will be guided[19]

In her *Weaving the Threads* exhibition at Neutral Ground in Regina in 2021, Murray foregrounds collaboration as a key aspect of her practice. Collaboration, though, resonates beyond the conventional sense of the term for Murray. Creating a work with her grandfather who has passed on, the concept of working with a partner takes on new meaning. "A lot of the time, I think people view collaboration as working with another person in real time. . . . Instead of using the object that he had made, I remade the object and that's a way of collaborating, because I'm working in the same ways that he would have been working, just on a different timeline."[20] Her grandfather's handmade billy club defies objectification, as does Murray's homage to him. Murray explains that *for hambone: metis billy stick* (Figure 7.4) reflects Michif ways of knowing because it is the remaking of an "object" her mooshum, Armand "Hambone" Fisher, made while he was living. The vitality of her life and his story is revealed in her remaking the club and beading the sheath that accompanies it.

Upending established notions of time and space by beading and making art with her departed grandfather, whose story remains very much alive, visually articulates the concept of wahkotowin. When I first met Audie, we discovered that our grandfathers, both from Fort Qu'Appelle, had been friends during their lifetimes. This connection offered me a way to more fully appreciate the sense of embodied generational collaboration she enacts through her process of art-making. Embodiment, here, is sensorial and spiritual, an active encounter that connects her and her grandfather through the act of making and remaking this work. Murray explains that this collaboration mirrors knowledge transmission through physical acts of making. Process, embodiment, and translation of story shape relational ways of knowing. Making this work *with* her grandfather shifts temporal realities, activating a concept of embodiment that allows the spirit of both Murray and Fisher to inhabit this work. While *for hambone* might be at first understood as an object, that characterization misses the significance of this work found in Indigenous ways of seeing.

New forms of collaboration are similarly at the centre of Dayna Danger's (they/their) *Kinship Medicine* (Figure 7.5). Danger is a 2Spirit/queer Métis/Saulteaux/Polish visual artist well known for their beaded matte black BDSM fetish masks. "I was just like wondering, what does a really collaborative mask look like?" The choice to collaborate with Kanyen'kehà: ka/Jamaican/Polish artist and midwife Kandace Price was a significant one. Danger explains that this mask is special "because it was way more collaborative than most of the other masks have been. . . . Mostly

FIGURE 7.4. Audie Murray, *for hambone: metis billy stick*, (2019), glass beads, leather, chain, wood, acrylic paint, 20 x 16 inches. Photo courtesy of the artist.

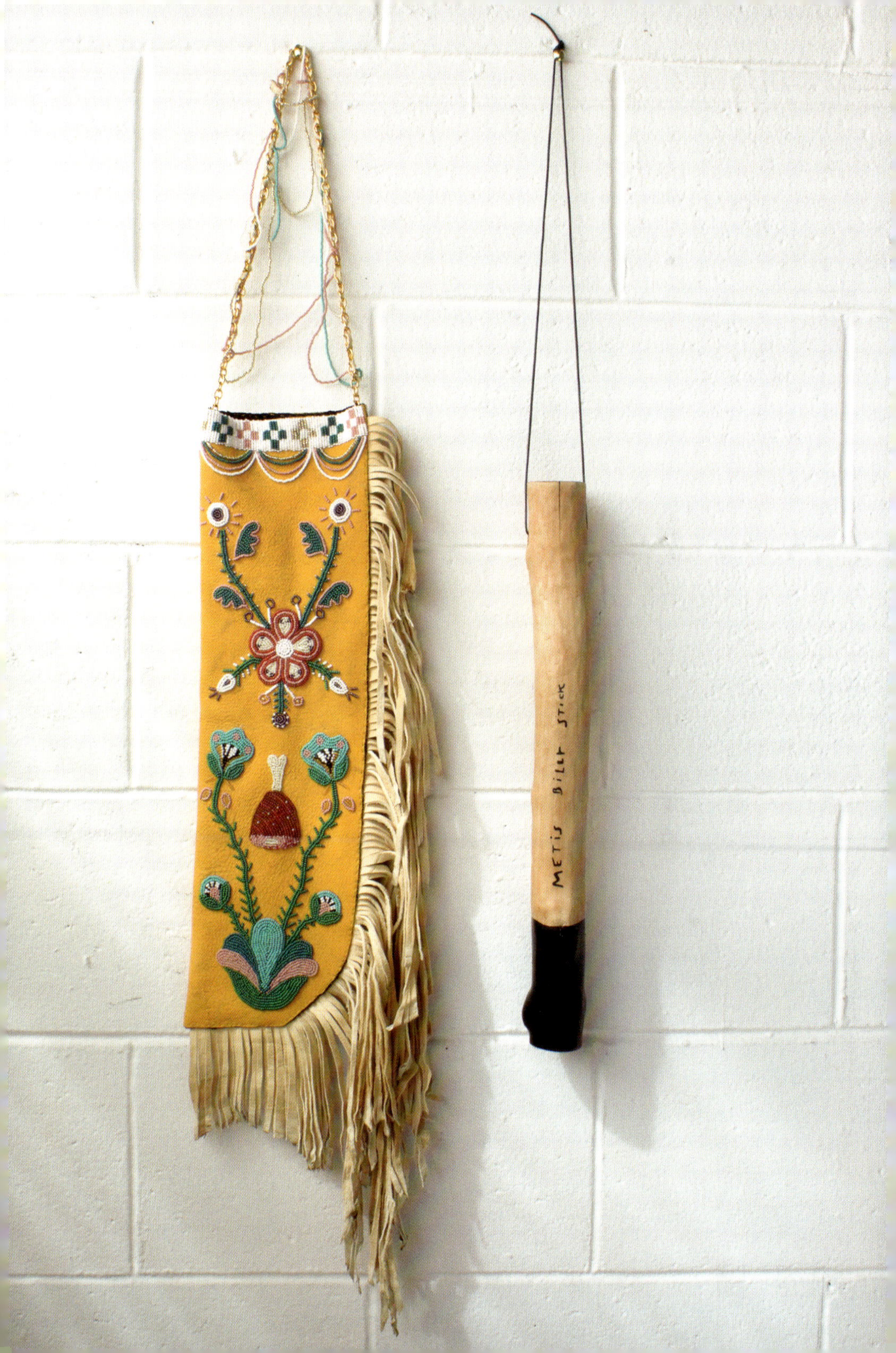
METIS BILLY STICK

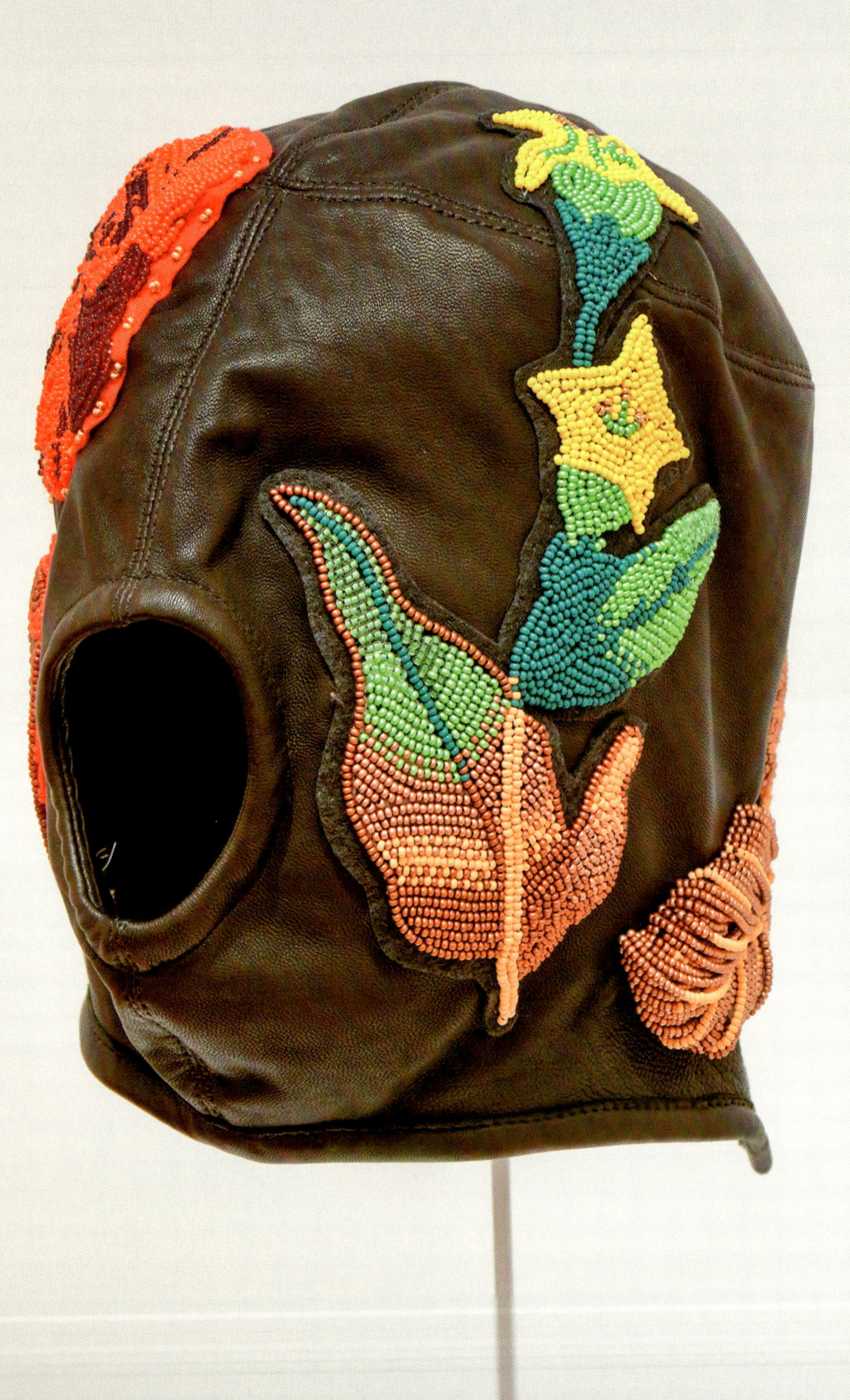

it's been me beading for other people, and so I've had this long relationship with Kandace as, like a friend, as a kin."[21]

Danger demonstrates how *Kinship Medicine,* from the series *Kinship Masks*, started a process of experimentation with the iconic mask form to make space for this collaboration, by "taking the eyes away, so now I have all this other surface area where eyes would have been and I really just kind of push it. I'm just wanting to change." Leaving more room for beading by removing the eyes from this mask combines beaded designs that reflect both artists' identities, building a sense of belonging.[22]

When I first visited *Kinship Medicine* at the *Àbadakone* exhibition at the National Gallery of Canada in 2019, I misread the beaded floral design as a Métis prairie flower and assumed the stem with two yellow blossoms that reach across the right side of the mask were specifically related to Danger's Flatland identity. Danger corrected me, explaining that both the tobacco flower and leaves reference sacred medicine derived from Kandace's Kanyen'kehà: ka teachings further east. The two yellow flowers of the traditional tobacco plant connect to the raised Mohawk-style beaded tobacco leaves on the mask beaded by Price. Danger, too, includes images sacred to their teachings on this mask: "One of the things that I thought about when me and Kandace first started this is that . . . if it's a collaboration, I really need to have myself in there, so that's why there's that red eagle and that pipe." Danger's representations of a red eagle and pipe connect to personal medicine teachings. In addition to connecting to ceremony, these powerful prairie images also reflect a personal and fluid or intuitive style of beading. "There is a kind of painterly quality that exists within everything I do, even though I don't see myself as a painter!"[23] To achieve a painterly fluidity through beading, Danger beaded the representation of the red eagle using a "mix of different reds to give it dimension . . . like if I'm painting." Danger admits

FIGURE 7.5. Dayna Danger, *Kinship Medicine* (2019), *Kinship Masks* series, beads, recycled goat leather, white and black bonded nylon, tobacco, smoked brain-tanned caribou hide, 24 x 17 x 25 cm. Photo courtesy National Gallery of Canada.

that this method reflects her larger practice because "I really like to lean into the mistakes and the 'not knowing things' because that's part of my journey."[24]

Danger provocatively captures Flatland and eastern ways of knowing as they stitch stories that expand the range of narratives typically shared openly in gallery spaces. *Kinship Medicine* was displayed at *Àbadakone/Continuous Fire/Feu continuel*, at the National Gallery of Canada (NGC) in 2020–2021, the second in a series of exhibitions following *Sakahàn* in 2013 dedicated to contemporary Indigenous art from around the world, featuring more than 100 works of art that shape ideas and forge "relationships with communities across boundaries," according to the museum's director, Sasha Suda.[25] Beadwork commanded a large presence in this latest iteration of the global exhibition, and included works by Ruth Cuthand, Dene artist Catherine Blackburn, Anishinaabe artist Barry Ace, Kanien'keha:ká artist Kathleen Kaweniieshon Dearhouse, and Danger's masks.

Swampy Cree and Welsh artist Marcy Friesen also explores masks in experimental works she created in 2021. In a provocative series of works, she covers her face in beads, forming an embodied story about fixing and unfixing identities. The beads help Friesen to grapple with such complex questions. Working with Ruth Cuthand as her artistic mentor, Friesen has been shifting her conventional beading practice, pushing herself in new and innovative directions that centre her art in more personal ways: "I am finding that I have a story to tell."[26] Applying beads directly to her face with adhesives—some with floral designs; others, such as Figure 7.6, using a jumble of colourful beads—relates to a healing narrative, stories held within her body that are transformative and central to Friesen's *Legacy* series of masks. "One morning I was sitting in my workshop, spinning in my chair, looking at my beads," and all of the sudden she hit on a new direction, "I used bead soup."[27] These works, which forego the use of a needle and thread, involve an arduous process nonetheless. After painstakingly applying beads to her body, she then very carefully drives from her farm into Carrot River to work with photographer Susan Stewart to document the outcomes.

Friesen comes from a long line of traditional beaders: her mom, her granny, her great-grandma. Marcy also beads in more conventional forms.

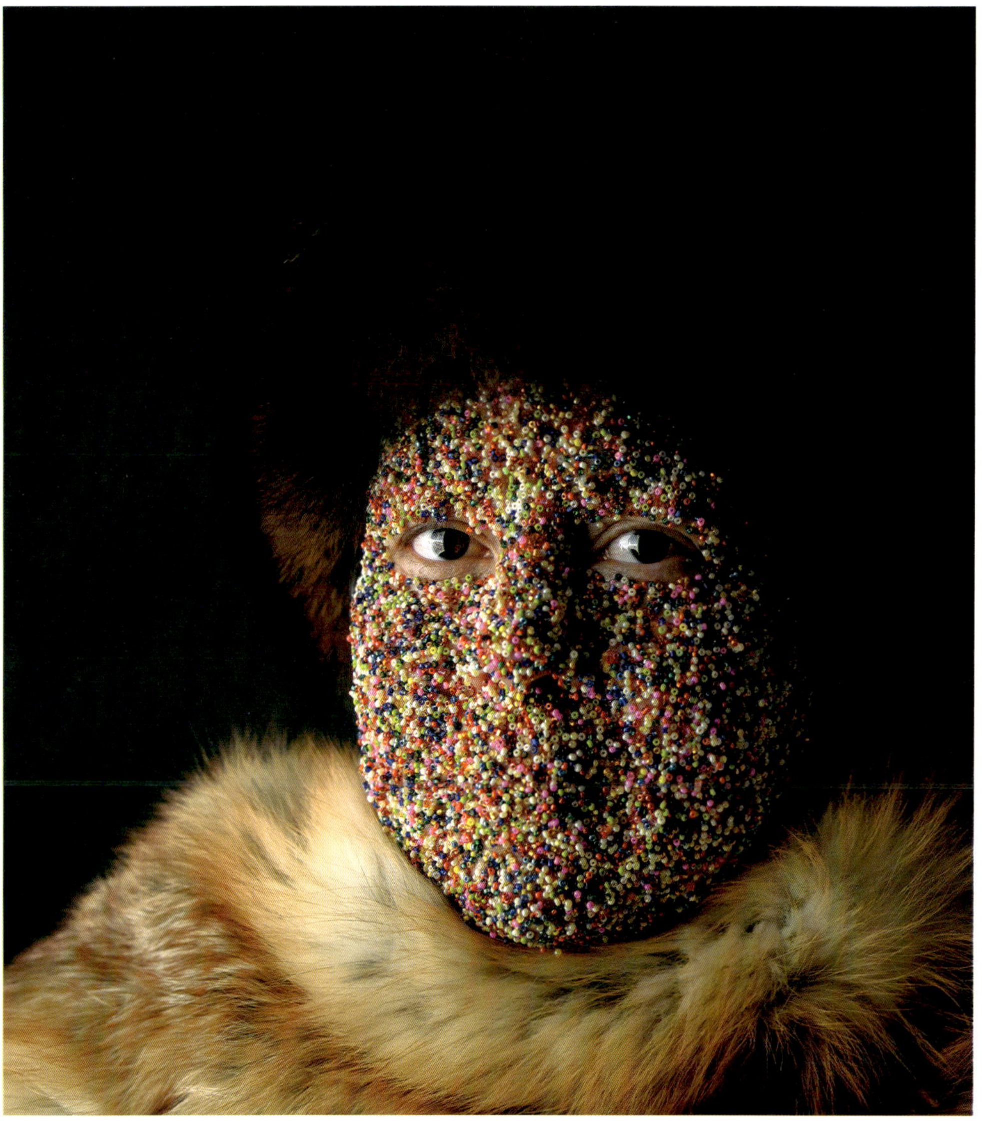

FIGURE 7.6. Marcy Friesen, *Who am I* (16 April 2021), beads, fur. Photo courtesy of Susan Stewart Photography.

Marcy is honoured to share her own gifts as a beader: "I found pride in reconnecting with my culture through beadwork."[28] For many years she focused on utilitarian projects until Cuthand prodded her to experiment with forms of beading that resulted in the creation of masks.

According to Friesen, photographic documentation for *Who am I* (Figure 7.6) reveals that she is "half-woman and half-bead, turning myself inside out, revealing my thoughts and opinions on topics such as racism, mental health, and acceptance."[29] "My skin colour was different than most everyone growing up and to this day. So beadwork for me has been very therapeutic," explains Friesen. Melding beading with her body has opened new ways of beading and thinking through story.

Friesen draws from the land and her relational connections, as she beads a wide range of artwork (more about Friesen's art can be found in her discussion with Cuthand in Conversation 2). "I love running my fingers over my beadwork, seeing if it's smooth or if I need to tack down a bead or two. And when I think about smooth, flat beadwork, I think about the Saskatchewan Prairies. I am a Flatlander. I love looking down the road for miles."[30]

QUEEN BEAD

Conceptually and through the process of sewing, we experience stories embedded in beads as we sit together in beading circles. Each piece of art described in this chapter brings together bodies and beads in different ways, but all reveal that Ruth Cuthand's impact on each of the noted beaders and scholars included in this collection cannot be underestimated. For this reason, the beaders featured in this book crown her "Queen Bead."

Many of the stories held by the beads in Ruth's works intersect with colonial narratives particular to the Plains but also to Indigenous/settler narratives beyond this territory. The stories of devastating loss held in her *Trading* series, the first body of work she created for a gallery setting, are countered by the realization that these beads also hold powerful stories of resilience and futurity.[31] Creating complicated works that defy easy understanding, her beaded works are also routinely horrific and mouth-wateringly beautiful.

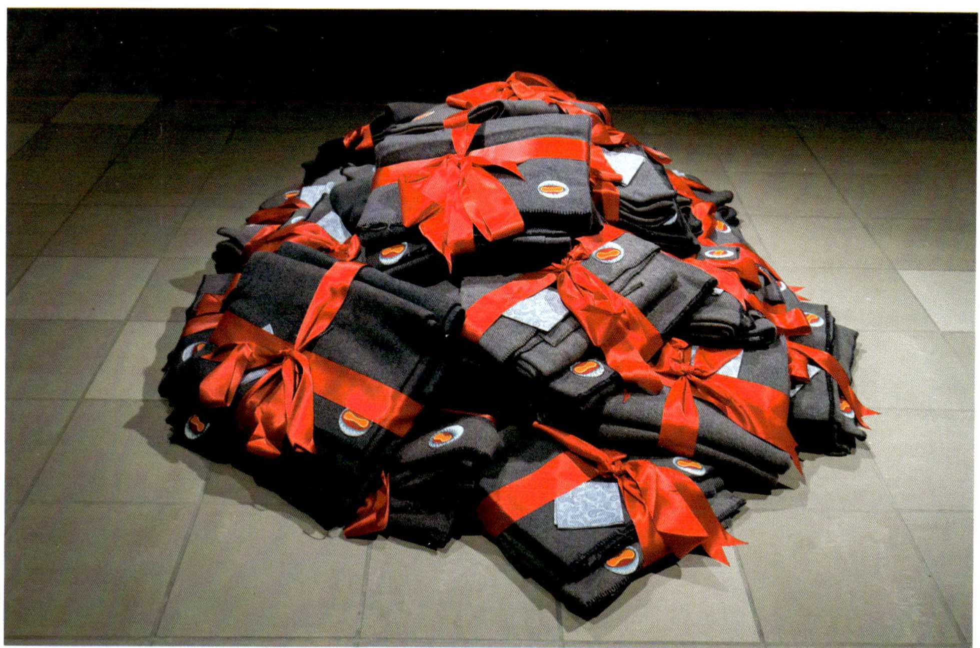

FIGURE 7.7A. Ruth Cuthand, *Extirpate this Execrable Race* (2018), wool blankets, cotton, ribbon, glass beads (each blanket approx. 50 x 40 x 14 cm). College of Art Galleries, University of Saskatchewan, Saskatoon. Photo courtesy of Carey Shaw.

Similarly, her beaded representation of COVID-19 (Figure 7.1) demonstrates the artist's ongoing efforts to bead diseases that resonate deeply with viewers. Cuthand declares: "Though humour softens the blow of a critical message, I have found that making work which confronts the most difficult truths about Canadian society and the impacts of colonization on Aboriginal people are made remarkably palatable when delivered in a strikingly seductive package."[32]

Combining stories of our colonial past with health issues faced by First Peoples today, Cuthand's 2018 installation, *Extirpate this Execrable Race* (Figure 7.7A and B) is one of her many works delivered in a seductive package—this one is literally tied up in a big red bow. The thought-provoking work takes its title from a direct quote found in a 1763 letter sent from Lord

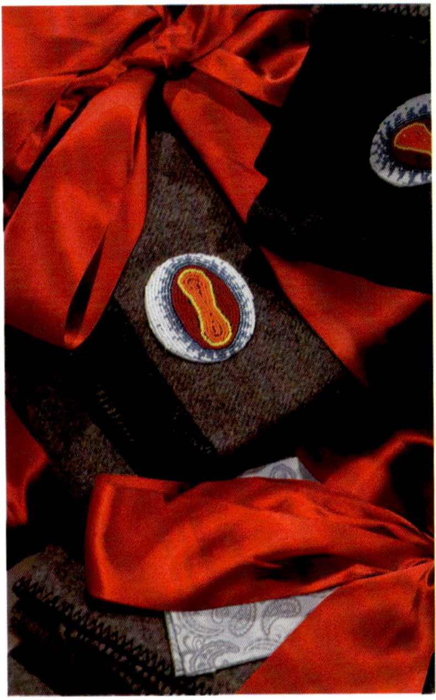

FIGURE 7.7B. Ruth Cuthand, detail of *Extirpate this Execrable Race* (2018), wool blankets, cotton, ribbon, glass beads, each blanket approx. 50 x 40 x 14 cm. College of Art Galleries, University of Saskatchewan, Saskatoon. Photo courtesy of Carey Shaw.

Jeffery Amherst, commanding officer of the British Forces in the American Revolution, to Colonel Henry Bouquet, at Fort Pitt (present day Pittsburg, USA) advocating that smallpox-infected blankets be employed as biological warfare.[33]

Building on Cuthand's award-winning *Trading* series, *Extirpate* holds traumatic stories of colonization and a disease that ravaged Indigenous populations throughout the Americas from the sixteenth century onward.[34] Yet this is not simply a work about historic atrocities, even though the grey army-surplus blankets can't help but remind viewers of the genocidal long game played by Britain and Canada that has continued into the present day. It is only when viewers pause to look past the full emotional impact of this horrific reality that other stories surface. The exquisitely beaded circles and the shiny ribbons stacked on the gallery floor demonstrate the care and love and resilience that this installation also embodies (Figure 7.7B).

Cuthand's art shares visual stories, and the beads and blankets keep the narratives in the minds of viewers. Her rich body of work situates story within bodies: beads hold stories, beads are bodies, bodies tell stories. Beads, therefore, are not simply objects, pretty as they may be, but living beings. The beauty of Cuthand's beaded works lies in part in the seductive beauty of the beads. The colours and patterns found in her beadwork draw us in. The teachings they hold are complex and unsettling—they cannot and should not easily be forgotten.

HONOURING/HEALING

Visiting with beads is love. Anyone who has sat in a group beading understands that. Moving beyond the beading circle into gallery spaces has given new forms of agency to beaded works. Beads share their embodied stories with diverse audiences, many of whom are only now learning this way of seeing beyond the object. Katherine Boyer's *The Grieving Bag* encompasses many of the elements found in the work by the other Aunties in that it emphasizes healing and honouring of our relations.

Made especially for her dad, *The Grieving Bag* (Figure 7.8A, B, and C) conceptually and ceremonially holds his life story. As in *Meet You Across the Medicine Line* (Figure 7.2) and *The Sky Vest* (Figure 3.1), this piece features emblematic beaded skyscapes on the bag's panels. Viewing the beaded skies as decorative elements belies their connection to place and story. These precise and localized representations of sky include one panel of sky seen from looking upward from the house where her father was born in Moose Jaw. The second beaded panel represents the sky above the house where he lives now, in Regina. The beaded panels enfold his storied life.

Boyer engaged in a collaborative decision-making process with her dad for the creation of the paracord strap for the bag, resulting in a design that reinforces connections to blood ties. The paracord strap and tassels that hang from the bag symbolize veins and blood lines. Other elements of the work also reinforce their solid bond. A section of 1920s fir derived from a renovation project they undertook together on Katherine's house serves as part of the apparatus from which the bag hangs. The solid dovetail joints of the truss structure similarly celebrate their unbreakable bond.

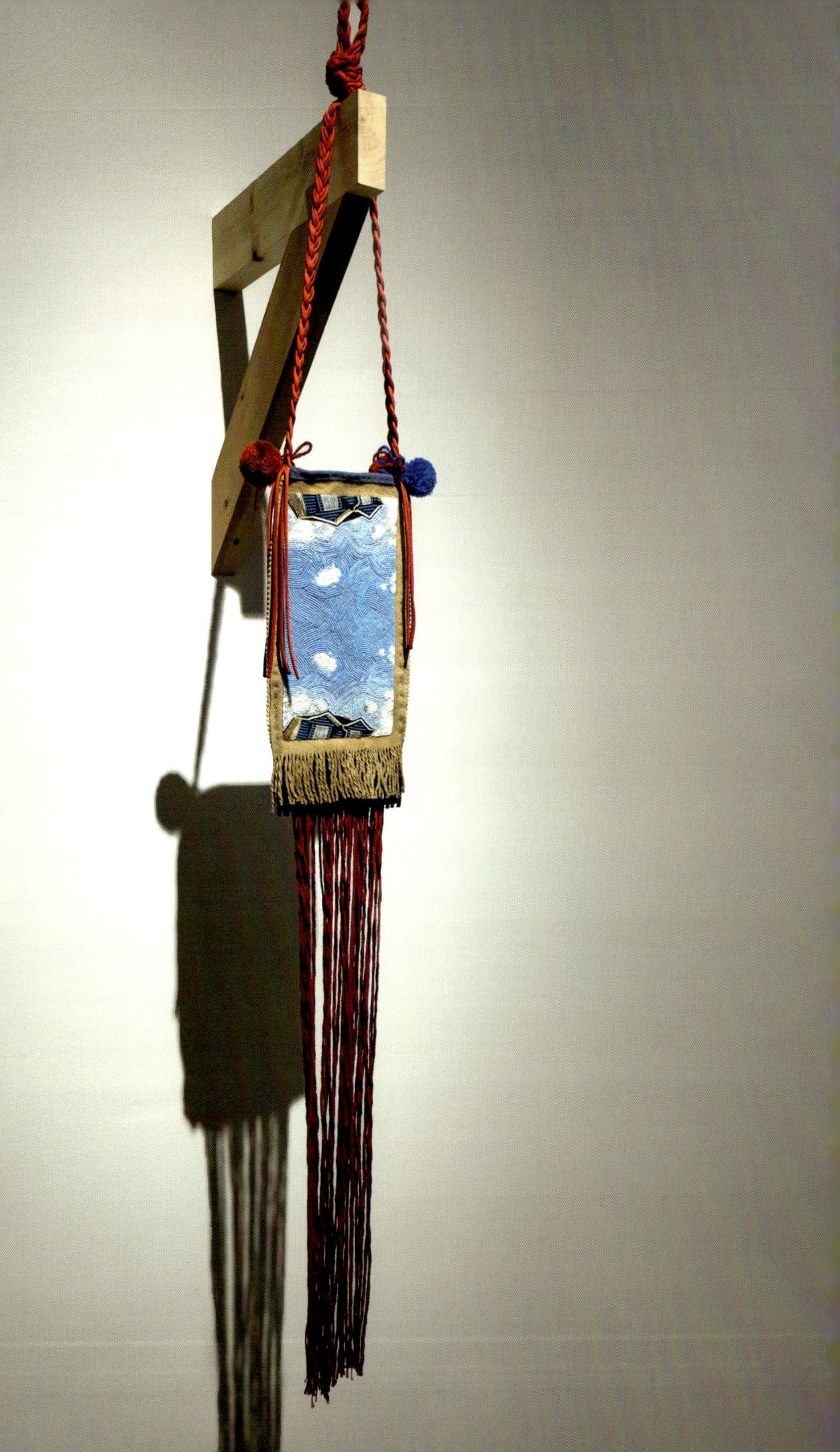

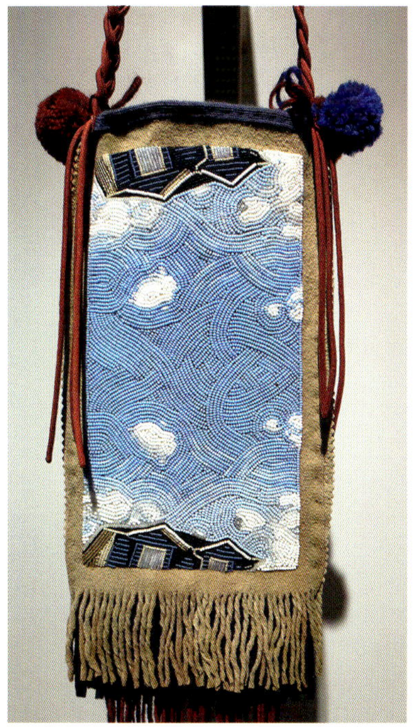

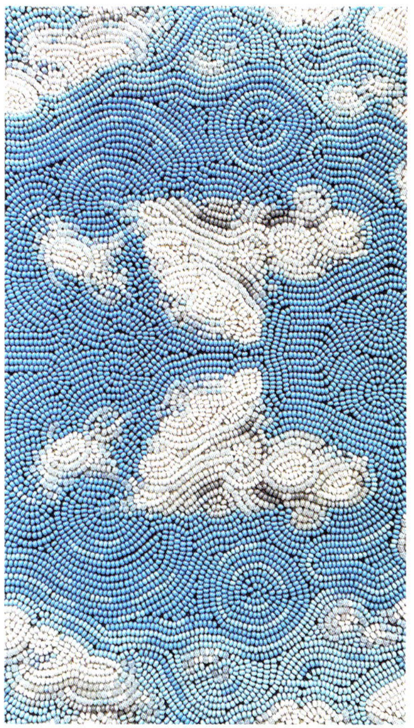

FIGURE 7.8A. Katherine Boyer, *The Grieving Bag*, full size, seed beads on moose hide, 2023. Photo courtesy of Gabriela Garcia-Luna.

FIGURE 7.8B. Katherine Boyer, *The Grieving Bag*, close-up, seed beads on moose hide, 2023. Photo courtesy of Gabriela Garcia-Luna.

FIGURE 7.8C. Katherine Boyer, detail of *The Grieving Bag*, seed beads on moose hide, 2023. Photo courtesy of the artist.

MITÁKUYE OYÁS'IŊ

Positioned with ties to the sky, the land, and the water, stories of places and relationships meld the diverse works of art featured throughout this essay. It is my honour to celebrate the works and ideas of these beaders whose teachings resonate far beyond the Flatlands. Visiting with the artists, seeing their projects realized, and hearing their stories bring a sense of oneness to my understanding of beads as beings.

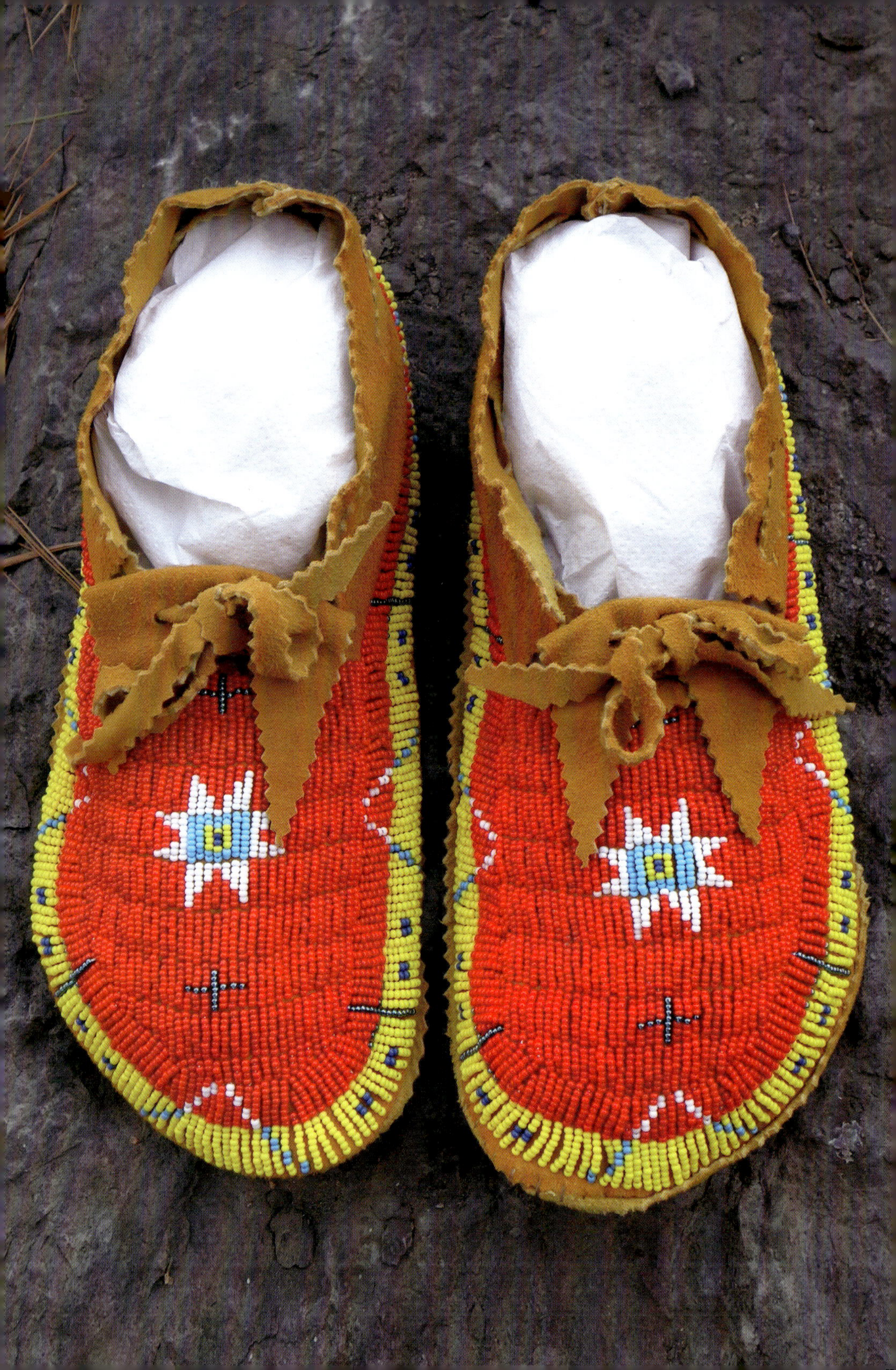

During COVID-19, I undertook a beading project, in part to better understand the labour and materials involved in making beaded art that the Aunties make so beautifully. I have no pretense of thinking I can do what the artists discussed above do with beads, yet I aim to locate the story of my relationships to my Indigenous and settler roots in the Qu'Appelle Valley through beads and stroud cloth. Beading in a Lakota/Dakota lane stitch-style to honour my matrilineal connections to Oceti Sakowin, I am visually and aesthetically working to sew together my diverse story of kinship within the valley. The work remains at present incomplete, though I prefer to think of it as underway. I persist. Inspired by the pair of beaded moccasins made for me by my cousin Paulete Poitras from Muscopetung First Nation (Figure 7.9), I better I appreciate how the lane stitch that Paulete used in creating these moccasins is a technique that, in addition to the colours and symbols, forms a bond or a link to our shared generations of kin. I invited my daughters, my mother, and my sister to add to my beading-in-progress, the embodied process of activating the beaded beings in ways that situate us within a larger tiospaye, the Lakota term for kinship. The activation of these stories takes form through the process of sewing and sometimes re-sewing each of my clumsy stitches.

Visiting kin opens up a web of creative makers of art and ideas held by the beads found in the work by the Aunties in this essay. Shared through the process of making, a dynamic system of relations that include animacy, spirituality, metaphysicality, and futurity informs these works and inspires new projects. The beads hold complex stories that help us to better understand and appreciate past, present, and future aspects of the interconnected spaces we share. Through these beaded works and their networks of story, we visit, share the beading circle, and learn from the teachings of the Aunties.

FIGURE 7.9. Paulete Poitras, beaded moccasins. Photo courtesy of Lisa Truong.

NOTES

1 Felicia Gay, *Beads in the blood: Ruth Cuthand, a Survey,* curatorial statement, Kenderdine Art Gallery, University of Saskatchewan, 22 January–10 April 2021.

2 Ibid.

3 I want to thank each of the artists featured in this essay for their generosity in sharing their stories, their time, and their labour. I aimed to write about their work in ways that would, I hoped, share some understanding of the Indigenous Prairies. The beading included here also shares stories that bring to life the interconnected ways Indigenous beaders sew together the past, present, and future of this territory.

4 Sherry Farrell Racette, "My Grandmothers Loved to Trade: The Indigenization of European Trade Goods in Historic and Contemporary Canada," *Journal of Museum Ethnography* 20 (2008): 78.

5 Peter Morin, "There are no Metaphors: A Proposal for Dreaming Indigenous Philosophies into Studio Arts Education," in *The Routledge Companion to Indigenous Art Histories in the United States and Canada,* eds. Heather Igloliorte and Carla Taunton (New York: Routledge, 2023), 228.

6 Katherine Boyer, *How the Sky Carries the Sun* artist statement, February 2022, Art Gallery of Regina, Regina SK, np.

7 The conversation in Chapter 4 between Katherine Boyer and Dayna Danger explores such issues in greater depth.

8 Brenda Macdougall, "Wahkootowin: Family and Cultural Identity in Northwestern Saskatchewan Metis Communities," *The Canadian Historical Review* 87: 431–62.

9 Brenda Macdougall, *One of the Family: Metis Culture in Nineteenth-Century Northwestern Saskatchewan* (Vancouver: UBC Press, 2010).

10 Maria Campbell, "We need to return to the principles of Wahkotowin," *Eagle Feather News* (November 2007): 5.

11 Nick Estes, *Our History Is the Future* (New York: Verso, 2019), 259.

12 Kim TallBear, "Dossier: Theorising Queer Inhumanisms," *GLQ: A Journal of Lesbian and Gay Studies* (2015): 235.

13 Colleen Cutschall, "Dresses, Designers, and the Dance of Life," in *Identity by Design: Tradition, Change, and Celebration in Native Women's Dress,* ed. Emil Her Many Horses (New York: HarperCollins, 2007), 71.

14 Lois Sherr Dubin, "North America," in *The History of Beads: From 100,000 B.C. to the Present* (New York: Abrams, 2009), 261–90.

15 Emil Her Many Horses, "Portraits of Native Women and Their Dresses," in *Identity By Design: Tradition, Change, and Celebration in Native Women's Dresses*. Exhibition catalogue published in conjunction with exhibition of the same title, organized and presented at National Museum of the American Indian, September 2008–February 2010 (Washington: Smithsonian/Collins, 2007), 15–64.

16 Farrell Racette, "My Grandmothers," 69–81.

17 Ibid., 78.

18 Judy Anderson, email conversation with author, 1 September 2021.

19 Audie Murray, poem shared during email conversation with author, 23 August 2021.

20 Ashley Martin, "Collaboration takes on new meaning in Audie Murray's artwork," *Regina Leader Post,* 11 March 2021, https://leaderpost.com/entertainment/local-arts/collaboration-takes-on-new-meaning-in-audie-murrays-artwork.

21 Dayna Danger, conversation, 17 January 2022.

22 Because of time constraints, Isanielle Enright also joined in to help bead the designs that Dayna and Kandace created.

23 Danger, conversation.

24 Ibid.

25 Sasha Suda, Foreword; Rachelle Dickenson, Greg A. Hill, Christine Lalonde (eds), *Àbadakone/Continuous Fire/Feu continuel*, exhibition catalogue (Ottawa: National Gallery of Canada 2020), 12.

26 Marcy Friesen, email conversation with author, 10 August 2021.

27 Ibid.

28 Ibid.

29 Ibid.

30 Ibid.

31 See Carmen Robertson, "Land and Beaded Identity: Shaping Art Histories of Indigenous Women of the Flatland," *Revue d'art canadienne/Canadian Art Review* 432, no. 2 (Fall 2017): 13–29; Ruth Cuthand and Chantal McStay, "Ruth Cuthand," *BOMB* 146 (Winter 2018–2019): 54–62.

32 Ruth Cuthand, artist statement, https://www.ruthcuthand.ca.

33 See Elizabeth A. Fenn, "Biological Warfare in Eighteenth-Century North America: Beyond Jeffery Amherst," *The Journal of American History* 86, no. 4 (2000): 1552–580. doi:10.2307/2567577.

34 For an analysis of how disease impacted Indigenous Peoples in the Prairie region, see James Daschuk, *Clearing the Plains: Disease, Politics of Starvation, and the Loss of Aboriginal Life* (Regina, SK: University of Regina Press, 2014).

8.

IF THE NEEDLES DON'T BREAK AND THE THREAD DOESN'T TANGLE: BEADING UTOPIA

SHERRY FARRELL RACETTE

> "UTOPIA: AN IMAGINED PLACE OR STATE OF THINGS WHERE EVERYTHING IS PERFECT."
> —OXFORD DICTIONARY

> "UTOPIA SHOULD BE THOUGHT OF AS A METHOD, RATHER THAN A GOAL."
> —RUTH LEVITAS (2003)

I teach, bead, and study stitch-based work in museum collections. I teach art history, curate exhibits, and engage with artists. Not unusual as things go. It can be a bit chaotic, but more often, my work provides rich intersections of ideas and experiences. I have been thinking about beading's impact on the maker for some time, initially puzzling over apparent contradictions between nineteenth-century Métis women's lives and their beadwork. Out of loss, war, and diaspora emerged stunning works of great beauty. I began to explore my own refuge-seeking in beadwork during times of difficulty and speak with other artists. Through good fortune I encountered other ideas.[1] First was Amber Berson's work on artist-run culture as an aspiration for feminist utopian spaces. She curated *Utopia as Method* in 2018, when I was teaching a graduate class on theory and methodology.[2] She shared her curatorial essay with me, and we discussed the exhibition's ideas on a quick phone call from an airport, of all places. I, in turn, shared her work with my students and dove into the work of sociologist Ruth Levitas.[3] One of the graduate students presented flow theory to their peers from music, visual art, film, theatre, and creative technology. The discussion—as you might imagine—was wide-ranging, with many examples of how notions of flow and utopian thinking manifest in a variety of arts practices. As the students made connections, I was making my own, madly writing notes and thinking (as ever) about beading.

In 2013, I taught an undergraduate class—Beadwork: An Interdisciplinary Study. I had ambitious plans. I imagined beading with students, sharing a meditative vibe. I actually did very little beading and spent a lot of time untangling thread. I told the students about the spiritual aspects and emotional benefits of beading. One afternoon, I paused outside the classroom and overheard this exchange: "God damn it!" said a frustrated voice. "That must be the spiritual part," was the response. Laughter ensued. Cue one slightly deflated professor. However, I noticed that, unlike any class I've ever taught, the students were always early. By the time I arrived, the beads were out, and students were working away. As they plopped into their seats, they often heaved a happy sigh. I didn't lose a single student, although some had serious struggles over the course of the semester. Métis artists Christi Belcourt and Jennine Krauchi visited our class. Making vamps for *Walking With Our Sisters* (*WWOS*, 2013–2019) became our primary focus. After Jennine visited, there was a significant shift to two-needle beading. We tested the curatorial concept for *WWOS* in the university gallery. Major projects were ambitious and well done.

Given the successful outcomes, I've come to realize how unrealistic my expectations were. The emotional and spiritual aspects of beading could not be experienced by students struggling to manage their thread and pick up beads. Skill development was a prerequisite, and we had to move beyond frustration and the desire to give up. I also became aware of inner emotions triggered by the gestures of beading. For some students, picking up the needle was a reconnection and reclaiming that addressed broken bonds and family trauma. Beading evoked a deceased mother, a grandmother never met. One international student dedicated her vamps to her sister who had died during a civil war. Another shared—at the very end of class—that her mother was among the missing and murdered we created vamps for. Our productive hum and meditative calm of beading together was hard earned. It emerged from our collective generative actions.

Beading as struggle, as aspirational gesture, and as just plain hard work has become something an increasing number of bead artists share on social media. Elias Not Afraid posts videos of ripping up beadwork that appears flawless to the viewer, but not to the maker. Jamie Okuma, who regularly posts works-in-progress photos and demonstration videos, shared a photograph of her bandaged, battered fingers with the caption, "according to my hands . . . it's one week until the Heard," referring to one of the most important annual American Indigenous art venues.[4] Other artists followed, posting bead spills, needle cuts, and the messy process behind often perfect final results.

Nadia Myre's *Meditation* series (2013–2017) was exactly that—an unstructured, contemplative process that resulted in monochromatic medallions she presented as large-scale photographs. Her *Orison* (2014) series showed the backs of her seminal *Beading the Indian Act* (1999–2002), exposing the rarely seen underbelly of beadwork: random stitches and untidy knots. Beading utopia isn't a state of perfection, rather it is the actions toward it.

LIVING OBJECTS

The first beads were painstakingly hand crafted from shell and small seeds. Indigenous languages remember these ancestors. In nēhiyawēwin and anishinaabemowin, variations of migis (shell) and manitou meness (spirit seeds) remember the raw materials of bead-making. Individual beads were treasured, and despite the labour-intensive process, thousands were amassed for creation and gifting. In 1997, a Cree woman's sixteenth-century grave was exposed by shoreline erosion on Nagami Bay, Southern Indian Lake, in northern Manitoba. kayasochi kikawenow (our mother from long ago) and her belongings were lovingly studied and reburied, resulting in a public education program and publication.[5] One remarkable find was thousands of tiny pin cherry beads that once adorned her hood. She also had bone hair pipes and beads of red pipestone. In the early seventeenth century, the Jesuits quickly realized that wampum was "the gold, diamonds and pearls of this Country."[6] In addition to the deeply significant belts and collars, the Jesuits documented the exchange of thousands of loose beads and the performative aspects of wampum use, describing the formal arrival of Kiotseaton, a famous Mohawk orator, standing in the prow of a canoe "almost completely covered with Porcelain beads."[7]

Beads were, and are, generally considered animate and precious. Most beaders are introduced to a range of beliefs and practices early in their learning that reflect a shared respect for beads. Tiny and unruly, beads are carefully gathered up, sorted, and never wasted. Preparing to bead is both a practical act of clearing space and the emotional work of clearing minds. We are cautioned to come to the beading table with a clear mind, putting aside negative thoughts. Artists disrupt perfection with an intentionally placed bead to remind ourselves and the viewer that only Creation is perfect.[8] We search for the "spirit bead" in historic work. How old are these ideas? How many generations of beaders have passed down these gentle protocols?

Anishinaabe artist Robert Houle translates manitoomaneskan (beadwork) as being "like a prayer," as one works in a meditative state with the living energy of natural materials.[9] Megis, manitou meness, and okawiy (quill) were initially stitched onto wayan (skin/hide), all animate nouns. Fine woollen broadcloth, introduced by the fur trade, was named manitou wayan to reflect wool's unique capacities. In addition to artistic techniques, meaning was transferred onto new materials, a grandmothering gesture to embrace and claim newness. Small seeds appear to have been quickly abandoned for new bead forms acquired through both Indigenous and fur trade networks. Traditional forms of wampum have persisted to the present, and introduced glass beads were adopted into wampum forms. Wampum beads are used for both new and ancient purposes.

KNOWLEDGE AS GESTURE

Looking at beadwork, particularly historic work, solely from a Western perspective of aesthetic contemplation misses the living knowledge embodied in the object. Beads are tethered to surfaces by thousands of tiny stitches, a gesture repeated over and over again. Beading is controlled, focused action. Cree scholar Keith Goulet emphasizes the importance of "doing" in relation to nēhiyawēwin concepts of knowledge and understanding, using the example of nisitootumowin (understanding), which has the root word itootu (doing) embedded within it. Understanding is doing knowledge.[10] When I asked the late Margaret McAuley of Cumberland House, Saskatchewan, to teach me to make pointed-toe moccasins, she initially refused, until I explained my frustrated attempts at learning, and she exclaimed, "they only told you, they didn't show you!" Under her strict supervision and highest standards, I repeated every action she showed me—she demonstrated, and I followed.

Beading knowledge is acquired through the struggle of doing. It is physically challenging. Any artist who works on large-scale beadwork projects knows the long hours, the backaches, blisters, needle pokes, and bandages the work requires. The site of struggle is the location of beadwork's key teachings: patience, problem-solving, solution-seeking, and persistence. Every accomplished bead artist has sojourned at this place and frequently revisits it. One common saying, "don't fight with the beads," speaks to the key role of patience. Needles will break and thread will tangle. Any time bead artists gather, the conversation invariably turns to materials and problem-solving. Artists find solutions to chronic problems and begin to enjoy the unravelling, understanding what went wrong, and knowing when they simply must start again. Persistence leads you to the feeling of accomplishment when a piece is finished to the last detail. It takes much, much longer than one anticipates. And persevering through to completion is one of the most powerful medicines of beadwork.

When we look at the accomplished beadwork of historic artists, we can see the control and intentionality of each stitch. Considering form, imagery, and gesture together, we can look more deeply into the role of beadwork in the lives of artists and their communities. Beadwork can be a form of prayer and devotional labour. One of the earliest documented examples is the wampum collar made by Wendat women in 1653.[11] It was for them a collaborative project in both the accumulation of the beads and execution of the belt. Each bead was earned by reciting the rosary, hundreds of individual acts of devotion to the Virgin Mary, with the purple beads possibly representing two rosaries: "We have recited as many rosaries, in the space of two months, as there are beads in the collar—one bead of purple porcelain being worth two of white. . . . It is a Collar full of hidden meaning. It is composed of our finest Pearls. It is inspired and enriched by the Utterance and the Greeting given you of old by the Angel Gabriel. We have nothing more precious in our hands, and nothing holier in our hearts."[12] Two later belts made by Wendat (1678) and Abenaki (1699) congregations carry a

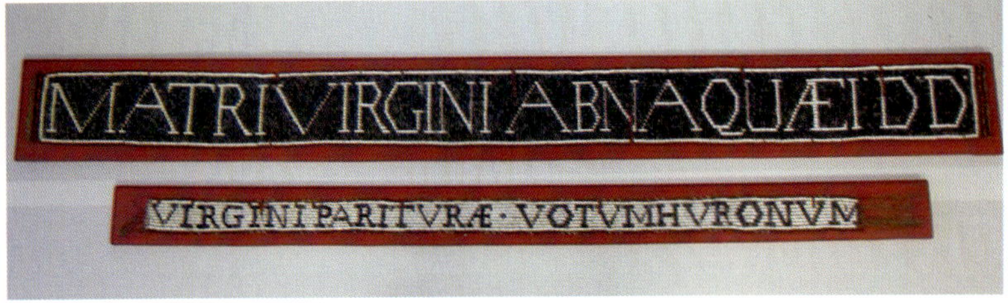

FIGURE 8.1. The Abenaki (1699) and Wendat (1678) devotional wampum belts were gifted to the Cathedral of Our Lady of Chartres and have been in Chartres, France, for more than 300 years. The top belt (2.18 m x 15 cm) is Abenaki. Large white letters, MATRI VIRGINI ABNAQUAEI D D, sit on a purple background. The bottom belt (1.445 m x 7 cm) is Wendat and has purple letters, VIRGINI PARUTURAE VOTUM HURONUM, on a white background. It is made of quahog (Mercenaria mercenaria), whelk, glass beads, leather, porcupine quills, and plant fibers. Photo courtesy of the CRoyAN project, musée du quai Branly-Jacques Chirac.

FIGURE 8.2. Lahkōta Artist, once known, cradle cover (c. 1885). Bequest of Dorothy Record Bauman, 74.63.5. Permission of Minneapolis Institute of Art.

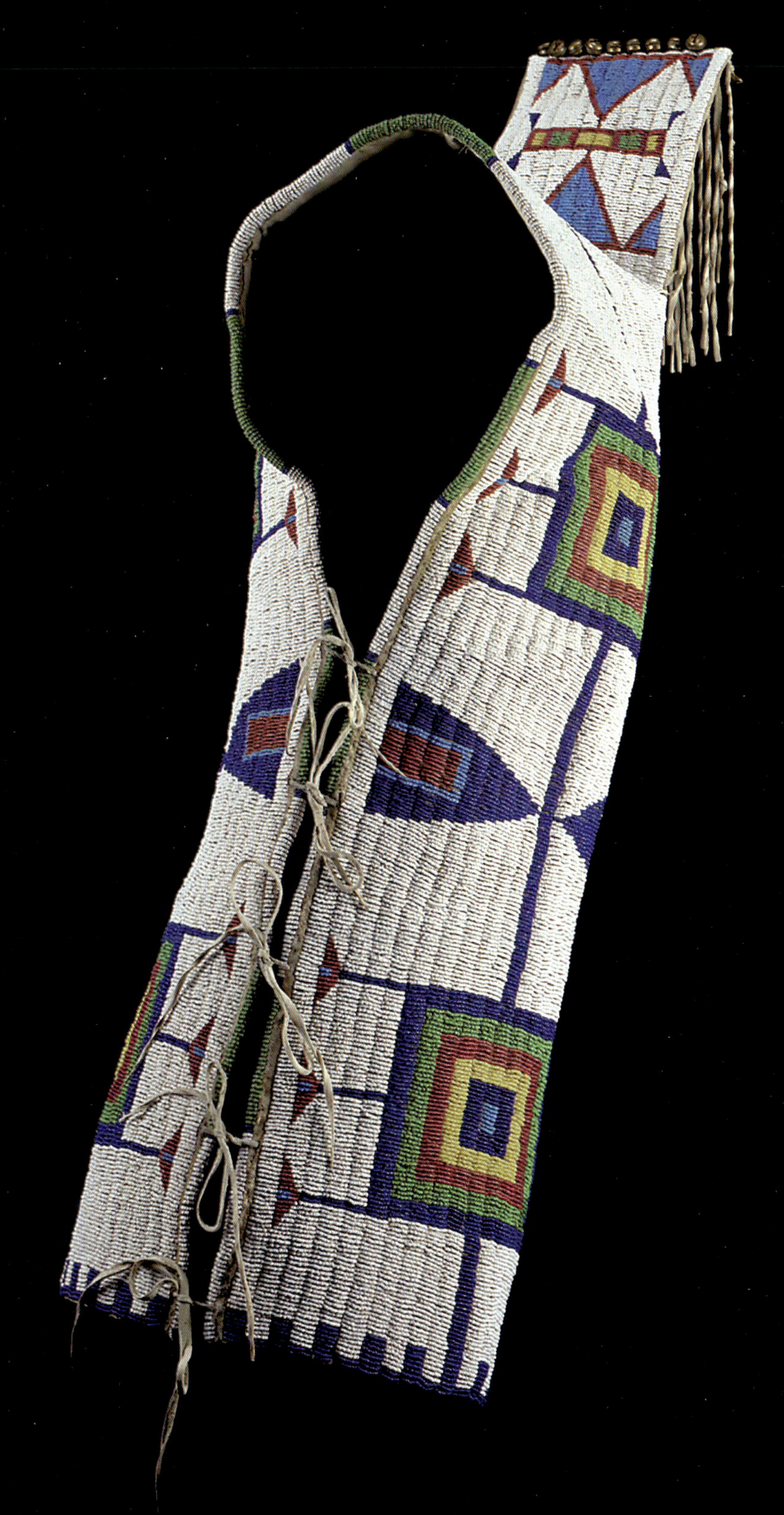

similar merger of Catholic devotion and ancient meaning. The belts were devotional gifts to the Cathedral of Our Lady of Chartres, where they now rest in Chartres, France.[13] As Nicole O'Bomsawin reflected, "The Chartres wampum belt isn't just something we made and gave away as a present: we were asking for Mary's protection through this artifact. We had been told that Our Lady of Chartres was a huge, magnificent Cathedral and . . . we wanted our gift to be worthy of her glory."[14]

Beaded containers enveloped sacred beings ranging from pipes to babies. The making was an act of dedication and discipline. Symbolic imagery communicated reverence or summoned protective forces. John Lame Deer, a Mineconjou Lakota Elder, described the number four "as the most wakan," representing the four corners of the earth and the four winds. On a cradleboard, it was a powerful protector. Lame Deer cautioned that, "to a white man symbols are just that: pleasant things to speculate about, to toy with in your mind. To us they are much, much more. Life to us is a symbol to be lived."[15] Beaded pipe bags and ceremonial regalia are examples of devotional labour so potent that they were banned by government policy and seized.

Beadwork is language, speech, and coded knowledge. Between 1849 and 1870, Lakota women began to cover dress yokes with solid blue beadwork with a distinct undulating line emulating a turtle shell. Some versions have a central "turtle emerging from the lake" motif, with blue representing water and various motifs that reference (but do not narrate) a story of turtle's role as protector of women's bodies and health.[16]

Similarly, a wall pocket made by Rosalie LaPlante Laroque is a love song to the rich ecosystem of the Qu'Appelle Valley in southern Saskatchewan. This was a functional piece, made by a skilled artist to beautify her own domestic space. It is sewn from rich velvet, once a deep crimson, now faded to brown. The wife of a Métis trader, Rosalie Laroque had access to an expansive palette of beads. With multiple shades of pink, green and blue, the

FIGURE 8.3. Rosalie LaPlante Laroque, wall pocket showing medicinal plants, water, fish, and a whooping crane (c. 1870), Laroque Collection. Permission from the Lebret Museum.

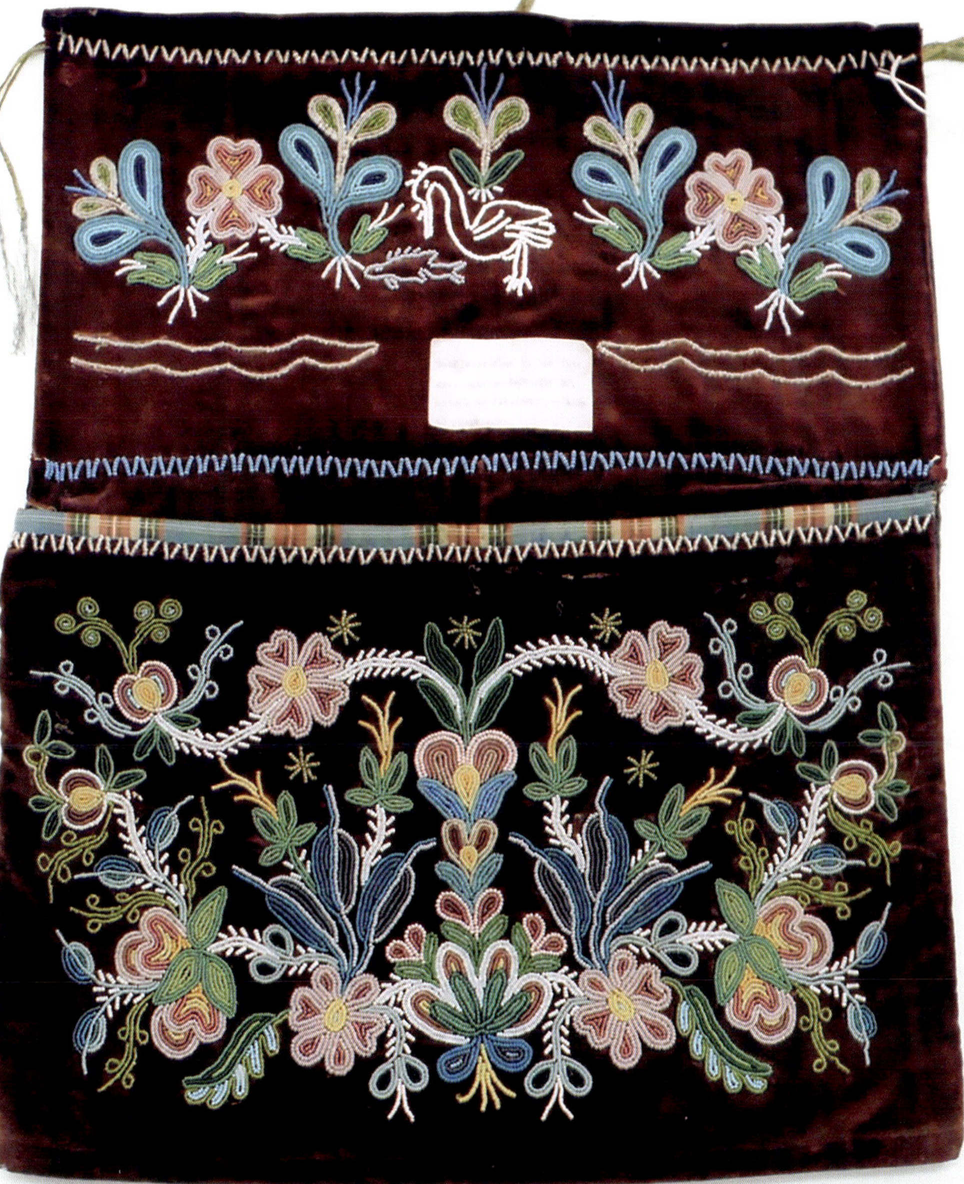

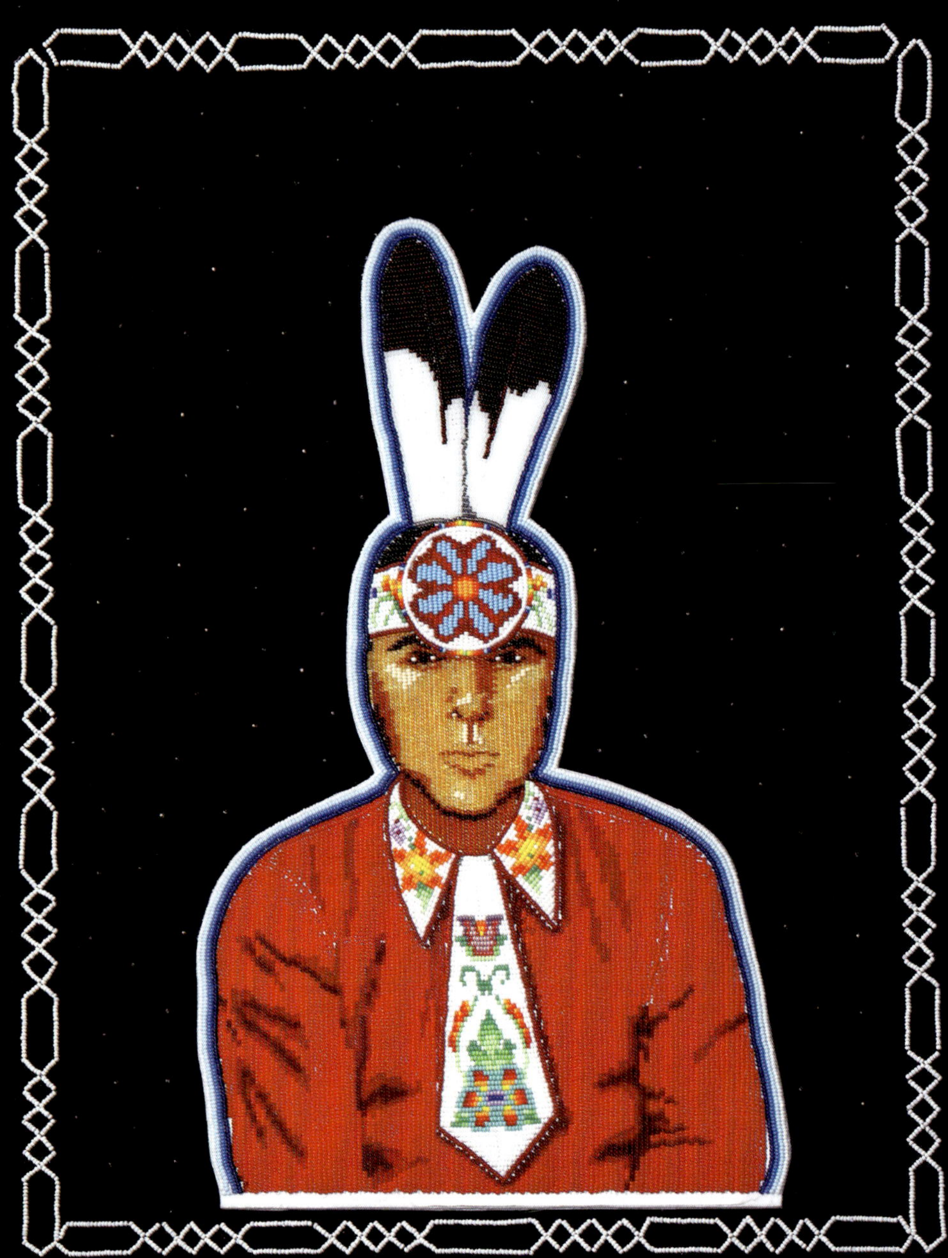

artist stitched a visual story of the land. The main pocket is embellished with a dense concentration of flowers and leaves, branching from a central axis of stacked flowers. The top of the wall pocket has a meandering river with vegetation along the shoreline, a whooping crane, and a fish. The narrow meandering Qu'Appelle River has cut deep rifts in the prairie silt. The valley has an unusually plentiful and varied range of medicinal plants growing on its arid hillsides and swampy lowlands. The bottom of the valley, with its network of coulees, shelters an abundance of animals, birds, and fish. The whooping crane, now endangered, was once common. The fish, freshly caught, is a buffalo fish: the Qu'Appelle River is its only Canadian habitat. During hard times, this valley kept people strong. As with all beadwork, the ability to decode the wall pocket's imagery has different levels of access. Those who know the Qu'Appelle Valley will recognize the symbols, and read it as descriptive, celebratory text. Others can feel its joy.

Beadwork can be a physical manifestation of hope: A beaded pad saddle, with elaborately beaded corners and complementary saddle blanket, honours the horse and rider but also the buffalo. It embodies hope for a beneficial hunt and safe return. Beadwork is also innovation and play: Beaded slippers are meant to dance. The designs on moccasins vamps were often placed to give visual pleasure to the wearer looking down at their feet. Unusual colour combinations and experimental forms open the practice of beadwork to growth.

The actions of beading can be a means to process shock, trauma, and personal loss. The term "healing" is somewhat overused, but beading helps. Perhaps it is the repetition of small gestures, focusing on something outside of yourself. During times of chaos and difficulty, I have often thought that bringing beads under my control gave me a sense that I could control some aspect of my life. It gave me a safe place. Creating something beautiful or creating something with a powerful message is medicine for the maker. A recent and powerful example of this is the multi-faceted creative ceremony

FIGURE 8.4. Justine Gustafson, *First Portrait* (2020). A work created in honour of her late brother for the *Piitwewetam: Making is Medicine* exhibition at the Thunder Bay Art Gallery.

undertaken by the Gustafson family of Thunder Bay to honour the memory of their son and brother, Jesse Piitwewetam Gustafson, who passed away in 2015.[17] Their collective ceremony was presented in the form of an exhibition that toured Ontario.[18] Each object in *Piitwewetam: Making is Medicine* will be gifted, and the exhibition itself is presented as an offering both to Jesse's memory and to extended networks of kin and community who supported Jesse during his life and his family after his passing. The works that emerged from their profound grief are both individual and collaborative, made by Ryan and Shannon Gustafson with their daughters Justine and Jade. Describing their weekly sessions around the kitchen table, Shannon said, "we sat as a family and worked on this project."[19] The assembled works are simultaneous expressions of love, vulnerability, and immense courage.

FLOW: TIME STOPS, ART HAPPENS

Most artists have experienced the sensation of entering a state of suspended concentration where time stops. Three hours can seem like five minutes. Given the contemplative aspects of beading and the deep meaning it often engages, we can speculate that certain works, both historic and contemporary, were created in a flow state. The beaded lines are lyrical, the imagery draws the viewer in, and the technical virtuosity is breathtaking.

The work of psychologist Mihaly Csikszentmihalyi is helpful when considering the aesthetic and transformational aspects of flow and rhythm in the context of beadwork. The state of flow has an element of transcendent joy. As Csikszentmihalyi describes, "the body or mind is stretched to its limits in a voluntary effort to accomplish something difficult and worthwhile."[20] Characteristics of the flow state will be familiar to those who have experienced it and helpful to those who seek it: complete concentration on the task, clarity of goals, transformation of time (either speeding up or slowing down); actions become effortless, self-consciousness recedes, and there is no fear of failure.[21] There are preconditions to achieving a state of flow: we cannot be interrupted, we must have space and a stretch of time, a foundation of skill and the element of challenge are fundamental. In

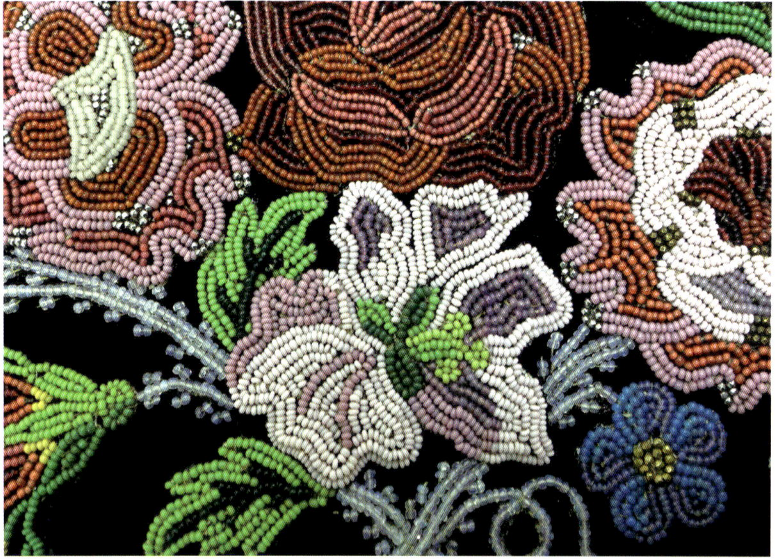

FIGURE 8.5. Marie Fisher Gaudet or her daughters Bella, Christine, and Dora, shelf valance detail (c. 1880–1890). Gift of Julien Gaudet, ME988.136.7. Permission of McCord-Stewart Museum.

terms of beadwork, it means managing beads, thread tension, stitching, and artistic concepts until gestures becomes effortless. Artists speak of "getting in the zone." The challenge level must be aspirational but achievable. It must take the artist further and higher to achieve heightened concentration. For the viewer, the response is one of awe.

BEADING UTOPIA

One utopian aspect of historic quill and beadwork has been imagery that represents the unseen powers fundamental to belief. Entire universes appear before our eyes, abstracted and essentialized, but conceptually complete. The ideal, unknown, and invisible are made visible. Many of the specifics have been lost as we seek to understand them, but their aesthetic power transcends the passage of time.

The struggles of doing are aspirational utopian gestures. The laughing, chatting, and rich silences around the beading table are nomadic utopian spaces—or at least they seek to be. Through beadwork we can literally sew ourselves back into the fabric of our communities, we can stitch the wounded parts of ourselves and mend broken chains of knowledge.

The works created by contemporary and historic artists in a state of flow are glimpses of utopia. I never get tired of contemplating Rosalie LaPlante Laroque's wall pocket (Figure 8.3), the imaginative florals of the Gaudet family, or the unknown Métis artist whose lyrical composition dances on a velvet pillowcase. At a recent exhibition, I watched an illustration of the power of flow as people fell into Katherine Boyer's *The Sky Vest* (discussed in Conversation 3).[22] Such works become portals to a place we want to go—if the needles don't break and the thread doesn't tangle.

NOTES

1 I include dates to anonymously acknowledge students and conversations that have contributed to the ideas in this essay, originally presented in public talks in 2016 and 2019.

2 Amber Berson, Curator's Text, *Utopia as Method* (2018), REGART: Centre d'Artistes en Art Actuel, Lévis, Quebec.

3 Berson's exhibition was inspired by Ruth Levitas, *Utopia as Method: The Imaginary Reconstitution of Society* (London: Palgrave Macmillan, 2013).

4 j.okuma, "According to my hands . . . it's one week until the Heard," Instagram, 22 February 2014, https://www.instagram.com/p/kuxlNwkQf5/. The Heard is the Annual Heard Museum Guild Indian Fair and Market, first organized in 1958, held at Heard Museum in Phoenix, AZ.

5 Kevin Brownlee and E. Leigh Syms, "Kayasochi Kikawenow: Our Mother from Long Ago (An Early Cree Woman and Her Personal Belongings from Nagami Bay, Southern Indian Lake," *Canadian Journal of Archaeology* 25 (2001): 137.

6 Ruben G. Thwaites, ed., *The Jesuit Relations and Allied Documents,* vol. 23 (Cleveland OH: Burrows Brothers, 1896–1901), 211. For more on wampum, see: Alexandra

Kahsenn:io Nahwegabow, "Islands of Memory" and "Places to Land: Haudenosaunee Beadwork in the Schreiber Collection," *National Gallery Review* 9 (2018): 1–21.

7 Thwaites, vol. 27, 247.

8 This is not a universal practice. Rather than intentionally place a spirit bead I usually let an error remain.

9 Robert Houle, "Indigenizing the Campus Through Art: Past and Future Perspectives," 26 April 2012, keynote address at the 100th Anniversary Symposium of the University of Manitoba School of Art, Winnipeg MB. https://umanitoba.ca/school-of-art-celebrating-100-years.

10 I have had many conversations with Cree scholar Keith Goulet but refer to my notes from his keynote address at the Frontier School Division Annual Conference, Winnipeg MB, February 15, 2013. See also Keith Goulet, "Animate and Inanimate: The Cree Nehinuw View," in *Material Histories: Proceedings of a Workshop Held at Marischal Museum,* ed. Alison K. Brown (University of Aberdeen, 2008), 7–19.

11 The distinction between belts and collars in the *Jesuit Relations* can be confusing.

12 Thwaites, vol. 41, 171–75.

13 Gratitude to Nicholas Renaud for sharing his research in a personal communication on 21 January 2022 and to Jonathan Lainey for sharing his important work with the Chartres Cathedral belts. See Jonathan Lainey, "Wampum in Quebec from the 19th Century to the Present Day: Appropriation, Loss, Identification," *Gradhiva* 33 (2022): 98–117, http://journals.openedition.org/gradhiva/6238. Note the international project bringing Wendat and Abenaki Knowledge Keepers into scientific collaboration to learn more about the belts, *Projet Introspect,* http://introspect.info/operationwampum/.

14 Nicole O'Bomsawin, Clémence Fort, Paz Núñez-Regueiro, Nikolaus Stolle, Leandro Varison, "Interview with Nicole O'Bomsawin: Wampum and Abenaki Culture Between Past and Present," *Gradhiva* 33 (2022): 132–43, https://journals.openedition.org/gradhiva/6269.

15 John (Fire) Lame Deer and Richard Erdoes, *Lame Deer Seeker of Visions* (New York: Pocket Books, 1972), 114, 117.

16 Emil Her Many Horses, *Identity by Design: Tradition, Change, and Celebration in Native Women's Dress* (Washington DC: National Museum of the American Indian, 2007), 98–100.

17 The Gustafson family are noted Anishinaabe artists, dancers, and cultural teachers.

18 Co-curated by Leanna and Jean Marshall, *Piiwewetam: Making is Medicine* was awarded Exhibition of the Year (budget under $20,000) by Galleries Ontario, https://theag.ca/piitwewetam/.

19 Shannon Gustafson, *Piiwewetam: Making is Medicine* Exhibition Video Tour, https://theag.ca/piitwewetam/.

20 Mihaly Csikszentmihalyi, *Flow: The Psychology of Optimal Experience* (New York: Harper and Row, 1990), 3.

21 Mihaly Csikszentmihalyi, *Creativity: Flow and the Psychology of Discovery and Invention* (New York: Harper Perennial, 1997), 113–17.

22 Katherine Boyer, *The Sky Vest* (2021) from her exhibition *How the Sky Carries the Sun*, at Art Gallery of Regina, Regina SK, 13 January–13 March 2022.

ACKNOWLEDGEMENTS

The foundations for ongoing expressions of beadwork were established by generations of Indigenous makers, artists, and Knowledge Keepers from across Turtle Island. Beading traditions and knowledge transmission that have emerged from the Flatlands are conveyed through stories, artistic practices, and technological innovations in ways that amount to bead love. We are indebted to our communities, to the artists known and no longer named whose painstaking efforts—whose determined efforts—have brought us to where we are today and have marked the paths for beading on the Flatlands going forward.

Carmen Robertson is grateful for the laughter, support, and care of the growing circle of Aunties who helped to bring this book together. This is Robertson's third book with University of Manitoba Press, and she remains thankful for the dedication and hard work of the editorial staff at the press. Her work has been shaped by the hills and waterways of the Qu'Appelle valley, the kinship ties, the wisdom of her Unci, grandma Jean, and her mom Collette, as well as countless family and friends who helped her to slow down and listen to the story keepers. Dagmar and Madelaine continue to inspire and amaze her every day. And to Mark, she appreciates the constant reminders of the wonder that life holds.

Judy Anderson is eternally grateful to Ka-nêwo-kaskwatêw (George Gordon First Nation). While she did not grow up there, she knows that she would not be where she is without the land to connect to and their unwavering support over the years. She also wishes to thank the relatives she could not meet who made unimaginable sacrifices (câpânak, nokohm, nisîmis) so that she could be where she is today, and to the relatives she was fortunate to grow up around and be influenced by (nimasôm, nikâwiy, nitôsisak, nisisak, nîtisân). She is also grateful for the Aunties who lovingly and hilariously walk this art road with her, teach her, and take chances with her. To Larry, who moves easily between being her partner and her assistant even though he'd rather just be retired. Finally, to her sons, Cruz and August, whose opinions matter most and remind her that there is always room to learn and grow.

Katherine Boyer is most grateful for family, in all its various shapes, across all timelines. She dedicates each stitch to her mom, Joan, and each joined piece of wood to her dad, Gary. The wild grasses would not smell as sweet without the support and encouragement of Auntie Yvonne, Uncle Merv, Erin, Jade, Kurt, and Kyle, Em and Jess, or the kids: Jasper, Hanna, Noa, and Lucille. She is grateful for Olivia and Kay, who are a force of kindness, love, and hilarity—so grounding that they could be land itself. She is also grateful for the sky, which reminds us that change is constant; and the wind, which, in case you thought you knew something, reminds us that change is constant. Lastly, she is grateful to the beads that each carry a thousand stories and more.

SPREADING THE BEAD LOVE FAR AND WIDE . . .

Most of the conversations for this project took place during the COVID-19 lockdown, as we mentioned in the Introduction. One of the positive outcomes of that otherwise difficult period was the explosion of beading that occurred! Social media and art galleries have become welcome spaces for beaders.

Our circle of beaders has been incredibly busy and the beading space has expanded in all directions as they spread the love.

JUDY ANDERSON exhibited her solo exhibition called . . . *Indigenized* at the Dunlop Art Gallery in Regina, Saskatchewan, and the Art Gallery of Swift Current, Saskatchewan, in 2023. This exhibition is made up of several multimedia installations that question what it is to "Indigenize" a place. Judy's work is also featured in *Radical Stitch*, which is now travelling to art galleries across Canada since it was first mounted in 2022 at the MacKenzie Art Gallery. Judy and Katherine are excited to finally be showing together in their own exhibition at the Nickle Galleries in 2024.

RUTH CUTHAND has been awarded the 2023 Senior Contemporary Art Fellowship at the Eiteljorg Museum in Indianapolis, Indiana. The fellowship will include a retrospective of her career that features a number of her beaded works and a catalogue with a companion essay by Carmen Robertson. Ruth has several beaded works included in *Radical Stitch*, which is now travelling to art galleries across Canada since it was first mounted in 2022 at the MacKenzie Art Gallery.

KATHERINE BOYER was included in *Révélations*, an International Craft Biennial in Paris, France, in the summer of 2023. Her work is also included in *Radical Stitch*, which is now travelling to art galleries across Canada since it was first mounted in 2022 at the MacKenzie Art Gallery. *How the Sky Carries the Sun* continues to show around Canada including, most recently, the Moose Jaw Museum & Art Gallery. Katherine is also excited to finally be showing alongside Judy in their own exhibition at the Nickle Galleries in 2024.

DAYNA DANGER was the artist in residence for the Department of Art History and Communication Studies and Mellon Indigenous Studies and Community Engagement Initiative (ISCEI), housed at McGill University, in Montreal in 2022. As of printing, they are pursuing a PhD at Concordia University that focuses on hide tanning practices from their great-grandmother, Madeline.

MARCY FRIESEN is represented (at the time of printing) by the Fazakas Gallery and has had work in several exhibitions since 2022 including *Radical Stitch*, which is now travelling to art galleries across Canada since it was first mounted in 2022 at the MacKenzie Art Gallery.

AUDIE MURRAY was the City of Regina Indigenous artist in residence in 2022 and had two solo exhibitions that year. Between 2022 and the time of printing, her work had been included in eight group exhibitions, including *Radical Stitch*, which is now travelling to art galleries across Canada since it was first mounted in 2022 at the MacKenzie Art Gallery. Oh, and she had a baby boy in 2022! Her art is featured in the North American compendium of Indigenous arts titled *An Indigenous Present,* edited by Jeffery Gibson (2023).

SELECTED BIBLIOGRAPHY

EXHIBITIONS

Anderson, Judy. *Indigenized*. Dunlop Art Gallery, Regina; and Art Gallery of Swift Current, Swift Current, 2023.

Beavis, Lori. *mazinigwaaso/to bead something—Barry Ace's Bandolier Bags*. Concordia University Gallery, Montreal, 2019.

Berson, Amber. Curatorial statement. *Utopia as Method*. Group exhibition. REGART, Centre d'Artistes en Art Actuel, Lévis, 14 September to 30 September 2018. http://www.centreregart.org/utopia-as-method/.

Boyer, Katherine. *How the Sky Carries the Sun*. Art Gallery of Regina, Regina, 13 January to 13 March 2022.

Campbell, Jesse, curator. *Catherine Blackburn: New Age Warriors*. Art Gallery of Guelph, Guelph, 12 January to 18 April 2021, and touring. https://artgalleryofguelph.ca/exhibition/catherine-blackburn-new-age-warriors/.

Doxtator, Deborah. Catalogue essay. *Basket, Bead and Quill*. Group exhibition. Thunder Bay Art Gallery, Thunder Bay, 8 September to 22 October 1995.

Falvey, Emily. Curatorial introduction. *Carrie Allison: Wâhkôhtowin*. Owen's Gallery, Mount Allison University, Sackville, 7 June to 14 August 2019.

Farrell Racette, Sherry, Michelle Lavellee, and Cathy Mattes, curators. *Radical Stitch*. Group exhibition. MacKenzie Art Gallery, Regina, 30 April to 25 September 2022. https://mackenzie.art/exhibition/radical-stitch/.

Gaucher, Karine, curator. *Beading Now!* Group exhibition. La Guilde, Montreal, 16 May to 21 July 2019.

Gay, Felicia. Curatorial statement. *Beads in the blood: Ruth Cuthand, a Survey*. Kenderdine Art Gallery, University of Saskatchewan, Saskatoon, 22 January to 10 April 2021.

Her Many Horses, Emil, ed. and co-curator. "Portraits of Native Women and Their Dresses." Exhibition catalogue. *Identity by Design: Tradition, Change, and Celebration in Native Women's Dresses*. National Museum of the American Indian, New York, 26 September 2008 to 7 February 2010. Catalogue published by Smithsonian/Collins, 2007.

Lavoie, Sophie, curator. *Cassandra Cochrane: Nindinawemaaganag: My Relations*. Muse Gallery, Kenora, 24 July to 5 September 2020.

Malbeuf, Amy. *Tensions*. Art Gallery of Southwestern Manitoba, Brandon, 28 February to 23 April 2019. https://agsm.ca/tensions-amy-malbeuf.

Marshall, Jean, guest curator. *Their Breath in Beads*. Group exhibition. Thunder Bay Art Gallery, Thunder Bay, 27 September to 10 November 2019.

Marshall, Leanna and Jean, co-curators. *Piiwewetam: Making is Medicine*. Group exhibition of work by Gustafson family. Thunder Bay Art Gallery, Thunder Bay, 27 February to 18 April 2021. Video tour by Shannon Gustafson. https://theag.ca/piitwewetam/.

Meyers, Lisa, curator. *Beads, they're sewn so tight*. Group exhibition. Textile Museum, Toronto, 10 October 2018 to 26 May 2019, and touring.

Nico Williams: Chi miigwech. Never Apart Gallery, Montreal, June 2021.

Robertson, Carmen. Catalogue essay. "Wâhkôhtowin—kinship—the way in which we relate to each other." *Carrie Allison, Wâhkôhtowin*. Owen's Gallery, Mount Allison University, Sackville, 7 June to 14 August 2019.

———. Exhibition catalogue essay. *Catherine Blackburn: New Age Warriors*. Art Gallery of Guelph, Guelph, 12 January to 18 April 2021, and touring. https://artgalleryofguelph.ca/exhibition/catherine-blackburn-new-age-warriors/.

Suda, Sasha. Foreword in exhibition catalogue. *Àbadakone/Continuous Fire/Feu continuel*. Group exhibition, curated by Rachelle Dickenson, Greg A. Hill, and Christine Lalonde. National Gallery of Canada, Ottawa, 8 November 2019 to 4 October 2020.

Warren, Daina. Curatorial statement. *Endurance . . . Patience*. Group exhibition. Urban Shaman Gallery, Winnipeg, 7 February to 21 March 2020. https://urbanshaman.org/exhibitions/endurance-patience/.

OTHER SOURCES

Ahmed, Sara. *Queer Phenomenology: Orientations, Objects, Others*. Durham: Duke University Press, 2006.

Allison, Carrie. Artist website. http://www.carrie-allison.com.

Anderson, Judy. Artist website. https://judy-anderson.com.

Anderson, Mark C., and Carmen Robertson. *Seeing Red: Natives in Canadian Newspapers*. Winnipeg: University of Manitoba Press, 2010.

Bol, Marsha. "Lakota Women's Artistic Strategies in Support of the Social System." *American Indian Culture and Research Journal* 9, no. 1 (1985): 33–51.

Boyer, Katherine "Viewpoints: The Foreground Is Blue." *Fold*, 2020. https://thisisthefold.org/viewpoints4.

Brownlee, Kevin, and E. Leigh Syms, "Kayasochi Kikawenow: Our Mother from Long Ago (An Early Cree Woman and Her Personal Belongings from Nagami Bay,

Southern Indian Lake." *Canadian Journal of Archaeology* 25, no. 1/2 (2001): 137–39.

Carter, Sarah, and Patricia Alice McCormack, *Recollecting: Lives of Aboriginal Women of the Canadian Northwest and Borderlands*. Edmonton: Athabasca University Press, 2011.

Csikszentmihalyi, Mihaly. *Creativity: Flow and the Psychology of Discovery and Invention*. New York: Harper Perennial, 1997.

———. *Flow: The Psychology of Optimal Experience*. New York: Harper and Row, 1990.

Cuthand, Ruth. Artist website. https://www.ruthcuthand.ca.

———. "From *Reserving* and *Don't Drink, Don't Breathe*." *The Capilano Review* 3, no. 27 (2015). https://thecapilanoreview.com/ruth-cuthand-reserving-dont-drink-dont-breathe/.

Cuthand, Ruth, and Chantal McStay. "Ruth Cuthand." *BOMB* 146 (Winter 2018–2019): 54–62.

Cutschall, Colleen. "Dresses, Designers, and the Dance of Life." In *Identity by Design: Tradition, Change, and Celebration in Native Women's Dress,* edited by Emil Her Many Horses, 65–94. New York: HarperCollins, 2007.

Daschuk, James. *Clearing the Plains: Disease, Politics of Starvation, and the Loss of Aboriginal Life*. Regina: University of Regina Press, 2014.

Dionne Prete, Tiffany. "Beadwork as an Indigenous Research Paradigm." *Art/Research International: A Transdisciplinary Journal* 4, no. 1 (2019). https://doi.org/10.18432/ari29419.

Dubin, Lois Sherr. "North America." In Lois Sherr Dubin, *The History of Beads: From 100,000 B.C. to the Present*, 261–90. New York: Abrams, 2009.

———. *North American Indian Jewelry and Adornment: From Prehistory to the Present*. New York: Harry N. Abrams, 1999.

Edge, Lois. "My Grandmother's Moccasins: Indigenous Women, Ways of Knowing and Indigenous Aesthetic of Beadwork." PhD diss., University of Alberta, 2011.

Estes, Nick. *Our History Is the Future*. New York: Verso, 2019.

Farrell Racette, Sherry. "Encoded Knowledge: Memory and Objects in Contemporary Native American Art." *Manifestations: New Native Art Criticism*, edited by Nancy Mithlo, 40–55. Santa Fe: Museum of Contemporary Native Arts. 2011.

———. "Historical Overview." In *Wapikwaniy: A Beginner's Guide to Métis Floral Beadwork,* edited by Gregory Scofield and Amy Briley, 3–8. Saskatoon: Gabriel Dumont Institute, 2011.

———. "Looking for Stories and Unbroken Threads: Museum Artifacts as Women's History and Cultural Legacy." In *Restoring the Balance: First Nations Women, Community, and Culture*, edited by Gail Valaskakis, Madeleine Dion Stout, and Eric Guimond, 283–312. Winnipeg: University of Manitoba Press, 2009.

———. "My Grandmothers Loved to Trade: The Indigenization of European Trade Goods in Historic and Contemporary Art." *Journal of Museum Ethnography* 20 (2008): 69–81.

———. "Sewing for a Living: The Commodification of Métis Women's Artistic Production." *Contact Zones: Aboriginal & Settler Women in Canada's Colonial Past,* edited by Katie Pickles and Myra Rutherdale, 71–146. Vancouver: UBC Press, 2005.

———. "Tuft Life: Stitching Sovereignty in Contemporary Indigenous Art." *Art Journal* 76, no. 2 (2017): 114–23. DOI: 10.1080/00043249.2017.1367198.

Fenn, Elizabeth A. "Biological Warfare in Eighteenth-Century North America: Beyond Jeffery Amherst." *The Journal of American History* 86, no. 4 (2000): 1552–80. DOI:10.2307/2567577.

Fournier, Lauren. "Métis Beading and Ancestral Knowledge: A Conversation with Katherine Boyer." *Canadian Art,* Interviews, 22 November 2018. Accessed 9 March 2020. https://canadianart.ca/interviews/metis-beading-and-ancestral-knowledge-a-conversation-with-katherine-boyer/.

Francis, Daniel. *The Imaginary Indian: The Image of the Indian in Canadian Culture.* Vancouver: UBC Press, 1992.

Friesen, Marcy. Artist website. http://www.marcyfriesen.ca/traplinecreations.html.

Fung, Amy. "Gay Liberation, Sex Dungeons, Gossip, and What We Want in Art: Writer Amy Fung joins artists Hazel Meyer and Cait McKinney for a deep lez bro down about a project at the Canadian Lesbian and Gay Archives." *Canadian Art.* Features, 13 September 2016. https://canadianart.ca/features/hazel-meyer-cait-mckinney/.

Gibson, Jeffrey, ed. *An Indigenous Present.* New York: DelMonico Books/DAP, 2023.

Goulet, Keith. "Animate and Inanimate: The Cree Nehinuw View." In *Material Histories: Proceedings of a Workshop Held at Marischal Museum,* edited by Alison K. Brown, 7–19. Aberdeen: University of Aberdeen, 2008.

Her Many Horses, Emil, ed. and co-curator. "Portraits of Native Women and Their Dresses." Exhibition catalogue. *Identity by Design: Tradition, Change, and Celebration in Native Women's Dresses.* National Museum of the American Indian, New York, 26 September 2008 to 7 February 2010. Catalogue published by Smithsonian/Collins, 2007.

Lainey, Jonathan. "Wampum in Quebec from the 19th Century to the Present Day: Appropriation, Loss, Identification." *Gradhiva* 33 (2022): 98–117. http://journals.openedition.org/gradhiva/6238.

Lame Deer, John (Fire), and Richard Erdoes. *Lame Deer Seeker of Visions.* New York: Pocket Books, 1972.

Levitas, Ruth. *Utopia as Method: The Imaginary Reconstitution of Society.* London: Palgrave Macmillan, 2013.

Macdougall, Brenda. *One of the Family: Metis Culture in Nineteenth-Century Northwestern Saskatchewan.* Vancouver: UBC Press, 2010.

———. "Wahkootowin: Family and Cultural Identity in Northwestern Saskatchewan Metis Communities." *The Canadian Historical Review* 87, no 3 (2006): 431–62.

Mattes, Cathy. "Artist Feature: Jennine Krauchi." *Pawaatamihk: Journal of Métis Thinkers* 1, no. 1 (2023): 44–48.

———. "Indigenous Littoral Curation: A Viable Framework for Collaborative and Dialogic Curatorial Process." PhD diss. University of Manitoba. 2021.

———. *Kwaata-Nihtaawakihk: A Hard Birth*. Interview, Winnipeg Art Gallery, 2 May 2022. https://www.wag.ca/art/stories/kwaata-nihtaawakihk-a-hard-birth.

———. "Wahkootowin, Beading and Métis Kitchen Table Talk: Indigenous Knowledge and Strategies for Curating Care." In *Radicalizing Care: Feminist and Queer Activism in Curating,* edited by Elke Krasny, Sophie Lingg, Lena Fritsch, Birgit Bosold, Vera Hofmann, 132–43. Publication Series of the Academy of Fine Arts, vol. 26. Vienna: Sternberg Press, 2021.

Mayer, Lorraine F. "A Return to Reciprocity." *Hypatia* 22, no. 3 (Summer 2007): 22–42.

Meyer, Hazel. Artist website. https://www.hazelmeyer.com.

Miner, Dylan A.T. "Mawadisidiwag Miinwaa Wiidanokiindiwag//They visit and work together." In *Makers/Crafters/Educators*, edited by Elizabeth Garber, Lisa Hochtritt, Manisha Sharma, 131–34. New York: Routledge, 2018.

Monture, Joel. *The Complete Guide to Traditional Native American Beadwork.* New York: Wiley, 1993.

Moore, Sandee. "New Age Warriors: Catherine Blackburn Creates Futuristic Regalia for Women Who Embody Strength and Fight Prejudice." *Galleries West*, April 8, 2019.

Jas M. Morgan [Lindsay Nixon]. "If You Don't Handle Me at My Best, You Don't Deserve Me at My Worst." In *Catherine Blackburn: with these hands, from this land*, 7 February–18 April 2020, Kenderdine Art Gallery, University of Saskatchewan. https://kagcag.usask.ca/exhibitions/2020/catherine-blackburn_with-these-hands,-from-this-land.php.

———. *nîtisânak.* Montreal: Metonymy Press, 2019.

Morin, Peter. "There Are No Metaphors: A Proposal for Dreaming Indigenous Philosophies into Studio Arts Education." In *The Routledge Companion to Indigenous Art Histories in the United States and Canada,* edited by Heather Igloliorte and Carla Taunton, 223–32. New York: Routledge, 2023.

Myers, Lisa. "Beads Need Threads." In *Becoming Our Future: Global Indigenous Curatorial Practice*, edited by Julie Nagam, Carly Lane, and Megan Tamati-Quennell, 193–204. Winnipeg: ARP Books, 2021.

Nahwegabow, Alexandra Kahsenn:io. "'Islands of Memory' and Places to Land: Haudenosaunee Beadwork in the Schreiber Collection." *National Gallery Review* 9 (2018): 1–21.

O'Bomsawin, Nicole, Clémence Fort, Paz Núñez-Regueiro, Nikolaus Stolle, and Leandro Varison. "Interview with Nicole O'Bomsawin: Wampum and Abenaki Culture Between Past and Present." *Gradhiva* 33 (2022): 132–43. https://journals.openedition.org/gradhiva/6269.

Pyle, Kai. "Métis, Queer, Trans and Two-Spirit Histories." Virtual presentation for the Mamawi Aachimotaak Project, 23 September 2021. https://www.facebook.com/themamawiproject/.

Robertson, Carmen. "The Beauty of a Story: Toward an Indigenous Art Theory." In *The Routledge International Handbook of Intercultural Arts Research,* edited by Pam Burnard, Liz Mackinlay, and Kimberly Powell, 13–28. London: Routledge, 2016.

———. "A Strikingly Seductive Package: Beaded Stories and the Art of Ruth Cuthand." In *UNSETTLE/Converge: Eiteljorg Contemporary Art Fellowship Exhibition 2024* (catalogue), 29–44. Indianapolis, 2024.

Robertson, Carmen, and Sherry Farrell Racette, eds. *Clearing A Path: new ways of seeing traditional Indigenous art*. Regina: Canadian Plains Research Center, 2009.

———. "Land and Beaded Identity: Shaping Art Histories of Indigenous Women of the Flatland." *RACAR: Revue d'art canadienne / Canadian Art Review* 42, no. 2 (2017): 13–29.

Simpson, Leanne. *A Short History of the Blockade: Giant Beavers, Diplomacy, and Regeneration in Nishnaabewin.* Edmonton: University of Alberta Press, 2021.

Smith, Monte, and Michele VanSickle. *Traditional Indian Bead and Leather Crafts: Bags, Pouches and Containers*. Liberty, UT: Eagles View Publishing Company, 1986.

TallBear, Kim. "Dossier: Theorising Queer Inhumanisms." *GLQ: A Journal of Lesbian and Gay Studies* (2015): 235.

Thwaites, Ruben G., ed., *The Jesuit Relations and Allied Documents.* Vol. 23. Cleveland: Burrows Brothers, 1896–1901.

Webb-Campbell, Shannon. "Reclaiming Indigenous Territories, Bead by Bead." *Canadian Art*, 27 June 2017. https://canadianart.ca/reviews/olivia-whetung-tibewh/.

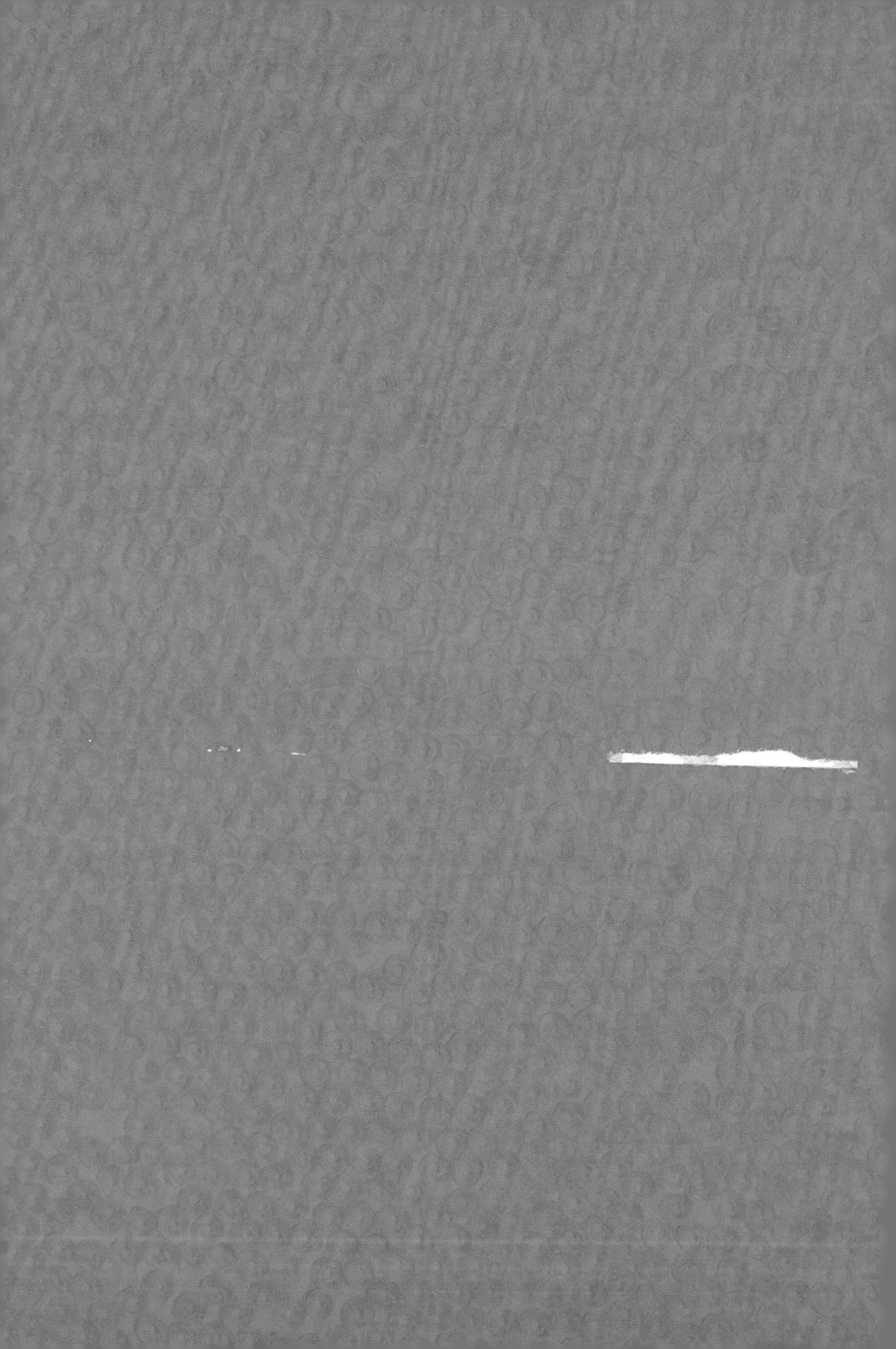